CANADIAN ROCKIES
ALBERTA & BRITISH COLUMBIA

Signpost
Guides

Titles in this series include:

For further information about these and other Thomas Cook publications, write to Thomas Cook Publishing, PO Box 227, Thorpe Wood, Peterborough PE3 6PU, United Kingdom

Signpost
Guides

CANADIAN ROCKIES
ALBERTA & BRITISH COLUMBIA

A journey into the wilderness and
majesty of Canada's great Rocky
Mountains taking in the cultural and
historical highlights of Alberta and
British Columbia

Donald L Telfer and Helena Zukowski

The
Globe
Pequot
press

Thomas
Cook
Publishing

Published by Thomas Cook Publishing
A division of Thomas Cook Holdings Ltd
PO Box 227
Thorpe Wood
Peterborough PE3 6PU
United Kingdom

Telephone: +44 (0)1733 503571
Fax: +44 (0)1733 503596
E-mail: books@thomascook.com

For further information about
Thomas Cook Publishing, visit our website:
www.thomascookpublishing.com

ISBN 1-841571-56-3

Published in the USA by
The Globe Pequot Press
PO Box 480
Guilford, Connecticut USA
06437

ISBN 0-7627-1250-3

Publisher: Donald Greig
Commissioning Editor: Deborah Parker
Project editor: Stuart McLaren
Proof-reader: Jan Wiltshire
Written and researched by: Donald L Telfer and
Helena Zukowski

Managing Director: Kevin Fitzgerald

About the authors

A writer, photographer and editor for the past 35 years, **Donald L Telfer** contributes to newspapers and magazines in Canada, the US and abroad such as the Toronto *Sun*, Vancouver *Province*, Edmonton *Journal*, Dallas *Morning News*, San Jose *Mercury News*, Hackensack *Record*, New York *Post*, *CNN Traveler*, *Going Places*, *Passport Newsletter* and *The Peak*, which is circulated in first and business class of Air France, Cathay Pacific and Lufthansa German Airlines. Prior to entering the exotic world of freelance travel journalism, Don was editor and publisher of the Humboldt (Sask.) *Journal*, a weekly newspaper founded in 1905 by his grandfather. He has travelled extensively around the world and throughout the neighbouring provinces of Alberta and British Columbia, though like many Canadians, this was his first visit to the remote and spectacular Cariboo Country. Between research trips, Don and his wife Mary Anne raised a family of two daughters and a son, the youngest two now studying to become teachers at the University of Saskatchewan in Saskatoon. They were inspired by visions of palm trees and laying on golden beaches but the fantasies evaporated quickly when they realised that teaching provided the opportunity for real vacations.

Helena Zukowski has logged more than 60 countries into her travelling career and has written about and photographed these for magazines and newspapers in Canada, the US and abroad. She has won numerous awards for her travel features and has had large cover stories in major newspapers all over the world. She is a member of The Travel Journalists Guild based in Chicago and is currently serving as president of that organisation. Born in Edmonton on a February day that was -47°C, she now makes her home just outside of Vancouver in the lush Fraser Valley where the temperature is much more agreeable. Her interests are broad and range from caring lovingly for a vast flower and vegetable garden to learning to make a perfect *oeuf en meurette* at La Varenne cooking school in Burgundy to scuba diving in Sipadan, one of the world's best underwater destinations. Her current project is to explore every part of Canada in addition to visiting exotic countries. She has lived in Toronto, Borneo, Montserrat and in Palm Springs where for six years she edited a glossy magazine called *Palm Springs Life*. 'In many ways, Palm Springs was the strangest and most exotic of them all', she says.

Contents

About Signpost Guides

Thomas Cook's Signpost Guides are designed to provide you wit comprehensive but flexible reference source to guide you as you to country or region by car. This guide divides the Canadian Rockies i 25 touring areas – one per chapter. Major cultural centres or ci form chapters in their own right. Each chapter contains eno attractions to provide at least a day's worth of activities – often mo

Star ratings

To make it easier for you to plan your time and decide what to every sight and attraction is given a star rating. A three-star rat indicates a major attraction, worth at least half a day of your tim two-star attraction is worth an hour or so of your time, and a one attraction indicates a sight that is worth visiting, but often of speci interest. To help you further, individual attractions within town theme parks are also graded, so that travellers with limited time quickly find the most rewarding sights.

Chapter contents

Every chapter has an introduction summing up the main attracti of the area or town, and a ratings box, which will highlight its app – some places may be more attractive to families travelling w children, others to wine-lovers visiting vineyards, and others to peo interested in finding historical sites, great restaurants, or view wildlife.

Each chapter is then divided into an alphabetical gazetteer, an suggested tour or walk. You can select whether you just want to vis particular sight or attraction, choosing from those described in gazetteer, or whether you want to tour the area comprehensively the latter, you can construct your own itinerary, or follow the auth suggested tour, which comes at the end of every area chapter.

The gazetteer

The gazetteer section describes all the major attractions in the are the ranches, towns, historic forts, national parks or museums that y are most likely to want to see. Maps of the area highlight all the pla mentioned in the text. Using this comprehensive overview of the a you may choose just to visit one or two sights.

One way to use the guide is to find individual sights that inte you, using the index, overview map or star ratings, and read what authors have to say about them. This will help you decide whethe visit the sight. If you do, you will find practical information, such the address and telephone number for enquiries and opening times.

Symbol key

ⓘ Tourist Information Centre

❷ Advice on arriving or departing

❸ Advice on getting around

➲ Directions

⓪ Sights and attractions

◖ Accommodation

● Shopping

⑨ Sport

◉ Entertainment

ctical information

practical information
he page margins, or
bar, will help you
te the services you
d as an independent
eller – including the
ist information centre,
parks and public
sport facilities. You
also find the opening
es of sights, museums,
rches and other
actions, as well as
ful tips on shopping,
-ket days, cultural
nts, entertainment,
ivals and sports
ities.

Alternatively, you can choose a hotel, with the help of the accommodation recommendations contained in this guide. You can then turn to the overall map on pages 10–11 to help you work out which chapters in the book describe the cities and regions closest to your touring base.

Driving tours

The suggested tour is just that – a suggestion, with plenty of optional detours and one or two ideas for making your own discoveries, under the heading 'Also worth exploring'. The routes are designed to link the attractions described in the gazetteer section, and to cover outstandingly scenic coastal, mountain and rural landscapes. The total distance is given for each tour, and the time it will take you to drive the complete route, but bear in mind that this indication is just for driving time: you will need to add on extra time for visiting attractions along the way.

Many of the routes are circular, so that you can join them at any point. Where the nature of the terrain dictates that the route has to be linear, the route can either be followed out and back, or you can use it as a link route, to get from one area in the book to another.

As you follow the route descriptions, you will find names picked out in bold capital letters – this means that the place is described fully in the gazetteer. Other names picked out in bold indicate additional villages or attractions worth a brief stop along the route.

Accommodation and food

In every chapter you will find lodging and eating recommendations for individual towns, or for the area as a whole. These are designed to cover a range of price brackets and concentrate on more characterful small or individualistic hotels and restaurants. In addition, you will find information in the 'Travel facts' chapter on chain hotels, with an address to which you can write for a guide, map or directory.

The price indications used in the guide have the following meanings:

$ budget level
$$ typical/average prices
$$$ de luxe

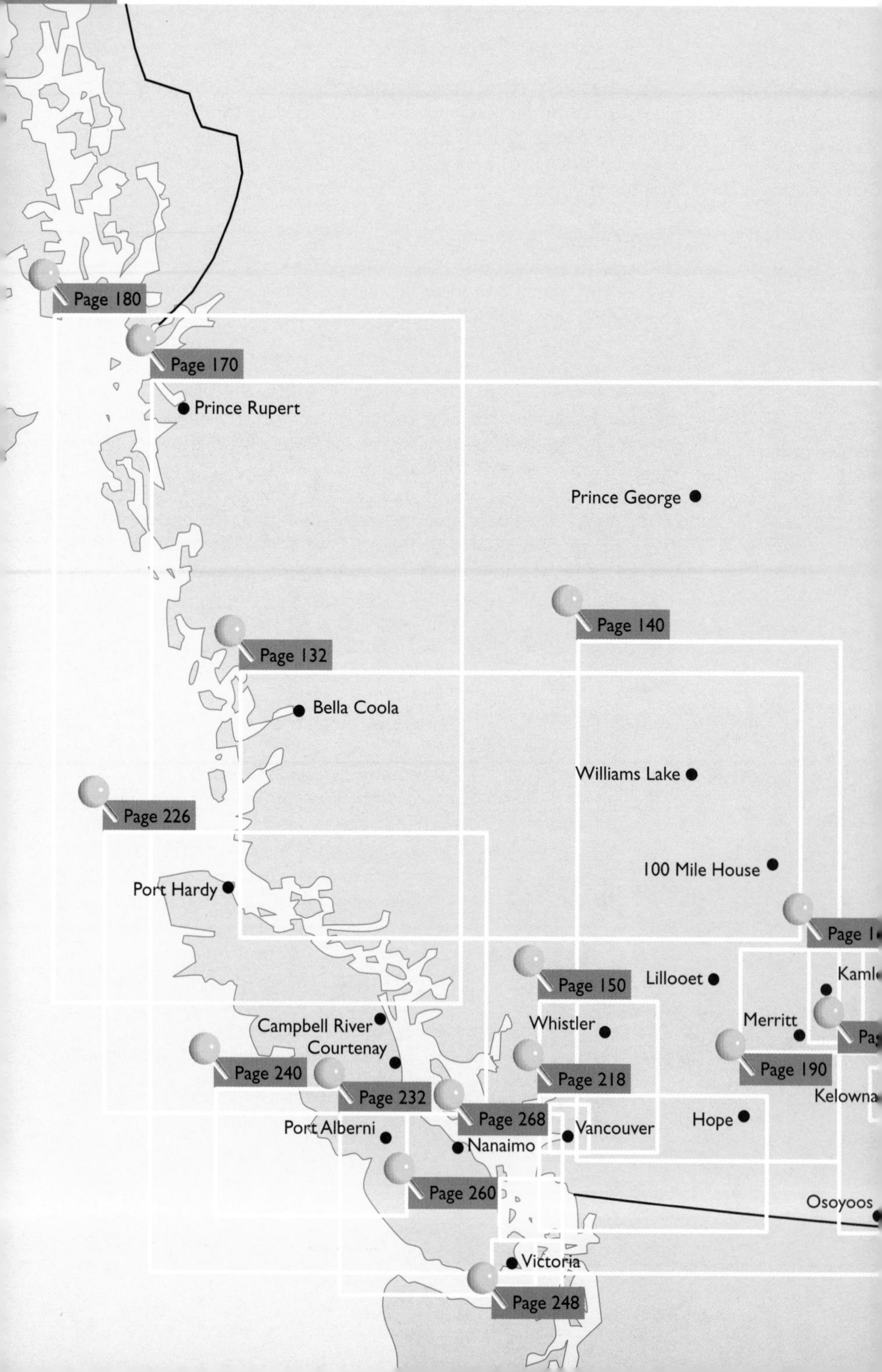

Page 180

Page 170

● Prince Rupert

Prince George ●

Page 140

Page 132

● Bella Coola

Williams Lake ●

Page 226

100 Mile House ●

● Port Hardy

Page 1◀

Lillooet ●

Kaml

Page 150

Whistler ●

Merritt ●

Pas

Campbell River ●
Courtenay

Page 190

Page 240

Page 218

Kelowna

Page 232

Port Alberni ●

Page 268

Hope ●

● Vancouver

● Nanaimo

Osoyoos

Page 260

● Victoria

Page 248

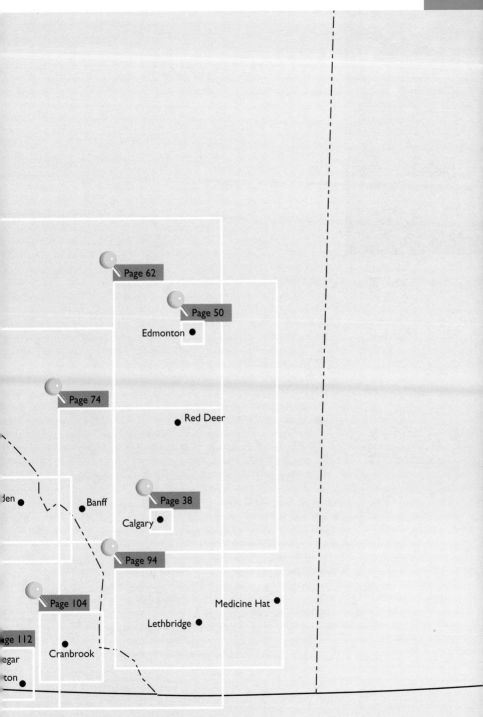

Introduction

One of Canada's more prolific authors, Pierre Berton, who on defined a Canadian as someone who could make love in a can couldn't have come up with a more apt phrase to describe weste Canadians. Albertans and the 'Lotus Landers' of British Columbia s their chunk of Canada as a large slice of paradise and will bore t knickers off anyone even *vaguely* hinting he might like to come a visit. Westerners firmly believe they live in the only part of Cana worth having and spend a good portion of their lives indulging in the scenic splendour around them. Beauty, they argue, makes up any economic rapids or recessionary waterfalls that swirl occasiona around their canoes.

Westerners have a lot of territory to brag about. You could Germany, France, Italy, Holland and all of the United Kingdom in the two provinces and still have more than 9 000 sq km left ov Mind you, most of this immense territory is unadulterated wilderne a vast expanse of trees, mountains, canyons, gorges, lakes and rive but according to British Columbians (who own the bulk of t wilderness) it's all just one massive virginal playground for natu loving eco-tourists.

Because of geography and climate, the population of both provinc is more or less a narrow band near the US border. The 3.987 milli fun-loving BC citizens are concentrated into the southwestern corr of the province, almost half of them in Vancouver. Step just fe beyond the city's most northerly fringe and you are immediate immersed in mountains and wilderness. Albertans tend to be spre out a bit more through the prairies that occupy about 90 per cent the province, but Edmonton and Calgary still account for more th half of Alberta's entire population.

While BC is largely trees and mountains and Alberta is prairie, t two provinces do have something in common: the Rocky Mountai that reach 12,000km northward from the US border and form divider between the two provinces. For two million years, glacie cataracts, streams and winds have sliced and sculpted the up-thr mountain range into an expanse of peaks, alpine lakes and meado of such beauty they set up double-decker lumps in the throat. T mountains hold many surprises: high-mountain hikers have actua found tiny marine fossils at altitudes of more than 3 000m above s level. These witnesses to yesterday are evidence that Alberta once at the bottom of a warm shallow sea that stretched from the Arc Ocean to the Gulf of Mexico. As millennia passed, layer upon layer shale, limestone and sandstone accumulated, creating deposits of wh would one day become a fortune in coal, oil and natural gas. The about 75 million years ago, tectonic plates clashed and the earth's crust buckled. At the point of collision, the young Rockies were pushed up, lifting the sedimentary layers embedded with the shells of tiny marine creatures from the great sea.

The mountains have meant different things to different people. For the early explorers seeking a Northwest passage, they were a challenge placed on earth by a legion of vengeful devils. For the aboriginals who had lived for thousands of years in undisturbed peace, the mountains were a greater protection than the most fortified castle built by European kings. When engineers finally broke through the barrier and newcomers began to pour through the mountain passes, prospectors rubbed their hands with glee. High-grade copper and silver deposits had been found and dreams of endless riches danced in their heads like sugar plums. So much of the beauty that still exists could have been lost forever to loggers and miners out to drain the resources if it hadn't been for a handful of greedy politicians and businessmen who saw a different kind of gold in 'them thar hills'.

The Rockies, with their emerald-tinted lakes and natural hot springs, were a perfect holiday spot for rich Easterners. They could travel out via the recently built railroad and stay in large hotels built by enterprising businessmen. To ensure that this natural beauty would remain unadulterated, politicians were pressured to create a park preserve in 1885, and two years later Canada's first national park, Rocky Mountain Park (later Banff National Park), was officially established.

It was just the beginning. Small wooden hotels grew into immense chateaux and tourists came in ever-increasing numbers to walk on the glaciers, visit the high alpine meadows, wallow in the hot springs and eventually ski the slopes of numerous great peaks. Not only the Rockies but BC as well would find itself plunged constantly into contradiction: for every government official or entrepreneur anxious to exploit a wealth of natural resources, there was a counter-balancing preservationist or environmentalist to stop him. The tug-of-war continues to this day and often spills out way beyond Canada as members of the international press and celebrities come to champion one environmental cause after another. The most memorable one was recently in Clayoquot Sound when loggers declared they intended to cut down old-growth trees that had been around since the Roman Empire. The response was explosive as more than 800 protesters were arrested for chaining themselves to trees and throwing themselves in front of logging trucks.

More than anything, people come to the West to experience its stunning beauty. They sample the 'good life' – the pure fresh cuisine, the produce from orchards and the wines from vineyards – but they take home something they didn't expect. The passion Westerners have for their land is contagious and visitors often go home forever infected by a need to return.

ow
ny Indian headdress,
nbow Museum

Above
Sinclair Canyon,
Radium Hot Springs

Travel facts

Accommodation

In most larger locations, there's a wide spread of accommodati
available from hostels to hotels, B&Bs, resorts, lodges, inns a
motels. In smaller areas or more remote locations, the best bet w
usually turn out to be one of the chain hotels and motels. In the la
cities, you definitely need a reservation during the peak seasons a
prices can be high. Expect to pay from $70–$200 in BC and $50–$1
in the Rockies and Alberta.

To book accommodation in BC, go directly to the tourism websi
or contact **Super**, **Natural British Columbia**, *tel (tollfree): (800) 4.
5622 or (250) 800-HELLOBC; web: www.hellobc.com* **Travel Alberta**,
(tollfree): (800) 661-8888 or (780) 427-4321, has lodging informati
but does not make bookings. Local tourist offices can provide lists
area accommodations.

Because of high demand during peak seasons, hotels in the cit
and major tourist resorts are often booked out months in advance
reservations as early as possible are advised. Cost of accommodati
can vary as much as 60 per cent from low and shoulder seasons
high season, usually mid-May–late-Sept and for the winter months
ski resorts.

Airports

For the Rockies, most international visitors fly into Calga
International Airport (YYC) for the major Rocky Mountain natior
parks and into Vancouver International Airport for West Coa
destinations. Both airports have recently undergone massive fac
lifting and are almost destinations in themselves with expand
facilities, shops and beautiful art work everywhere. For information
flights and bookings, contact individual airlines at loc
numbers or on the Web, not the airports. Trolleys a
available free in the baggage area upon arrival f
international passengers; smaller airports usually ha
pay trolleys for around $1–$2. Major airports ha
currency counters for exchange and banking services,
well as a range of major car hire/rental counter
Vancouver airport charges an airport-improvement tax
$10 for North American flights and $15 for internatior
flights upon departure unless passengers have same-d
flight connections. Both Calgary and Edmonton airpo
have airport-improvement fees of $10.

Below
First Nations artist
in Vancouver

Children

Because of reported child abductions, immigration officials may ask for identification for children such as a passport or birth certificate. A child travelling with a solo parent may be asked for a letter of permission from the absent parent. Divorced parents with shared custody should carry legal documents establishing their status.

Climate

International visitors are often surprised at the range of temperatures in Alberta and BC and the many micro-climates. Summers in BC are warm and dry, with rain confined mostly to the winter months; Vancouver Island is milder with less rain, while the Gulf Islands have the least rain of all. In the interior, the Okanagan Valley has hot summers and cooler winters. The Rocky Mountain areas tend to have pleasant summers and abundant snowfall in the winter, while Calgary frequently experiences warm winds called chinooks as a break from heavy snowfalls. Edmonton is hot in the summer and extremely cold in the winter with lots of snow.

Currency

Even though rumour circulates about Canadians adopting the US 'greenback', it's unlikely to happen soon. Current Canadian bills come in denominations of $1 coins (called Loonies) and two-colour $2 coins (sometimes called Toonies), as well as $5, $10, $20, $50 and $100 notes (bills). These vary in colour but are a uniform size. There are 100 cents (¢) to the dollar and the coins are: 1¢ (penny), 5¢ (nickel), 10¢ (dime), 25¢ (quarter), $1 and $2.

As travellers are advised anywhere, it's best to carry travellers' cheques and debit and credit cards. Since many smaller businesses may only accept one or two credit cards, it's best to carry several, with the most popular ones being: **Visa**, **MasterCard** (**Access**) and **American Express**. Usually hotels and car hire companies will ask for a credit card upon registration even if payment has been in advance or is to be settled in cash: for hotels, this is usually to cover mini-bar purchases and for security.

ATMs (automated teller machines) offer the best currency exchange rates and never close. Star and Cirrus are the most common international ATM networks, but check with your card issuer before leaving home to ensure that you have the proper four-digit PIN (personal identification number) for Canadian outlets. International airports have currency exchange facilities in the international terminal that are open long hours. Domestic terminals and smaller airports have no exchange facilities at all. US dollar and pound sterling travellers' cheques from Thomas Cook and other major issuers are

Thomas Cook
4, 4338 Main Street
Whistler, BC
V0N 1B4
Tel: (604) 938-0111

Electricity

Canada uses 110v 60Hz current with two- or three-prong plugs. Power and plug converters are seldom available in Canada so buy them before you leave home. Beware of buying electrical equipment: while some are dual voltage many won't operate on the 220v 50Hz power elsewhere. Exceptions are battery-operated items such as radios, cameras and portable computers. Be equally wary of pre-recorded videotapes since Canada uses the NTSC format while other countries are on the PAL or SECAM. When buying pre-recorded videos, check the box for compatibility. If no system is listed, it's probably NTSC.

Festivals

Each community has a long list of festivals that range from fall fairs and harvest events to wine festivals and stampedes. Numerous cultural festivals are devoted to music and there are many First Nations events visitors can attend. Some of the festivals are just downright silly (but fun), like the annual bathtub race from Vancouver Island. For a full list, check with the local tourism office.

accepted almost everywhere, but travellers' cheques in oth currencies must generally be cashed at a bank. Eurocheques a personal cheques drawn on banks outside Canada are generally accepted.

Thomas Cook Travellers' Cheques free you from the hazards carrying large amounts of cash. Thomas Cook foreign exchan bureaux are listed in the side column. They all provide full fore exchange facilities and will change currency and travellers' cheq (free of commission in the case of Thomas Cook Travellers' Chequ They can also provide emergency assistance in the event of loss theft of Thomas Cook Travellers' Cheques. To report Thomas Co Travellers' Cheque losses and thefts, *tel (tollfree, 24-hour service): (8 223-7373*.

Most banks are open Mon–Thur 1000–1500 and Fri 1000–17 Some banks open Sat morning and all are closed on Sun and natio holidays.

Customs allowances

Visitors to Canada may bring 1.14 litres of spirits or wine, 24 35 cans of beer or ale, 200 cigarettes, 50 cigars and 200g of loose tobac Any alcohol or tobacco in excess of this is subject to duty, provinc fees and taxes.

Drinking laws

The minimum drinking age is 19 in British Columbia and 18 Alberta; this is strictly enforced and youthful looking visitors may asked for identification. Unlike the US, beer, wine and spirits are o available in BC Government Liquor Stores or in some places at spe beer and wine stores. Alberta also has provincially licensed Liq Stores for the sale of beer, wine and spirits. Opening hours vary.

Eating out

A few decades ago, western Canadians rarely dined out but today t love their many restaurants, bistros and ethnic specialities as much anyone. West coast cuisine concentrates on fresh fish and seafc (particularly salmon, Pacific halibut and Dungeness crab), distinct local produce and 'fusion' dishes that marry the many eth influences in the two provinces, such as presenting wild game with Asian flair. In better restaurants, you will see exotic meats and of rare regional specialities such as barnacles and sea asparagus.

Prices tend to vary from the super-budget chain restaurants to ul expensive fine dining with portions from lumberjack-hearty minuscule and artfully arranged. Many restaurants have menus pos outside so you can avoid finding yourself in a champagne eatery w a beer wallet.

8

neral Tourism
rmation

**urism British
lumbia** *PO Box 9830,
Prov Govt, Victoria, BC
V 9W5; tel: (800) 435-
*2 (HELLOBC) or (240)
-1642; or 3 Regent St,
don, England, UK SW1Y
5; tel: (020) 7930 6857;
: www.travel.bc.ca*

avel Alberta *999 8th
et southwest, Calgary,
erta T2R 1J5; tel: (403)
-2700; fax: (403) 297-
8; web:
w.discoveralberta.com; e-
l: info@travelalberta.com*

ks Canada (National):
tish Columbia *PO Box
, 23433 Mavis Ave; Fort
gley, BC V1M 2R5; tel:
4) 666-1280; fax: (604)
-4798;* **Alberta** *Room
, 220 4th Ave southeast,
gary, Alberta T2G 4X3;
(800) 748-7275 or
3) 292-4401; fax: (403)
-4408; web:
w.parkscanada.psch.gc.ca*

Parks (Provincial) *800
son St, Victoria, BC V8V
4; tel: (250) 387-4550;
:
w.elp.gov.bc.ca/bcparks*

ow
*eloader in Stanley Park,
couver*

The coffee house is a recent phenomenon and particularly popular out west since the craze started in Seattle. Chains such as Starbucks and Second Cup are everywhere and feature a wide range of speciality coffees (at hefty prices). Coffee served in restaurants is closer to the American style (that is, weaker than in Europe) but most will serve espresso, cappuccino and similar brews.

Entry formalities

Except for US citizens whose proof of citizenship can be a birth certificate, voter registration, baptismal certificate or a passport, non-Canadian citizens require a passport, visa (if stated) and proof of return travel before departing for Canada.

Canada's firearms laws are considerably stricter than the US so all handguns, semi-automatic or fully automatic weapons and self-defence sprays such as mace or pepper spray are prohibited. Hunters bringing in rifles and shotguns must declare these upon entry. Failure to declare firearms will result in their seizure and criminal charges. Since 1 January 2001, new regulations require visitors to have a confirmed 'Firearms Declaration' to bring any guns into Canada. A fee of $50 will apply and be good for one year.

Narcotics and certain pharmaceutical products may not be imported. Carry documentation such as a doctor's prescription to prove that medications are legitimate.

Food

Alberta beef is quite famous (and Albertans will tell you this proudly) but the province also serves buffalo and wild meats such as venison, caribou, wapiti (elk), moose and quail. Portions are usually hearty. On the West Coast, salmon comes in many species with the best being sockeye and coho served barbecued, grilled or raw. Shellfish here is the best with excellent mussels, clams, geoducks and oysters served steamed or baked. Sushi has become a huge favourite with restaurants everywhere on the coast, where fish comes straight from the ocean. BC particularly promotes organic and healthy food so that even chain supermarkets have sections with everything from soya milk to goat feta cheese. On Vancouver Island and in the Gulf Islands, small boutique farms have sprung up everywhere, each farm specialising in some quality product such as sheep cheeses or fine balsamic vinegar aged in the Modena process.

Health and insurance

The main number to remember in case of a medical emergency is 911: this will bring the police, fire engines or an ambulance. If a life is at stake, treatment is swift and professional as government-run health

Language

Canada is officially bilingual in English and French; all public signage and documents will be in both languages.

Maps

The Canadian Automobile Association (CAA or BCAA in BC) prints useful road maps in conjunction with the American Automobile Association (AAA) free to members at CAA offices. The RAC and other automobile clubs have reciprocal agreements with the CAA. **MapArt** *70 Bloor St East, Oshawa, Ontario L1H 3M2; tel: (905) 436-2525,* produce easy-to-use regional and city maps. Detailed, 3-D maps of Rocky Mountain national parks are designed by **Gem Trek Publishing** *Box 1618, Cochrane, Alberta T0L 0W0; tel: (403) 266-2523.*

Museums

Most museums charge an entrance fee and are closed one day a week. Entrance fees are generally low with discounted prices for children, students and seniors. In tourist areas, museums have seasonal times for opening with many open all week in peak season.

programmes cover everyone. Non-Canadians will be expected to for treatment in both emergencies and non-emergencies; as in m countries, the former can be costly so travellers are highly advised carry good medical insurance. Most travel agents selling internatio travel offer travel insurance policies.

Be sure to bring all prescription medications for the entire trip a few extra days. Carry a copy of the prescription showing the gen (chemical) name and formulation, not just a brand name since th differ widely from country to country.

Canada is basically a healthy place with no inoculations requir Visitors should eat sensibly and avoid drinking from mount streams no matter how clear they look since they may be infec with *Giardia lamblia*, an intestinal bacteria that causes severe infect of the gut. Water served in restaurants is completely safe but in r areas and some small towns it is wiser to stick to bottled water. Dr lots of water or non-alcoholic liquids, especially in warm weather.

Since parts of BC and Alberta can become very hot in the summ sunglasses, wide-brimmed hats and good sunscreen will prevent bu sunstroke and heat prostration.

National parks

National parks and historic heritage sites charge daily entry fees person, with camping fees extra. If you plan to visit several parks region, you can save on park fees by buying a multi-park pass. **Great Western Annual Pass** ($35) allows entry to 11 parks (exclud Gwaii Haanas National Park). BC provincial parks' fees vary depend on the park and season. Alberta has the **Alberta Federal a Provincial Historic Sites Pass**.

Opening times

Standard office and business hours are Mon– 0830/0900–1640/1700. Banks are open Mon–Fri 1000–1500/1700 Sat mornings. ATMs are open 24 hours but doors may require a ba card to open. Shops are generally open Mon–Wed and 0900/1000–1800 and Thur & Fri until 2100, but this may vary (m large discount stores such as Wal-Mart are open until 2200). Sun h are 1100/1200–1700. Convenience stores are generally open 24 h a day.

Tourist offices outside Vancouver and Victoria have limited hours are closed from mid-Sept–mid-May. Petrol (gas) stations are open l hours but may close between 2200–0630. Pub, saloon and restaur hours vary widely depending on the season and location. For servi at churches, synagogues, temples or mosques, check local ph directories for numbers.

Packing

With the exception of luxury resorts and 5-star hotels in cities that require at least business attire, dress in the West is casual and practical. Since rain can fall at any time in BC, some kind of coat or fold-up plastic cover is recommended along with a good fold-up umbrella. At higher altitudes even in the summer the weather can turn cold suddenly so at least one change of warm clothing is important (sweater/pullover and jacket). For any kind of hiking, sturdy weatherproof shoes are important: and throw in some bug repellent for wilderness walks. A backpack, essential for trips involving hiking, can be brought or purchased at excellent Western outdoor stores for reasonable prices. Stock this with a hat, sunscreen (at least PF 15), insect repellent and sunglasses.

Postal services

There are **Canada Post/Postes Canada** buildings usually centrally located in all cities and towns, but many chemists (pharmacy/drug stores) will also have small postal counters at the back of the store (post offices are listed in the phone directory blue pages). Most post offices are open Mon–Fri 0900–1700 but drug store outlets will sell stamps after hours. Hotel concierges, tourist shops and some markets also sell stamps.

Letters or parcels sent abroad should go airmail to avoid delays, but for guaranteed fast service it's best to send by courier. Check the yellow pages under 'courier'. Rates for first class stamps are 47¢ per 30g within Canada; 60¢ per 30g to the US for letters and postcards; $1.05 per 20g internationally for letters and postcards.

ow
:ouver trolley bus

Public transport

Most large towns and cities have a local bus system; contact numbers can be found in the local phone directory. For transit between towns check under the **Greyhound Bus** (coach) listing. Vancouver also has a quick and efficient SkyTrain that links Surrey, Coquitlam and Vancouver. For local transit information in BC contact **BC Transit**, *web: www.transitbc.com* In Calgary contact **Calgary Transit**, *tel: (403) 262-1000; web: www.calgarytransit.com* Adult bus rates begin at $1.75, day pass is $5, which is good on all buses and the LRT. In Edmonton contact **Edmonton Transit Service**, *tel: (780) 496-1600; web: www.edmontontransit.com* Adult bus charges start at $1.75; day pass is $6, valid on all buses and the LRT.

Seniors

Canada has a considerable number of discounts for seniors (over 65) but to qualify you must mention your senior-citizen status up front when booking hotel reservations and before you are seated in a restaurant. Car hire agencies also have special rates for seniors, but often current value promotions may be less.

Taxes

BC has a 7 per cent provincial sales tax; Alberta has none. Most goods and services are subject to a Canadian Goods and Services tax (GST) of 7 per cent, although purchases of goods, including accommodation over $50 per transaction, will be rebated upon application to *Revenue Canada Visitor Rebate Program, Summerside Tax Centre, Summerside, Prince Edward Island C1N 6C6*; tel: (800) 668-4748 or (902) 432-5608. Both provinces charge a room tax.

Time

Most of British Columbia is on Pacific Standard Time (PST), GMT-8. Alberta and the Rocky Mountain section of BC are on Mountain Standard Time (MST). Both provinces jump ahead to Daylight Time (PDT) GMT-7/ (MDT) GST-6, from the first Sun in Apr until the last Sun in Oct.

For **BC Ferries**, *tel: (250) 386-3431 or (888) 223-3779; w www.bcferries.bc.ca*

For rail information, call **BC Rail**, *tel: (800) 339-8752; w www.bcrail.com; e-mail: passinfo@bcrail.com*

Reading

- *Best Places Vancouver*, Kasey Wilson, Sasquatch, Seattle, US, 2000.
- *The Big New Beautiful British Columbia Travel Guide*, Bryan McGill al, Beautiful British Columbia, Vancouver, 1999.
- *The Canadian Rockies Guide to Wildlife Watching: The Best Place: See and Appreciate Animals in their Natural Habitat*, Michael K Fifth House, Toronto, 2000.
- *Day Trips from Vancouver*, Jack Christie, Douglas & McInty Vancouver, 1997.
- *Gardens of Vancouver*, Christine Allen and Collin Varner, Rainco Vancouver, 2000.
- *Handbook of the Canadian Rockies*, Ben Gadd, Corax, Jasper, Albe 1995.
- *Outlaws and Lawmen of Western Canada*, Heritage House, Surrey, 1999.
- *Switchbacks: True Stories from the Canadian Rockies*, McClelland Stewart, Toronto, 2001.
- *Tell Me a Good Lie: Tales from the Chilcotin Country*, Paul St Pie Douglas & McIntyre, Vancouver, 2001.
- *A Traveler's Guide to Aboriginal BC*, Cheryl Coull, Whitec Vancouver, 1996.
- *A Traveler's Guide to Historic British Columbia*, Rosemary Neeri Whitecap, Vancouver, 1993.
- *The Way We Were: BC's Amazing Journey to the Millennium*, staff the Vancouver Province, Harbour, Vancouver, 2000.
- *West by Northwest: BC Short Stories*, David Stouck and M Wilkinson, eds, Raincoast, Vancouver, 1998.

Safety and security

- Dial 911 on any telephone for free emergency assistance fr police, fire and medical authorities.
- Never discuss travel plans or valuables in public. Walk w assurance in well-lit places and give the impression that you are worth robbing; for example, don't wear costly jewellery or h expensive cameras hanging around your neck. A wallet in a b pocket or an open handbag is an invitation to theft. Rep incidents to local police immediately and get a report for y insurance company.
- Unwatched luggage can vanish in an instant. Most airports and or train stations have lockers; guard the key and memorise

ping

and service charges
not usually added to a
in Canada. In general,
er cent of the total bill
more for exceptional
ice) is recommended
estaurant servers, taxi
ers and beauty salon
spa personnel. Bar
ders get 50¢ per drink.
cers usually get $1 a
(or more if he shows
your room) and maids
$3 per day. Tips for
parking vary
ending on how
ensive the restaurant,
el etc.

lets

adians refer to them as
hrooms; restroom,
room and toilet are
used. Men's and
nen's facilities will
lly be differentiated by
mbol of a man and a
nan. Parks and
eational areas plus
e ultra-trendy bars
have unisex
hrooms.

locker number. Hotel bell staff may keep guest luggage for a few days, but always get receipts.

- If your car breaks down, turn on the flashing emergency lights, raise the bonnet (hood) and wait inside the vehicle. Have your keys out to unlock car doors before entering a car park on foot, and check around and inside the vehicle before entering. Don't pick up hitchhikers and never leave the car with the engine running.

- Lock room doors, windows and sliding glass doors from the inside. Ground-floor rooms are convenient but easier to break into. When leaving the room at night, leave a light on. When someone knocks at the door, use the peephole to see who it is. If someone claims to be on the hotel staff, check with the front desk. Money, cheques, credit cards, passports and keys should be with you or in the hotel safety deposit box. Photocopy the important pages of your passport and visas. Carry the copies and extra passport photos separately from the documents themselves.

- When hiking or camping in the back country, you must register with the nearest park warden's office to ensure that if you need help it will come. Be wary of natural hazards and avalanche conditions in the winter. Pay attention to warnings about aggressive animals and follow instructions issued by park authorities.

Telephones

Public telephones (pay phones) are marked by a white telephone on a blue background. Dialling instructions are posted on the telephone or in the local telephone directory white pages. Local calls cost 25¢; tollfree (800, 877 and 888 area codes) and 911 emergency calls are free. To talk to an operator, dial 0. To locate local numbers, dial 411. For long-distance information, dial 1 + area code + 555-1212. There is a charge for information calls; there is no charge for local information from pay phones.

Talking Yellow Pages, tel: *(local area code) 299-9000* in both provinces, has free information on time, road conditions, weather, news and entertainment.

Many hotels and motels add steep surcharges to the cost of phone calls, even calling tollfree (freephone) numbers from rooms. Use a pay phone in the lobby; prepaid phone cards are available at many local outfits. The costs for phoning overseas on these cards can vary widely so ask about the most economical.

For international enquiries or assistance dial 00. For international calls, dial 011 (access code) + country code + city code (omit the first zero if there is one) + local number.

Driver's guide

Automobile clubs

The RAC and other touring clubs have reciprocal agreements with the Canadian Automobile Association (CAA), which in turn has reciprocal agreements with the American Automobile Association (AAA) in the US. Ask for CAA discounts on accommodation, car hire and attraction/museum admission. Road maps are provided free.

Accidents

Canadians drive on the right-hand side of the road. If involved i collision, stop immediately and exchange contact informati drivers' licences and insurance numbers with the other drive involved in the accident. Get the names, addresses and phc numbers of any witnesses, including passengers in other vehicles. 1 regulations stating if police are to be called vary from place to pla but usually police are not called unless there is personal inju requiring an ambulance, if the accident is blocking a ma intersection or if there is a criminal act involved such as alcol impairment.

Accidents must then be reported to your car-hire company a insurance company. Vehicle accidents registered in British Colum must be reported to the province's **Insurance Corporation of Brit Columbia** (ICBC), *tel: (800) 663-3051 or (604) 520-8222*. In Albe motorists carry private, not governmental insurance.

Breakdowns

Pull as far off the road as possible, turn on the flashing hazard lig and raise the bonnet. Use flares at night. Change tyres only when v away from the road and traffic. Dial 911 from any telephone police/RCMP for medical assistance, but not for a breakdown lc (tow truck).

CAA or other auto club membership usually includes a free tow service to the nearest garage for repairs. Most car-hire compan either pay for repairs directly or reimburse the cost shown on rep receipts. If a hire car will be out of service for more than a few hot ask the hire company for a replacement vehicle.

Camper vans, caravans and recreational vehicles

Recreational vehicles or RVs (camper vans and caravans) are a popu way to travel in western Canada, though hire companies restrict acc to some highways and may limit cross-border travel to the US. I options include a choice of daily mileage limits and seasons; h season is July–Aug.

The cost of hiring and operating an RV is offset by savings accommodation and meals plus the convenience of not packing a unpacking at every stop. RVs are cramped, however, and savin evaporate if gas (petrol) prices are high and you yield to temptation of eating out. Extra shopping, cooking and cleaning a

cuments

ur home-country
er's licence or an
rnational Driver's
ence is valid in BC and
erta. Always carry it
le driving, along with all
icle registration
uments and proof of
ility insurance. The
imum legal driving age
6, but most car-hire
npanies require that all
ers be at least 21,
ally 25. For RVs there
y be a maximum age
t of 70 or 75.

nking and driving
s

l, driving under the
ience of alcohol or any
er drug, is illegal. The
ninal blood alcohol limit
08mg and strict
orcement permits a
ce officer to take
ath samples on the
t. Police often establish
dom checkpoints
ticularly near winery
ing rooms, popular
dside restaurants and
ertainment venues.
vays appoint a
signated driver' who
not enjoy wine tasting
day.

eat into holiday time. Be sure to pack old clothes to wear while crawling underneath the vehicle when hooking up and disconnecting.

Get operating manuals and a full demonstration for all systems before leaving the car hire office with the RV. These vehicles drive more like lorries (trucks) than cars and are viewed as lorries by traffic laws. They are buffeted by wind more than cars, are taller and wider and therefore more inclined to roll over: be particularly careful at gas stations and car parks with low-hanging trees or signs.

To book a spot in BC Parks, call **Discover Camping**, *tel: (800) 689-9025; web: www.discovercamping.ca* Mar–mid-Sept.

Car hire

Car categories vary, but most hire companies offer subcompact, compact, economy, mid-sized, full-sized, luxury and sport utility vehicles (SUV). Reserve well in advance to ensure getting the type and size vehicle you need. Standard features usually include automatic transmission, air-conditioning and unlimited mileage. Some hire companies restrict travel east of Saskatchewan or into the US, and/or charge beyond a certain number of kms. Check the contract carefully.

It's usually cheaper to pick up a vehicle at an airport than in the city centre. A surcharge, or drop fee, may be levied for leaving the vehicle in another city. Ask about RV one-way rates if you aren't planning to arrive and leave from the same place.

All drivers must be listed on the hire contract. If an unlisted driver has an accident, you will probably be required to pay for repairs yourself. Most car-hire companies require a credit card deposit, even if the hire has been prepaid. Before leaving, be sure you have all necessary registration and insurance documents and that you know how to operate the vehicle.

Driving conditions

In the West, pedestrians always have the right of way at zebra crossings and intersections. When cars arrive at an intersection at the same time, the vehicle to the right proceeds first. Stop when a school bus lowers its red and white Stop sign or flashes its lights and do not pass. Oncoming traffic on narrow roads is required to let the uphill driver proceed.

If stuck in mud or snow, gently rock the vehicle by changing from forward to reverse gears. Winter driving experts also advise carrying a bag of kitty litter in the car to sprinkle on the snow under tyres for traction. In winter away from the coast, blowing snow can reduce visibility to zero and slow or halt traffic for hours. Highways require mandatory use of chains or other traction devices 1 Nov–30 Apr, and the speed limit becomes 40–50kph. If you're planning mountain driving in winter, ask the car-hire company to include chains or buy your own (under $50). When chains are required, gas station

Above
Old-style trucking at the Ukrainian Cultural Heritage Village

Fuel

Petrol and diesel are sold at gas stations in litres. Most vehicles take unleaded which comes in regular, premium and super grades. Buy regular unless the car-hire company specifies otherwise. Most stations are self-service although some offer a higher priced full-serve alternative. Pump prices include all taxes. Gas stations generally accept credit cards and $20 travellers' cheques but will not take $50 or $100 bills because of counterfeiting concerns. Many stations at night hours require that you pay before pumping your gas.

attendants and roadside workers will install them for about $20. Ca warm clothing and food in case of traffic delays and always keep gas tank at least half-full. Useful items include a blanket and can for warmth, an ice scraper and a small shovel. Snow-bound c should be equipped with a front engine compartment plug to po the engine block heater when temperatures fall to -10°C (14°F). extreme temperatures, an anti-freeze gas additive is recommenc when you fill your tank with petrol.

Information

BC Ministry of Transport and Highways InfoLine, *tel: (900) 4. 4997 (75¢),* and the **Alberta Motoring Association** (AMA), *tel: (8 642-3810,* have recorded road conditions. Local radio stations a broadcast weather and driving information. In urban areas most ra stations have regular traffic reports during morning and evening ru hours. **Government of Canada Weather Information** is in the pho directory blue pages. For weather online: www.weatheroffice.com

Insurance

Canadian and US drivers may be covered by their own insurance their premium credit cards) but other renters are strongly advised purchase coverage beforehand or accept the collision damage wai (CDW), sometimes called loss damage waiver (LDW), offered by h companies. Without the waiver, renters are personally liable for t full value of the vehicle. CDW is often required as part of a fly-dr package or for RV hire.

curity

ɔid vehicles with hire
npany decals or logos
ɔle since thieves prey
these. Whether it's an
or a car, lock your
icle when you're in it as
l as when you leave.
eck for intruders before
:ing in, especially at
ht and in RVs at any
ie. Never leave the
ine running when the
er is not in the car and
ays park in well-lit
as or in secure parking
s.

eed limits

e highway speed limit is
ally 80–100kph for cars,
ted for less for lorries
RVs (on some super
ways the limit will go
to 110kph). Slow down
owns and cities where
limit is 50kph or
er. If driving conditions
poor, drivers are
uired to keep to a safe
ed, no matter how
w. Police use radar and
oplanes to track, stop
ticket speeders, but be
rt even when traffic
mally flows at least
kph above the posted
ted.

lls

:ept for the 210km
quihalla Highway (Hwy
om Kamloops to Hope)
h a $10 toll, there are
other toll roads in
tish Columbia or
erta.

Parking

Parking garages, parking lots and parkades (car parks) are indicated by a white P on a blue background. Prices are posted at the entrance and some urban parkades accept credit cards. Outdoor parkades have metres that require either cash or credit cards paid in advance. Kerbside parking is usually limited, either by posted signs or by coin-operated parking metres, where the per-hour rate may be higher than in lots and parkades. Parking within major cities can be very expensive, particularly in the downtown area.

Kerbs may be colour-coded: *red* is no stopping or parking at any time; *white* is for passenger loading/unloading only; green is limited time parking (usually 10 minutes); *yellow* is a commercial loading zone; *blue* is special permit handicapped parking. Some streets are designated for residents of that street only. Parking is not allowed within 5m of a fire hydrant, near a disabled kerb ramp, at bus stops, intersections or zebra crossings (crosswalks), sidewalks (pavements) or on freeways. Fines levied against hired cars are charged against the hirer's credit card.

Police

Local police or the RCMP (Royal Canadian Mounted Police) signal drivers with flashing red and blue lights, sirens and loudhailers. Pull off the roadway as quickly as possible, turn off the engine and roll down the driver's side window. Stay inside the vehicle unless asked to step out. Have your driver's licence and vehicle registration ready for inspection and be prepared to give a breath sample to test your blood alcohol level.

Road signs

European-style road signs are widely used but there are differences in style. A black chequer board surrounding a number on a yellow sign for example indicates a speed limit change in non-urban areas. Car hire companies will have free road maps that will illustrate the most common road signs. In Canada, all signs use metric and give directions in both English and French.

Seat belts

The driver and all passengers must wear seat belts; police will issue fines if belts are not worn. Children under the age of six or weighing less than 18kg (Alberta) must ride in approved child-safety restraint seats. Safety seats can be hired with a car, or purchased for under $100 in a discount store. In an RV, passengers riding behind the driver's seat need not wear belts but should be safely seated.

Getting to the Rockies and British Columbia

Travellers with disabilities

While federal and provincial laws require that public business and services be readily accessible by handicapped persons, not all are. For specific information, contact **SATH** (Society for the Advancement of Travel for the Handicapped), 347 5th Ave, Suite 610, New York USA NY 10016; tel: (212) 447-7284. **RADAR** 12 City Forum, 250 City Rd, London EC1V 8AF; tel: (020) 7250 3222, publishes a useful annual guide, Holidays and Travel Abroad, with details of facilities for the disabled in different countries.

Wheelchair accessibility information is free from the **Canadian Paraplegic Association** 780 southwest, Marine Dr., Vancouver, BC V6P 5Y7; tel: (604) 324-3611; fax (604) 326-1227. **Access Canada** Tourism BC, Box 9830, Stn Prov Govt, 300 1803 Douglas St, Victoria, BC V8W 9W5, certifies agility, mobility, vision and hearing-impaired, disabled-designated accommodations, Canada-wide. **SPARC**, 106 2182 west 12th Ave, Vancouver, BC V6K 2N4; tel: (604) 736-4367, provide disabled parking permits.

Unless you live within driving distance of Alberta and British Columbia, flying is the most practical way to get there, with rail a close second. **VIA Rail**, tel: (800) 339-8752, and **BC Rail**, tel: (800) 3 8752, have had a recent 'rebirth' and now offer a number of different routes from major centres into tourism areas on both luxury and economy trains. These sightseeing trains operate during the summer months and usually involve stops at night to ensure the best possible views of dramatic mountain scenery during the day. Contact the railroads for specific routes (see also pages 170–9). There is also a ferry service from Seattle and other cities in Washington State to Vancouver and Victoria as well as a rail service from the US via **AMTRAK**. Motor coach travel is possible, though slow and cramped. Air travel is actually even more cramped since airlines try to squeeze in as many passengers as possible into economy; the trade-off is a major time saving.

To reach the Rocky Mountains first, the best airport is Calgary, Alberta with Edmonton second. Banff is two hours by car from Calgary compared to 12–14 hours of driving from Vancouver via Hwy 1, the TransCanada Highway. If you choose to drive from Vancouver consider overnighting in Revelstoke, about halfway to Banff. Some Rockies resorts such as Kananaskis are a one-hour drive from Calgary.

No matter whether you're flying to Vancouver or Calgary, don't let airline flight schedules mislead you into a full first day of touring. Vancouver may be only 10–12 air hours from much of Europe or Asia but jet lag intensifies the effects of long-distance air travel. Expect to arrive fatigued, disorientated, short-tempered and otherwise not ready to drive.

Overnight flights are attractive because they seem to offer an extra day of sightseeing upon arrival. Resist the temptation. Most travellers do better by timing their flights to arrive in the late afternoon or early evening, then getting a good night's sleep before tackling the sights. Since many airport-area hotels and motels offer a free shuttle service to and from the airport, you can take a shuttle to the hotel, sleep off the flight, shuttle back to the airport the next morning and pick up the rental car at no additional cost.

Jet lag cures are legion but the most effective seems to be to expose your body to as much light as possible as soon as you arrive in order to adjust to the new time zone. Experts suggest drinking as much water as possible on the flight over and avoiding alcohol and overeating.

ove
ding home to Nimmo Bay
kayak

There are also medications available such as Melatonin that seem to help some people.

Many fly-drive programmes offer what looks like an easy first-day drive such as Vancouver International Airport to Whistler resort, north of Vancouver. It looks easy on the map but in reality two hours of driving time can stretch into half a day if traffic is bad or if there is an accident on the 2-lane highway. Also on your return to the airport, allow extra time beyond the recommended two hours before an international departure. Unexpected traffic or bad driving conditions can leave you stranded on a freeway as your plane takes off overhead. Allow a safety margin by spending your last night in Canada near the departure airport, or at least in the same city.

Try to arrive with a few dollars in Canadian currency and coins. Luggage trolleys are free at larger airports such as Vancouver International but must be paid for in some domestic airports. Some trolley stands accept credit cards, usually Visa or Access/MasterCard, but other stands require cash and currency exchange facilities are located outside the arrivals area. Tips for porters may also be necessary.

Canadian airports do not have duty-free shopping for incoming travellers, but it's no great loss. Prices for alcohol and other duty-free items are almost always lower in Liquor Stores, supermarkets and discount stores than in duty-free shops.

Car-hire companies usually have cars at the major airports or nearby, but others require that you take a coach to an off-airport facility to pick up your hire car. Be sure to ask when making your reservation.

If hiring an RV ask the hire company about airport pickup and drop-off when making your booking. Most hire companies provide free transport to and from their offices, which are usually located some distance from the airport.

Setting the scene

The land

While the nature of many European countries is shaped largely
their history, for Canada, and especially the West, the defining forc
geography. Because most of the northern parts of Alberta and Brit
Columbia are wild, hostile, unforgiving and brutally cold in
winter, European explorers were defeated by the landscape
aboriginal people retained control of the land much longer th
elsewhere. Most of today's cities are less than 150 years o
photographs of Edmonton, for example, taken in 1871 show the to
as a trading post surrounded by a palisade.

The south coast of BC on the other hand is warmed by beni
currents and fertile soil piled up over aeons by the Fraser River,
living for the First Nations people was easy. For coastal tribes such
the Haida fish were so abundant and food so easily grown that th
was time to develop a complex and richly artistic culture. East of
Rockies, great plains provided grazing for millions of buffalo so t
Plains tribes, when they needed meat, had simply to stampede
herds over cliffs. This would provide enough meat to keep the tr
fed over the long winter.

Today, the two provinces claim perhaps the most diverse geograp
on earth: mountains, valleys, sea coast, plateaux, glaciers, tund
prairie and even a desert. During the Pleistocene Age, nearly the ent
area was blanketed in ice and from that time thousands of glaciers s
remain. In the northern part of BC these run side by side, separat
only by rivers, while those in the Rockies now form one of the are
most popular tourist attractions. Most of BC is ribbed by paral
ranges that are considered one of the world's major mount
systems. The Rocky Mountain Trench is No
America's longest valley, extending 1 600
from BC's northern border to Montana in
US. This is the birthplace of BC's most import
rivers including the Peace, Columbia and Fras

While cities were springing up in the East
early as the 17th century, the West remain
terra incognita, a place where there be drago
The forbidding Rocky Mountain range was
impenetrable obstacle that challenged a
usually defeated those seeking a passageway
the western ocean. The most romantic events
Canadian history come from the explorers w
fought enormous obstacles to find that passag

Below
Sculpture honouring the
cowboy and his horse at
Cochrane

The history of the West

While anthropologists now believe that wandering Asians migrated here as far back as 60,000 years ago, European settlement is barely a hiccup in the span of history. As one English visitor commented on viewing BC's historic buildings, 'I've got moss on my roof older than that'. Little more than 50 years ago, when officials had to take the census in northern Alberta, they went in with trains of mules, killing their own food as they went along. Vancouver, 150 years ago, was wilderness.

Alberta, named after a daughter of Queen Victoria, became a province in 1905 but remained a rugged place where bushy buffalo roamed freely through vast rolling grasslands. Homesteaders from Europe began trickling in to tame the prairies and turn them into wheat fields, in the process enduring unbelievably harsh conditions. The glaciers had left a landscape of muskeg bogs and bug-laden swamps so that these early pioneers, living in sod houses, broke both the land and their backs at the same time. Alberta's future changed one blustery February afternoon in 1947 when a crowd gathered in a

ow
aine Lake

Above
Stump Lake tepee

field near Edmonton and shou
'Here she comes!' As oil gushed fr
the ground everyone knew t
something very big, very import
had happened. Today Alberta
Canada's *wunderkind*, a province t
seems to be able to do no wro
economically speaking at lea
Calgary, Canada's energy capit
continues to be a boom town.

There are tales of exploration al
the BC coast that go back to an ea
Chinese manuscript dated 220 BC, a
Asian shipwrecks dating back to
5th century AD seem to confirm t
Sir Francis Drake was thought to h
visited the coast on his 1579 voyage
well, but Juan de Fuca, a Greek sail
from Spain in 1592, is credited as
first outsider to officially visit BC. It was the search for the Northw
passage to China (and a prize of £20,000 to the discoverer) that lu
explorers to challenge the mountains and rivers. Alexander Macker
was the first White to cross the continent north of Mexico, making
way to the mouth of the Bella Coola River in 1793. David Thomps
in trying to open trade with the Indians west of the Rockies, crea
the first comprehensive maps of the West as a result of
explorations, and Simon Fraser in 1808 struggled through the peril
canyons and rapids on to the mouth of the river that would be nam
after him.

The course of BC's history was changed by two things: gold and
railroad. During the first half of the 19th century, development
slow, consisting primarily of fur trading at various Hudson's
Company posts such as Fort Langley, Kamloops and Fort George.
as the California goldfields were trickling out, vast quantities of
precious substance were found in the sandbars along the lower Fra
River in 1857. Thousands of fortune hunters flooded in from all o
the world, crowding into a wholly inadequate Victoria demand
picks and shovels and permits. With wagon trains and on foot,
gold seekers walked the tributaries of the Fraser, striking major find
gold. Barkerville became a gold boom town with a population
25,000, making it the largest town east of Chicago and north of
Francisco. With greed the motivating factor, chaos ensued. In orde
maintain some order, the British established the mainland colony
British Columbia in 1858 under James Douglas, the governor
Vancouver Island.

No gold field lasts forever, and by late 1859 the sandbars of
Fraser were pretty thoroughly picked over all the way to Lillooet m

than 200 miles upriver. Prospectors drifted on and merchants selling prospecting supplies in Victoria had little to do but 'stand by their doors and project idle spittle into the streets'. Then in the fall of 1860, electrifying news hit: gold was found by the ton in the Cariboo. By the time the ice broke up on the Fraser in the spring of 1861, all the prospectors who left were surging back again: from New York, Australia and Liverpool. This time there seemed to be enough gold to go around and Victoria began to boom again. By the fall of 1861, it was estimated that more than $5 million in gold had been taken out.

By the time the Fathers of Confederation sat down to create a country, they realised they wanted the gold- and resource-rich territory on the Pacific Ocean to be a part of it. Since BC was toying with the idea of either joining the US or declaring independence, the British were panicked that the crucial last link in their much-desired safe land route to India might slip from their hands. To lure British Columbia into the family of Canada, it was promised a transcontinental railroad to link it to the East. In a country as diverse as Canada, the railroad proved to be one of the few real national bonds: it not only created a dependable physical link in a territory usually cut off by snow, rampaging rivers, mountains and landslides, but an emotional link as well. The story of the building of the transcontinental railway is one of Canada's great legends well told in Pierre Berton's book *The Last Spike*. It not only created 'a dominion from sea to sea' but shaped the ethnic diversity of the province as well.

The people

Until the 20th century, Canada received most of its immigrants from either Britain or France, but the opening of the prairies required a different kind of settler. One official, Clifford Sifton, Minister of the Interior in 1896, laid out the specifications: 'I think we require a stalwart peasant in a sheep-skin coat, born on the soil, whose forefathers have been farmers for ten generations, with a stout wife and a half-dozen children of good quality.'

t
Park beach, Kelowna

To meet this demand, thousands who fitted this description floo
into the plains from the Ukraine, Scandinavia, Germany, Holland a
Poland, lured by the offer of 160 acres (64.8ha) of 'virgin farmland'
free. Most were bitterly disappointed to find a brutal landscape fi
with trees and bogs. Western Canada became the promised land foi
sorts of religious dissidents as well, looking for peace, freedom a
hope. Mennonites and Doukhobors came from Russia, as wel
Jewish survivors of tsarist pogroms; Mormons and Hutterites ca
from the US. Later, refugees from other countries fighting oppress
governments came in waves: in 1956 Hungarians after th
revolution, Czechs after the Prague Spring and thousands of He
Kong Chinese fearful of the China take-over. Unlike in the US wh
immigrants found themselves dropped into a 'melting pot', the
Canadians held onto their languages and customs, forming instea
'mosaic' of people.

The Chinese were here even before this, drawn to the frontie
labourers to pound in the spikes on the great transcontiner
railroad. Today parts of Vancouver are densely Asian (in Richmond
per cent of the residents are Chinese), but the history of Chir
immigration and the treatment of the Japanese have left a so
historical blot. Until the mid-20th century, the Chinese were sub
to a 'Head Tax' and the families of Chinese male immigrants were
allowed to join them. During the Second World War Japanese v
were born in Canada were sent to concentration camps in the Inte
as 'undesirable aliens', their possessions confiscated.

Like any place with a frontier history, BC and Alberta have
more than their fair share of colourful characters. During the g
rush days, a Cornish sailor named Billy Barker jumped ship in Vict
and headed into the Cariboo to seek his fortune. Billy made
biggest strike ever in 1862, led a lusty life and died in pove
'Hanging Judge' Begby brought law and order to the restless fron
and one of BC's most colourful bank robbers was an ageing g
haired desperado called 'The Grey Fox'. Vancouver's unofficial 'fat
was a drunken publican named 'Gassy Jack' Deighton who arrived
the wooded shores, set up a sawhorse and a barrel of whiskey
thereby opened Vancouver for business. Politics has been a magnet
colourful characters in BC, especially Premiers. When he was elec
as premier, John Smith decided his name was too plain for such a le
position so he legally changed it instead to Amor de Cosmos (Love
the Universe). In more recent history, one of the longest reign
Premiers was known as 'Wacky' Bennett, and three Premiers in a
following him were thrown out of office because of scandals. Cabi
ministers have been equally colourful, such as 'Flying Phil' Gagla
Minister of Transportation, who clocked up an astounding numbe
speeding tickets while he was in office. We don't even want to
onto the subject of hucksters and charlatans: suffice to ment
Brother XII, a charismatic character who started a cult near Nanai

Below
Gassy Jack Memorial,
Vancouver

and left just hours ahead of the law with a fortune in gold stuffed in jam jars conned from his devoted followers.

First Nations

As in the United States, Central and South America and Australia, the historical relationship of aboriginal people and the newcomers is a blemished one full of shame and tragedy. It is only within the last few decades that some of the historical wrongs have been addressed and the many aboriginal communities, formerly called 'Indians', have assumed their rightful place as Canada's First Nations. All through BC and Alberta, treaty negotiations have taken place to restore lands and establish self-government to the people, reclaiming their languages and identities as Gitxsan or Dakelh or Quw'utsun'.

Canadians in recent years have become more aware of aboriginal landscape, issues and history, and to build on this First Nations communities have been opening their doors and inviting guests to learn from them. More and more First Nations cultural centres are opening up along with interpretative tours, art galleries and special events. At Duncan's Cowichan Native Village, for example, visitors hear traditional stories around a smoking fire, listen to the songs, watch the dance performances and get to dine on a traditional feast of pit-barbecued salmon, venison and clams. At Xa:ytem National Historic Site outside Mission, Sto:lo guides share lessons taught by the Transformer, Xexa:ls. *A Traveler's Guide to Aboriginal BC see* (*Reading, page 20*) provides an excellent guide to places where visitors can share in the stories and cultural events.

The wildlife

Of all the reasons people are drawn to the Rockies and BC, a chance to experience wilderness and its animals – and to test oneself in a multitude of wilderness activities – probably places first. There are more resident wild animal species here than anywhere else in Canada. It's said that more than three-quarters of Canada's wildlife species actually breed here. On the coast, there are resident pods of whales and among the regular visiting species, nearly all of the world's 24,000 Pacific grey whales swim past the length of BC's coast in the spring and fall. Sea lions, dolphins, seals and porpoises are full-time residents; in fact BC's coastal waters are so alluring to sea mammals and fish that they are considered by scuba divers as some of the best in the world. Visibility is phenomenal and many species come in 'industrial size': the world's largest octopus and sea urchins are here, as well as mussels so huge, one alone would make a chowder.

The Rockies are home to grizzly and black bears, cougars, wolves, coyotes, mountain goat, bighorn sheep, caribou, elk and moose just to name a few. Banff National Park has 53 species of mammals alone,

Above
Black bear

ranging from the pygmy shre
weighing a fraction of an oun
to huge bison. Many of the lar
animals will be spotted j
grazing by the side of the ro
There are in fact more big-ga
species here than in any ot
place on earth.

Birdlife is even more abunda
from tiny chickadees to regal b
eagles. More than a million bi
migrate on the Pacific flyway a
hundreds of thousands stop
rest. For bird watchers, t
western wetlands are filled with

endless procession of waterfowl: trumpeter and whistling swa
pelicans, loons, Canada geese and snow geese. To make things ea
for visitors, provincial wildlife viewing programs have been set up
that people may observe wildlife in their natural habitats. For deta
write to **BC Wildlife Watch**, *Box 7394, Stn Prov Govt, Victoria, BC V*
9M4 or *tel: (250) 387-9737.*

The sporting life

Next to wilderness and wildlife, the biggest lure in the West is spc
the more active the better. The Rockies and BC have become wo
famous not only for the quantity but also the quality of skiing terr
available to all levels and types of skiers. Whether downh
snowboard, cross-country, helicopter or powder-cat skiing, the resc
are fully equipped, the snow is plentiful, the scenery grand and the
as fresh as it can be. Banff, Jasper and Lake Louise are long-ti
favourites in the Rockies, but Kananaskis is coming up hard a
family favourite and Kicking Horse Pass nearby plans to be 'the n
Whistler'. In BC, Whistler/Blackcombe is world-famous for
extraordinary runs and scenery but many of the Okanagan ski resc
are equally good, cheaper and less crowded.

'Watching' has become one of the West's hottest sports. B
watchers have been around for aeons but the latest favourites .
whale watching, bear watching and now storm watching. Just driv
through wilderness areas can be a non-packaged watching event
moose, herds of deer, bighorn sheep and elk nibble beside the road.

Guest ranches have sprung up all over, with visitors encouraged
take an active part in rounding up cattle, sheep shearing and day-
day ranch chores. In the Cariboo, guest ranches or outfitters prov
horseback riding trips on a daily basis or on lengthy forays into
wilderness. A new twist on this is llama-trekking where hiki
becomes a novel experience when you have a llama as a companion

Provincial parks have hundreds of miles of trails for the fit and experienced or the casual stroller, some easy walks for a few minutes, others for hours and days. Among the most challenging and popular are the West Coast Trail that takes 5–7 days along Vancouver Island's west coast and the 25-day Nuxalk–Carrier Heritage Trail in the Cariboo to trace aboriginal footsteps. A number of outfitters also take people heli-hiking where a helicopter lifts you from a plateau near a wilderness lodge up to the highest peaks and alpine meadows for unparalleled walking experiences.

Fishing also draws passionate anglers to cast for giant halibut, lingcod and BC's five salmon species found along thousands of kilometres of shoreline or in remote rivers and streams. Trout fishing is also huge in the myriad freshwater lakes all through the West.

There's more: caving in some of the thousands of charted and explored caves, particularly on Vancouver Island; mountain biking through the Rockies; scuba diving along the entire BC coast and its islands; gold panning in the Cariboo, mountaineering and rock climbing that is among the best in the world; and for something a little different, soaking in a remote cove on the edge of the world in hot water bubbling up from the core of the earth.

w
s bison graze in Elk Island
onal Park

Highlights and touring itineraries

Top ten sights

These are not the most frequently visited places but are certainly some of the best:

- **Barkerville Historic Town** (*page 140*)
  Where the Cariboo Gold Rush began.
- **Fort Steele Heritage Town** (*page 107*)
  A frontier town that has brought the 1890s vividly back to life.
- **Fraser Valley Canyon and Hell's Gate** (*page 144*)
  Raging rivers and spectacularly rugged landscapes.
- **Heritage Park, Calgary** (*page 42*)
  The largest historical village in Canada recreates pre-1915 life in western Canada.
- **Head-Smashed-In Buffalo Jump, Fort Macleod** (*page 96*)
  A UNESCO World Heritage Site that tells the story of how Plains Indians ingeniously harvested buffalo.
- **Kettle Valley Railway** (*page 210*)
  The KVR runs all through the Okanagan and is a masterpiece example of 'recycling'.
- **Nelson** (*page 118*)
  The entire town is quaint, friendly and a favourite with movie makers from Hollywood.
- **The Royal BC Museum, Victoria** (*page 254*)
  Rated one of the 10-best museums in the world for its permanent holdings and its highly imaginative special shows.
- **The Royal Tyrrell Museum of Palaeontology, Drumheller** (*page 67*)
  Some of the most stunning reconstructed dinosaur skeletons in the world stalk the museum.
- **Stanley Park, Vancouver** (*page 274*)
  This is just about the perfect city park and a monument to foresight by the original city planners.

The best of Alberta and BC

Two of these three circular tours start and (in Calgary and one begins and ends Vancouver. Suggested overnight stops shown in bold type.

Two weeks

This is the Best of the West, a journey w coastal activities as its theme.

Day 1	Arrive in **Vancouver** (*see page 268*)
Day 2	**Vancouver**.
Day 3	BC Ferries to **Mayne Island** (*see p 261*).
Day 4	BC Ferries to **Salt Spring Island** *page 263*).
Day 5	BC Ferries to **Victoria** (*see page 248*)
Day 6	**Victoria**.
Day 7	Hwy 1 to the **Cowichan Valley** *page 234*).
Day 8	Take Hwy 1 and 19 to **Campb River** (*see page 227*).
Day 9	**Strathcona Park** (*see page 230*) ; drive via Hwy 9 and 4 to **Uclue** (*see page 245*).
Day 10	**Ucluelet** and **Tofino** (*see page 242*)
Day 11	**Tofino**.
Day 12	BC Ferries to **Vancouver Nanaimo**, then drive via Hwy 1 **Fort Langley** and **Harrison F Springs** (*see page 221*).
Day 13	Return to **Vancouver**.
Day 14	**Home**.

Three weeks

See most of Alberta, from the Rockies to prairies.

Day 1	Arrive in **Calgary** (*see page 38*).
Day 2	**Calgary**.
Day 3	TransCanada Highway (Hwy 1) Brooks, then Hwy 550/544/876 Dinosaur Provincial Park. Follow F

876 to TransCanada Highway and continue on to **Medicine Hat** (*see page 98*).

y 4   Crowsnest Highway (Hwy 3) to **Lethbridge/Fort Macleod/Head-Smashed-In Buffalo Jump** (*see pages 96–7*).

y 5   Hwy 2 to Cardston, then Hwy 5 to **Waterton Lakes National Park** (*see page 99*).

y 6   **Waterton Lakes National Park.**

y 7   Cowboy Trail (Hwy 6) to Pincher Creek, then Hwy 22 to **Rocky Mountain House** (*see page 78*).

y 8   Hwy 11 to Red Deer/Innisfail/Olds then Hwy 27/21/837 to **Drumheller** (*see page 67*).

y 9   Hwy 56/26/2A to Stettler/Wetaskiwin/Leduc/Devon, then Hwy 60/16 to **Edmonton** (*see page 50*).

y 10 **Edmonton.**

y 11 Yellowhead Highway (Hwy 16) to **Jasper** (*see page 87*).

y 12 **Jasper.**

y 13 Icefields Parkway (Hwy 93) to **Columbia Icefields/Lake Louise** (*see pages 86, 88*).

y 14 **Lake Louise.**

y 15 Bow Valley Parkway (Hwy 1A) to **Banff** (*see page 84*).

y 16 **Banff.**

y 17 TransCanada Highway (Hwy 1) and Hwy 40 to **Kananaskis** (*see page 76*).

y 18 **Kananaskis.**

y 19 Continue on Hwy 40/541/22 to **Bragg Creek** (*see page 74*).

y 20 Return to **Calgary.**

y 21 **Home.**

ur weeks

m mountains to ocean, this covers a lot of ritory.

y 1   Arrive in **Calgary** (*see page 38*).

y 2   **Calgary.**

y 3   Hwy TK to **Drumheller** (*see page 67*) and then Hwy TK to **Head-Smashed-In Buffalo Jump** (*see page 96*).

Day 4   Return to **Calgary** and Hwy TK for **Kananaskis** (*see page 76*).

Day 5   Take Hwy TK to **Banff** (*see page 84*).

Day 6   Continue up Hwy 93 for **Lake Louise** (*see page 86*).

Day 7   Follow Hwy 1 to **Revelstoke** (*see page 126*).

Day 8   **Shuswap Lakes** (*see page 160*).

Day 9   Take Hwy 97B to **Vernon** and **Kelowna** (*see pages 205, 210*).

Day 10 The **Okanagan Valley** tourings (*see page 198*).

Day 11 Follow Hwy 97C to **Merritt**, then 5A to the **Nicola Valley** (*see page 194*).

Day 12 The **Nicola Valley.**

Day 13 Follow Hwy 5A north via **Kamloops** to **Williams Lake** (*see page 137*).

Day 14 Take Hwy 97 south for the **Gold Rush Trail** (*see page 140*) to join Hwy 1 south to **Hope** (*see page 223*).

Day 15 Continue on Hwy 1 through the **Fraser Valley** (*see page 218*) and Fort Langley.

Day 16 Hwy 1 to **Vancouver** (*see page 268*).

Day 17 **Vancouver.**

Day 18 BC Ferries to the **Gulf Islands** (*see page 260*).

Day 19 BC Ferries to **Victoria** (*see page 248*).

Day 20 Take Hwy 1 north to the **Malahat and the Cowichan Valley** (*see page 234*).

Day 21 Follow Hwy 1 then 19 to **Parksville**, then 4 to **Ucluelet** (*see page 245*).

Day 22 **Tofino** (*see page 242*) for eco-adventures.

Day 23 Take Hwy 4 west and 19 north to **Campbell River** (*see page 227*).

Day 24 Continue on to **Port Hardy** for BC Ferries to **Prince Rupert** (*see page 184*).

Day 25 Follow Hwy 16 west to **Jasper** (*see page 87*).

Day 26 **Jasper.**

Day 27 Drive to **Calgary.**

Day 28 **Home.**

Calgary

Ratings

Children	●●●●●
Entertainment	●●●●●
Food and drink	●●●●●
Museums	●●●●●
Restaurants	●●●●●
Shopping	●●●●●
Outdoor activities	●●●●○
Scenery	●●●○○

Bounded by the Rocky Mountains on the west and t
vast wheat fields and rangeland on the east, Calg;
sprawls over the largest landscape of any Canadian city. T
financial centre of Western Canada, downtown Calgary i
Lego-size Manhattan with towering skyscrapers housi
banks, insurance firms and oil companies. Despite its si
openness and party atmosphere, 'Cowtown' is a clean, s;
and friendly city. The fastest-growing city in Canada
regarded as one of the world's finest: UNESCO has rat
Calgary one of the best in the world to live in. There ;
numerous parks, a world-class zoo and the famous Stampe
held every July. The 1988 Winter Olympics not only help
Calgary emerge from relative obscurity but also chang
Calgarians. Visitor numbers increased, especia
international travellers who introduced new expectations
fine galleries, *haute cuisine* and comfortal
accommodation, without changing the loveable cowb
image.

Arriving and departing

**ⓘ Calgary
Convention and
Visitors Bureau**
*Stephen Avenue Walk, 220
8th Ave southwest; tel: (403)
263-8510, tollfree (800)
661-1678; web:
www.tourismcalgary.com
Open daily 0800–2000 in
summer, 0900–1700 in
winter.*

Canada's fourth busiest airport, **Calgary International Airport**
(403) 735-1200, provides non-stop service from London, Amsterd;
and Frankfurt as well as many points in Canada and the US. A $
airport-improvement fee is added to tickets for domestic a
international flights. Roving volunteer 'White Hatters' greet arriv;
answer questions and solve problems. A 20-minute drive to the c
centre, **Airport Shuttle** $ *tel: (403) 509-4799*, operates door-to-door
hours a day; **Banff Airporter** $$ *tel: (403) 762-3330*, provides door-
door service to Banff; taxi $$ to downtown. Many hotels ha
courtesy shuttles.

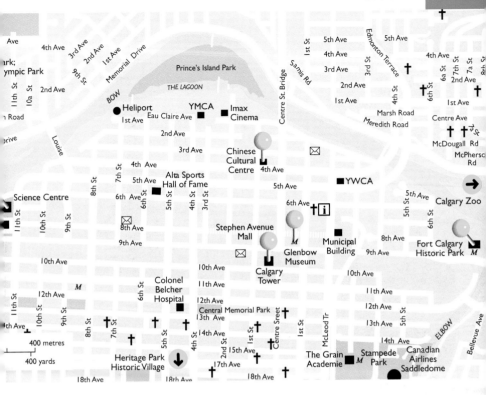

Getting around

Calgary International rport. *Arrivals Level en daily 0010–2200; partures Level open daily 00–2400 in summer, 00–2300 in winter.*

ewster Banff *(403) 762-6700, tollfree 0) 661-1152; web: w.brewster.ca* e Graylines Sightseeing sion provides airport vice between Calgary d Banff. With over 80 tor coaches, Brewster s been in business for er a century.

Breeze through the city on the C-Train light-rail transit (LRT) or hop aboard a Calgary Transit bus, with free transfers from bus drivers with an all-day pass ($5). Easy access is provided for all passengers with priority seating for wheelchairs and scooters. Calgary has an extensive bike path system of some 300km of well-groomed paths. Afternoon bike rentals are available at cycle shops.

Sights

Calaway Park✧✧✧
Western Canada's largest outdoor family amusement park, Calaway Park is a 20-minute drive west of Canada Olympic Park. Among the 26 rides are the Corkscrew Rollercoaster, Mountain Scrambler, and the Rocky Mountain Rail. Spectacular musical productions are performed at the Showtime Theatre and Celebration Stage.

Calgary Chinese Cultural Centre✧✧
Modelled on the 1420 Temple of Heaven in Beijing, the Chinese Cultural Centre was built by artisans from China using traditional

Above
Saddledome and downtown
Calgary

tools. Centrepiece is the Hall of Prayers of the Temple of Heaven, 21m-high dome ceiling decorated with 40 phoenixes and 561 dragon. Situated in the heart of Chinatown, the ornate Centre contains a cr shop, cultural museum, herbal medicine store and restaurant.

Calgary Science Centre✦✦✦

Holograms, frozen shadows, and laser beams delight visitors at the , plus hands-on exhibits. The latest in computer graphics are featured the Discovery Dome, all brought to life on the huge domed scree The stars are observed Fri evenings through the observatory's hig powered telescope.

Cardinal Coach Lines
*732 41 Ave northeast; tel:
(403) 531-3940, tollfree
(800) 661-6161.* Has
scheduled airporter
service to downtown
hotels as well as individual
motorcoach tours with
step-on guides.

Calgary Tower✦✦

It may not be the tallest structure in the city, but the Calgary Tower the most recognisable outline on the horizon. The 190.8m scept shaped edifice provides stunning views of the city, the vast plains a the rugged Rocky Mountains from the Observation Terrace. Two , passenger elevators whisk visitors to the top in 62 seconds, or if y feel energetic, try the 802-step staircase. After the Olympian worko dine at the revolving Panorama Dining Room.

Greyhound Canada
*tel: (403) 260-0877, tollfree
(800) 661-8747; web:
www.greyhound.ca*
Provides service to
numerous points in
Alberta and BC. Canada's
largest inter-city bus
company. Greyhound also
operates motorcoach
charters.

Calgary Zoo, Botanical Garden and Prehistoric Park✦✦✦

Home to over 1400 animals in their natural habitats, the zoo i world-renowned institution containing many rare and endanger

Arrow Motorcoach
9 Ave southeast, tel:
3) 531-0350, tollfree
0) 232-1958; web:
.redarrow.pwt.ca
vides a de luxe, daily
ress service between
gary, Red Deer,
nonton and Fort
Murray, offering
plimentary snacks and
eshments, fold-down
k tables and laptop
-ins.

species. Situated on St George's Island in the middle of the Bow River in downtown Calgary, the Prehistoric Park teems with 22 life-size dinosaur models, giving visitors an opportunity to step back in time to a world when T. Rex shook the earth. The Canadian Wilds, the Aspen Woodlands and the Canadian Rockies exhibits each represent a slice of Canada's wilderness.

Canada Olympic Park✧✧✧

Canada's premier Olympic venue is a busy year-round site with locals and visitors who ride the chairlift for stunning views of Calgary and the Rockies, and travel down the thrilling Bobsleigh Road Rocket at 95kph. Site of the 1988 Winter Olympics, visitors may opt for the 1-hour bus tour that goes around, under and over the ski jumps and bobsleigh and luge tracks.

ve
ada Olympic Park

Fort Calgary Historic Park✧✧✧

Amid a sea of scarlet jackets and thundering hooves, 'F' Troop of the North West Mounted Police crossed the Bow River in 1875 to build Fort Calgary. Now, the reconstructed Fort Calgary brings history to life on the 40-acre (16.2ha) park on the banks of the Elbow River. Across the river, enjoy lunch, dinner or a murder mystery evening at the elegant Deane House. Behind the building is the Hunt House, the

Calaway Park $$
*TransCanada Highway
West; tel: (403) 240-3822.
Open May–Oct; web:
www.calawaypark.com*

**Calgary Chinese
Cultural Centre $**
*197 1 St southwest; tel:
(403) 262-5071.
Open year round.*

**Calgary Science Centre
$$** *701 11 St southwest; tel:
(403) 221-3700; web:
www.calgaryscience.ca
Open Tue–Thur
1000–1600; Fri–Sun
1000–1700.*

Calgary Tower
*101 9 Ave; tel: (403) 266-
7171. Open daily
0800–2300.*

Calgary Zoo $$
*1300 Zoo Road northeast;
tel: (403) 232-9372. Open
daily 0900–1700.*

Canada Olympic Park $
*88 Canada Olympic Rd
southwest; tel: (403) 247-
5452; web: www.coda.ab.ca*

**Fort Calgary Historic
Park $**
*750 9 Ave southeast; tel:
(403) 290-1875. Open
May–Oct daily 0900–1700.*

Glenbow Museum $
*130 9 Ave southeast; tel:
(403) 268-4160; web:
www.glenbow.com
Open daily 0900–1700;
Thur–Fri 0900–2100.*

**Heritage Park Historic
Village $**
*1900 Heritage Dr.
southwest; tel: (403) 259-
1900. Open mid-
May–Labour Day weekend
0900–1700; weekends
Labour Day–Thanksgiving.*

oldest structure in Calgary, built
by the Hudson's Bay Company
in 1876.

Glenbow Museum*
Visitors to the vast Glenbow
Museum journey into the
heritage of the Canadian West
and the richness of First Nations
cultures. There are exhibits of a
Blackfoot tepee, elegant
quillwork of the Plains Cree, and
the hard-won comforts of a
settler's cabin. Permanent
displays are laid out over four
floors, with the top floor
provided for military history.
The Museum Shop offers a
variety of unique souvenir items,
while the Lazy Loaf and Kettle
café offers snacks and quick,
fresh meals.

Heritage Park Historic Village*
Recreating all the sights and sounds of pre-1914 life in West
Canada, Heritage Park is the largest living historical village in Cana
The park contains dozens of structures collected from across the W
including outhouses and a two-storey hotel. The SS *Moyie* sternwhe
takes visitors on a 30-minute cruise around the Glenmore Reserv
while electric streetcars provide rides to and from the front ga
Thundering steam trains and horse-drawn buses add to
atmosphere. During summer, there is a free breakfast 0900–1000 w
regular paid admission.

Accommodation and food

Calgary has a wide selection of accommodation that ranges fr
budget to de luxe. Vacancies are tight June–Sept and prices are high
As Calgary is a convention city, reservations well in advance
recommended year round.

Fairmont Palliser $$$ *133 9 Ave southwest; tel: (403) 262-1234.*
former Canadian Pacific Railway hotel is the *grande dame* of Calg
hotels situated in the heart of downtown.

posite
Calgary Historic Park
e

Hampton Inn and Suites $$ *2231 Banff Trail Northwest; tel: (403) 289-9800.* Conveniently located on the TransCanada Highway, has a superb recreation area with a rainforest theme.

Calgary Westways B&B $$ *216 25 Ave southwest; tel: (403) 229-1758.* A delightful downtown B&B located in a 1912 heritage home.

Carriage House Inn $$ *9030 Macleod Trail South; tel: (403) 253-1101.* Located close to Heritage Park, about a 10-minute drive from downtown.

Calgarians and visitors enjoy a variety of fine cuisine, cooked over an open fire or served on the finest linens. Flapjacks, buffalo burgers and Alberta beef are renowned but locals also enjoy dim sum, grilled tuna and New Zealand lamb.

Calgary Tower $$$ *101 9 Ave; tel: (403) 226-7171.* Has the best views of Calgary and the Rockies from atop the revolving Panorama Dining Room.

Inn on Lake Bonavista $$$ *747 Lake Bonavista Dr. southeast; tel: (403) 271-6711.* Overlooks a man-made lake where guests enjoy New Zealand lamb or grass-fed Alberta beef.

La Chaumière $$$ *139 17 Ave southwest; tel: (403) 228-5690.* One of Calgary's finest restaurants; choose a fine wine from the 11,000-bottle cellar to go with the caviar, seafood and Alberta beef.

Owl's Nest $$$ *Westin Hotel, 320 4 Ave southwest; tel: (403) 266-1611.* Has superb prime rib with Yorkshire pudding in the formal yet friendly dining room.

Conservatory $$ *Delta Bow Valley, 209 4 Ave southeast; tel: (403) 266-1980.* Has an outstanding chef's menu which changes weekly.

Joey Tomato's $$ *Eau Claire Market; tel: (403) 263-6336.* Is packed with good humour, from the Auntie Pasta sign over the kitchen to the Italian flag-wrapped pillars. **Eau Claire Market** *2 St and 2 Ave Southwest; tel: (403) 264-6460; web: www.eauclairemarket.com*

River Café $$ *Prince's Island Park; tel: (403) 261-7670.* Prepares organic and locally-grown ingredients such as Saskatchewan venison chops, Saskatoon berries and crispy risotto cakes.

Teatro $$ *200 8 Ave southeast; tel: (403) 290-1012.* Located downtown in a former bank building, the Italian cuisine prepared in a traditional wood-burning oven.

Lazy Loaf and Kettle $ *9001 130 9 Ave southeast; tel: 403-266-1002.* Has wonderful sandwiches and take-out picnic lunches.

Right
Old City Hall clocktower

Shopping

Competition and variety provide shoppers with good value.
overhead pedestrian walkway, Plus-15, connects over 600 sto
through 16km of downtown. Bankers Hall has three levels of special
stores and one-of-a-kind boutiques. Canadian Wilderness featu

Albertan- and Canadian-made souvenirs, clothing and native art. Alberta Boot Co. has the best selection of men's and women's cowboy boots, all made in Calgary. The Bay has the famous Hudson's Bay point blankets as well as international gift foods, cheeses and fashions. The Wine Cottage has an inviting atmosphere with an extensive selection of wine, scotch and speciality beer.

The *Eye Opener*

The hard-drinking, cigar-smoking editor of the *Eye Opener*, Robert Chambers Edwards, was one of Canada's most colourful newspaper men. With an unmatched reputation for his wit and scathing editorials, Bob Edwards's itinerant newspaper was published 'semi-occasionally' from 1902 until his death in 1922. Born in Edinburgh, the lampooning journalist waged war on big business, self-righteous individuals, and hard-line social institutions. The targets of his strong social conscience – politicians, politics and organised religion – were lambasted for their pomposity and pretension. He faced legal action when he called the three biggest liars in Alberta: 'Robert Edwards, Gentleman; Hon. A L Sifton (Premier); and Bob Edwards, Editor of the *Eye Opener*'. The suit was dropped when similar suits were filed on behalf of Robert Edwards and Bob Edwards. His favourite inspiration was the Alberta Hotel and its Long Bar, reputed to be the longest drinking beam between Winnipeg and Hong Kong.

ht
al in downtown Calgary

Suggested tour

Total distance: 55km.

Time: Allow 1.5 hours for driving, longer during rush hour, to drive the circuit, which cannot be reversed because of one-way streets.

Links: The TransCanada Highway (Hwy 1) runs from the Saskatchewan boundary to the east, and Banff to the west. The C&E Trail (Hwy 2) links with Calgary from the north and Macleod Trail (Hwy 2) from the south. Hwy 1A runs in a northeasterly direction toward Cochrane, then angles southwesterly to Canmore.

Route: Exit Tower Centre parkade near the **CALGARY TOWER ❶** onto 10 Ave southwest and go right for half a block. Turn right on 1 St southwest for one block and right again past Calgary Tower on 9 Ave southwest for three blocks. Go left onto Macleod Trail southeast, staying in the left lane. Turn left on 6 Ave southeast and go west 13 blocks. Go left on 11 St southwest one block to 7 Ave southwest and the right-hand entrance to the **CALGARY SCIENCE CENTRE ❷**.

Continue south on 11 St southwest. Go left on 9 Ave southwest, then turn right on 5 St southwest and go under an overpass. Turn right onto 17 Ave southwest, Uptown 17 Avenue, nine blocks of trendy eateries, coffee houses, galleries, bookstores and boutiques. Turn left on 24 St southwest. Two blocks beyond, 24 St southwest veers left into Crowchild Trail. Take the Flanders Ave turn to cross over Crowchild Trail. Go right on Arras Dr. following signs to the Museum of the Regiments.

Return to Crowchild Trail and continue south. Follow signs to go left on Glenmore Trail, crossing a short causeway over Glenmore Park Reservoir. Go right on 14 St southwest and look for the Canadian Pacific locomotive on the right at the entrance to **HERITAGE PARK ❸**.

Calgary Stampede

Billed as 'The Greatest Outdoor Show on Earth', the world-famous Calgary Exhibition and Stampede in July was born in 1912, instigated by an American trick roper, Guy Weadick, who envisioned a big rodeo in the heart of cattle country. Interrupted by the First World War, chuckwagon races were introduced a decade later, which now see 4-horse teams and four mounted outriders racing for more than $350,000 in prize money. But the biggest draws are the rugged saddlebronc and bull riding events, the cowboys competing for a purse of over $500,000. **Stampede Park** *tollfree (800) 661-1260; web: www.calgarystampede.com*

osite
ry Stampede,
wagon racing

Leave Heritage Park at Heritage Dr. turning right to go 4km south
14 St southwest. Turn left on Canyon Meadows Dr., which winds
around the northern side of Fish Creek Provincial Park, Cana
largest urban park. Turn right 2.5km on Bow Bottom Trail to
Valley Ranch. Return north 4km on Bow Bottom Trail to go left
on Anderson Road southeast. Turn right onto Macleod Trail and
7.5km north to the main entrance of Stampede Park.

Continue three blocks north on Macleod Trail, then turn right on
Ave southeast. **FORT CALGARY HISTORIC PARK** ❹ and
Interpretive Centre are three blocks east on 9 Ave southeast. Conti
east, crossing the Elbow River via the 9 Avenue Bridge, otherv
known as the 'Duck' Inglewood Bridge. Go right onto 8 St south
across the railway crossing, then turn right to go up 17 Ave south
to Scotman's Hill. Turn left onto Salisbury St for a panoramic viev
downtown highrise buildings, with the Elbow River below. Stamp
Park and the saddle-shaped Saddledome are below to the left.

Go around the block on Ramsay Dr. and return to 17 Ave southe
Go right, then turn left on 8 St southeast. Go right on 9 Ave south
to the shops and pleasant restaurants of the Inglewood District. T
left on 12 St southeast, crossing over two Bow River bridges to
CALGARY ZOO, BOTANICAL GARDEN and PREHISTORIC P
❺ .

Leave the zoo on Memorial Dr. West, continuing 3.5km tow
downtown. Take the exit for 4 Ave southeast into Chinatown, and
right on Centre St. Before reaching the imposing stone lions flan
the Centre Street Bridge, turn left onto 2 Ave southwest. Go right
St southwest for one block, then left onto Riverfront Ave southw
and left one block on 2 St southwest to Eau Claire Market.

Turn right onto 2 Ave southwest for one block. Barclay Parkade is
the right. Go left on winding 3 St southwest, south along the Bar
Mall. Turn left on 9 Ave southwest, passing a regal Canadian Pa
locomotive engine and the Fairmont Palliser Hotel on the right
return to Calgary Tower.

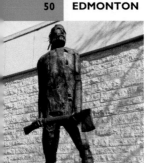

Edmonton

Ratings

Children	●●●●●
Entertainment	●●●●●
Food and drink	●●●●●
Historical sights	●●●●●
Museums	●●●●●
Outdoor activities	●●●●●
Scenery	●●●●●
Shopping	●●●●●

ⓘ **Edmonton Tourism Administration Office**
*9797 Jasper Ave northwest,
tel: (780) 426-4715 or 800-463-4667; web:
www.tourism.ede.org
Open Mon–Fri 0800–1700
year round.*

Opposite
Edmonton Space Centre

Edmonton spans a deep valley along the meanderi North Saskatchewan River. Overlooking the verda valley setting are a greenbelt of ravines and beautifu landscaped parks, golf courses and woodland trai highlighted by the majestic Alberta Legislature, the striki glass pyramids of the Muttart Conservatory, and the histo Fort Edmonton Park. The capital of the province a thriving oil capital of Canada, Edmonton is best known visitors as the home of the gargantuan West Edmonton Ma one of the biggest tourist draws in Canada. The abundar of water, timber and wildlife drew semi-nomadic hunte and gatherers here for several thousand years. Settleme occurred in 1795 when the Hudson's Bay Company and t North West Co. built a series of fortified trading posts, a Edmonton House, named after the English birthplace o Hudson's Bay Company clerk, became the most importa post in Western Canada.

Arriving and departing

By air: Edmonton International Airport, located 19km fr downtown, is Canada's fifth busiest airport, providing non-stop serv in summer from London and many points in Canada and the US. A $ airport-improvement fee is added to tickets for domestic a international flights originating in Edmonton. **Airport Shuttle Bus** has service to downtown, west end and University of Alberta; taxi $$ downtown is about a 30-minute drive, depending on traff Independently operated **Sky Shuttle $$** to Fantasyland Hotel at West Edmonton Mall, located on the first floor of the airport, runs ev 45 minutes weekdays and hourly on weekends. Courtesy shuttles also available to many hotels. Conveniently located in the heart Edmonton, **City Centre Airport** (locals fondly call it the 'Muni'), *(780) 477-1992*, is a hub for regional carriers providing service to sma centres in Alberta, Saskatchewan and the Northwest Territories. M passenger services use the Esso Aveitat Passenger Lounge.

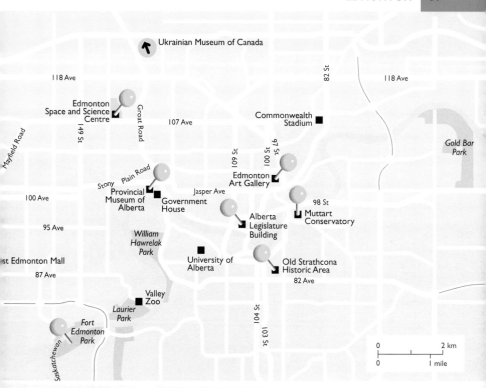

Ukrainian Museum of Canada

118 Ave

82 St

118 Ave

Edmonton
Space and Science
Centre

Groat Road

149 St

107 Ave

Commonwealth
Stadium

Gold Bar
Park

Mayfield Road

Stony   Plain Road

Provincial
Museum of
Alberta

Government
House

Jasper Ave

97 St

100 St

106 St

Edmonton
Art Gallery

98 St

Muttart
Conservatory

100 Ave

Alberta
Legislature
Building

95 Ave

William
Hawrelak
Park

st Edmonton Mall

87 Ave

University of
Alberta

Old Strathcona
Historic Area

82 Ave

104 St

103 St

Valley
Zoo

Laurier
Park

Fort
Edmonton
Park

Saskatchewan

0   2 km

0   1 mile

ⓘ Edmonton Tourism Visitor Information Centre
2404 Gateway Blvd (formerly Calgary Trail); tel: (780) 496-8400, tollfree (800) 463-4667. Open May–Sept daily 0800–2100; Oct–Apr Mon–Fri 0830–1630, Sat–Sun 0900–1700.

🛫 Edmonton International Airport Information Booths *Arrivals Level, North and South Terminals; tel: (780) 890-8382. Open Mon–Fri 0730–2400, Sat 1200–2400, Sun 0900–2400 year round.*

VIA Rail *12360 121 St; tollfree (800) 561-8630; web: viarail.ca*
Provides national rail service. The transcontinental 'Canadian' provides service three times a week to Toronto, Jasper and Vancouver.

Greyhound Canada
10324 103 St; tel: (780) 413-8747, tollfree (800) 661-874; web: www.greyhound.ca
Has service to numerous points in Alberta and British Columbia. Canada's largest inter-city bus company, Greyhound also operates motorcoach charters.

Red Arrow Motorcoach
Howard Johnson Motel, 10014 104 St, tollfree (800) 232-1958; web: www.redarrow.pwt.ca
Offers a de luxe, daily express service between Calgary, Red Deer, Edmonton and Fort McMurray, offering complimentary snacks, fold-down work tables and computer plug-ins.

By car: Highway access is Hwy 16 (Yellowhead Highway) from east and west, and Hwy 2 (Calgary Trail and Gateway Blvd Edmonton) from the north and south.

Getting around

**Downtown Info
Centre** Central LRT
ɔn, Street Level, 100A St
lasper Ave; tel: (780)
1600. Open Mon–Fri
ⁱ–1700 for tickets,
es and route maps.

  route information
780) 496-1611, is
ɔble Mon–Fri
ⁱ–2230, Sat
ⁱ–1800, Sun
ⁱ–1730.

**Edmonton Art
Gallery** $ 2 Sir
ston Churchill Square;
780) 422-6223. Open
–Fri 1030–1700, Thur
2000; Sat–Sun
0–1700; closed public
lays.

nonton Space and
ɔnce Centre** $
11 142 St; tel: (780)
-3344. Open Tue–Sun
ⁱ–1800, closed Mon
Christmas Day.

t Edmonton Park
x Dr. and Whitemud
el: (780) 496-7381.
n May–June Mon–Fri
0–1600, Sat–Sun
0–1800; July–Aug,
1000–1800.

Public transport

A quick, easy and inexpensive option throughout the city is Edmonton Transit Service (ETS). LRT (light rail transit), trolleys and buses cover Edmonton but not the airport. Billed as a trip across the world's highest streetcar bridge, **High Level Streetcar**, tel: (780) 437-7721, follows a 2.5km route across the old CPR rail line from Old Strathcona across the High Level Bridge to the Grandin LRT Station, adjacent to the Legislature Building.

Sights

Edmonton Art Gallery**

The gallery with an open central stairway contains an extensive, high-quality collection of works of art by regional, national and international artists. The Children's Gallery contains interactive exhibits. There is also a delightful coffee bar and gallery shop.

Edmonton Space and Science Centre***

The largest planetarium in Canada, the complex contains an IMAX theatre, interactive exhibits, an observatory, the Dow Computer lab, a ham radio station, and Environment, Forensics and Health galleries.

Fort Edmonton Park***

A reconstruction of the fur trading fort, Fort Edmonton Park is set in a ravine of the North Saskatchewan River. The vast living history museum is an adventure through four time periods. Guides in period costume recreate the atmosphere and perform the daily duties of the early days. Nostalgic steam train and street car rides are included in the price of admission.

Legislature Building**

Alberta's foremost historic structure, the stately, domed Legislature Building has a prominent setting on the verdant banks of the North Saskatchewan River. The yellow sandstone building is graced with beautifully landscaped grounds in summer, and a huge skating rink in winter. Opened in 1912 on the site of the original Fort Edmonton, the building contains a portrait of Princess Louise Caroline Alberta, daughter of Queen Victoria and wife of the Governor-General of Canada 1878–83, after whom the province is named.

Muttart Conservatory***

Four spectacular glass pyramids contain some 700 species of plants and flowers collected from around the world. Explore a steaming ′ jungle, trek across a sun-baked desert, and stroll through the scents of

osite
son's Bay Company fort

**Legislature
Building** 10800 97
; tel: (780) 427-7362;
: assembly.ab.ca
en May–Oct, Mon–Fri
30–1700, Sat, Sun and
lic holidays 0900–1700,
rs on the hour
)0–1200, every half hour
30–1600; Oct–Apr,
n–Fri 0900–1630, Sat,
 and public holidays
)0–1700; tours on the
r 0900–1200, on the
 hour from 1200–1600.

ttart **Conservatory**
626 96A St; tel: (780)
6-8755. Open Mon–Fri
)0–1800, Sat, Sun and
lic holidays 1100–1800,
sed Christmas Day.

d **Strathcona
storic Area $**
4th St and Whyte (82nd)
; Old Strathcona
ndation; tel: (780) 433-
56 for information. Open
y.

a floral paradise. One-hour guided tours for groups should be booked two weeks in advance. Refreshments, light lunches and after-hour visits are available.

Old Strathcona Historic Area***

Restored houses and shops line Whyte Ave (82nd) and 104th St on the south side of the river, the early town of Strathcona before it was amalgamated with Edmonton in 1912. Wide streets and low buildings give it an Old West atmosphere, a good place to walk around and browse through the museums, theatres, restaurants and Saturday farmers' market.

ht
 Strathcona shops

posite
ttart Conservatory

**Provincial Museum
of Alberta** $ 12845
102 Ave; tel: (780) 453-
9100. Open weekdays
0900–2100, weekends
0900–1700, closed
Christmas Day and Boxing
Day.

**Ukrainian Museum of
Canada** 10611 110 Ave;
tel: (780) 483-5932. Open
May–Aug Mon–Fri
0830–1630, Sun and
Sept–Apr by appointment
only.

Provincial Museum of Alberta❖❖❖

Highlight of the museum is the stunning Syncrude Gallery
Aboriginal Culture which showcases native artefacts in North Ameri
Other galleries include Habitat and Natural History, and the live F
Room. Tour menus are available for breaks, lunch and dinner in
restaurant.

Ukrainian Museum of Canada❖❖

Edmonton's rich Ukrainian heritage is celebrated with displays
colourful costumes, dolls, tapestries, paintings and Easter eggs.

st Edmonton Mall
2 170 St; tel: (780) 444-
0. Open daily. Individual
action's hours vary; call
nformation.

West Edmonton Mall✧✧✧

Billed by the *Guinness Book of Records* as the world's largest indoor playground and shopping complex, the West Edmonton Mall is a destination in itself. Alberta's No 1 destination has over 800 retail stores, 100 eating establishments, and such varied attractions as World Waterpark, the high-tech Playdium and a replica of Christopher Columbus's *Santa Maria*.

Accommodation and food

Edmonton has variety of accommodation, from budget to de luxe. Most hotels can be booked through Edmonton Reservations: *tel: (780) 464-3515, tollfree (800) 884-8803; web: www.edmontonreservations.com*

Fairmont Hotel Macdonald $$$ *10065 100 St; tel: (780) 424-5181.* Edmonton's foremost hotel with sweeping views of the North Saskatchewan River valley.

Fantasyland Hotel $$$ *17700 87th Ave; tel: (780) 444-3000.* Part of the West Edmonton Mall and has regular and theme rooms such as Polynesian, Victorian and Roman.

Union Bank Inn $$$ *10053 Jasper Ave; tel: (780) 423-3600.* Has an art deco look, located in the heart of downtown Edmonton in a restored bank building.

Glenora B&B Inn $$ *12327 102 Ave; tel: (780) 488-6766.* Has full breakfast, and is located in a historic building near the Provincial Museum of Alberta.

Edmonton is a multicultural city and its culinary expertise shines at the 1700 restaurants, offering traditional fare to Ukrainian and Russian delicacies.

The Crêperie $$$ *10220 103 St; tel: (780) 420-6656.* Has a cosy, romantic ambience. Located in downtown Edmonton, The Crêperie is widely regarded as the best French restaurant in the city.

Bourbon Street $$ *West Edmonton Mall.* Has a collection of restaurants in a New Orleans atmosphere such as Albert's (Montreal-smoked meat), Hooters (scantily-clad waitresses), and Sherlock Holmes (great selection of imported beer).

Century Grill $$ *3975 Calgary Trail; tel: (780) 431-0303.* Features Canadian dishes such as rack of lamb, herb roasted chicken and fine Alberta beef.

Unheardof Restaurant $$ *9602 82nd Ave; tel: (780) 432-0480.* Located in an old house in Old Strathcona. This popular eatery (the owner's name is 'Heard') is noted for its 5-course *prix-fixe* (fixed price) dinners.

Vue Weekly
307, 10080 Jasper Ave;
tel: (780) 426-1996, and
See Magazine *222, 8625*
109 St; tel: (780) 430-9003,
are free distribution
publications which provide
information on local
events, cultural attractions,
performances, cinemas and
other happenings.

The Front Page
10356 Jasper Ave; tel:
780-426-1206, for books,
magazines and newspapers:
carries an extensive
selection at its downtown
location.

Gourmet Goodies
10665 109 St; tel: (780)
438-1234, for picnic
lunches to go.

**Wine and Spirits
Warehouse – Cost Plus**
11452 Jasper Ave; tel: (780)
488-7973, for wine and
spirits.

Shopping

Edmonton has a variety of shopping centres such as the downtc
Eaton Centre, Edmonton Centre and ManuLife Place, all connected
tunnels above and below, and street-level pedways. Over 800 stc
and services are tucked into the huge West Edmonton Mall. Boutiq
restaurants and the Saturday farmers' market line Old Strathcona.

Suggested tour

Total distance: 53km.

Time: Allow 1.5 hours to drive the circuit, longer during rush h
which limits the route to the direction indicated because of the o
way streets.

Links: The Yellowhead Highway (Hwy 16) links with Edmonton fr
the Saskatchewan boundary to the east and Jasper to the west.
C&E Trail (Hwy 2) connects from the north and south. 1
Poundmaker Trail (Hwy 14) runs in a southeasterly direction
Wainwright and the Saskatchewan boundary

Route: Begin at the Edmonton Tourism Visitor Information Cen
9797 Jasper Ave northwest. Turn left onto 97 St and continue to 1(
Ave and turn left again, heading west. **EDMONTON ART GALLF**
❶ is on the right. To the right on 99 St, also called Rue Hull, is (
Hall's fountain/winter ice rink, pyramid and carillon. Turn left at
St and cross Jasper Ave; the landmark Hotel Macdonald is on the lef

Continue down McDougall Hill and over the Low Level Brid
following signs for the **MUTTART CONSERVATORY** ❷ via east
Ave through a circular spaghetti maze of roads, then turn right on S
St. Go east on 97 Ave, turn right onto Cloverdale Rd, and at the
turn right onto Connors Rd. Go right on 85 St to Whyte (82nd Ave
OLD STRATHCONA HISTORIC AREA ❸, a delightful place to get
and wander.

Continue along Whyte (82nd Ave) and follow the sign for the 114
exit then turn at 71 Ave/Belgravia Rd and veer right onto Fox Dr. T
right onto Fort Edmonton Park Rd to the reconstructed **FO**
EDMONTON PARK ❹. Leave Fort Edmonton Park and retrace
route to 71 Ave/Belgravia Rd. Half-way around the traffic circ
continue east on 72 Ave. Turn left on 111 St, go right one-half bl
on University Ave, then left on 110 St. Turn left onto Saskatchew
Dr. Rutherford House Provincial House is on the left, with
handsome University of Alberta campus ahead.

Opposite
Alberta's Legislature Building

Go left onto 111 St then to 87 Ave, left on 109 St. Take a sharp rig
onto Saskatchewan Dr. East. Just beyond the Strathcona Informati
Caboose turn left onto Queen Elizabeth Dr. and cross Walterdale I
and turn left onto the 105 Street Bridge, veer right onto 103 St. Go I
on 97 Ave, left again on 106 St, then right on 96 Ave and right on F
Way Dr. to the lovely and picturesque **LEGISLATURE BUILDING ❺**

Take Fort Way Dr. around the legislature grounds through t
gracious park. Fort Way Dr. becomes 107 St as it turns north. T
striking pillars and modern architecture of Grant MacEw
Community College are straight ahead. Drive on Jasper Ave to 1
Street, turning right to browse nine blocks of art galleries. Go left
111 Ave to 142 St and the **EDMONTON SPACE AND SCIEN**
CENTRE ❻.

Continue west of 111 Ave as it becomes Mayfield Rd. Go south at 1
St to the **WEST EDMONTON MALL** (WEM) ❼. Exit WEM and go
87 Ave, then left on 149 St and right to Stony Plain Rd which tu
into 102 Ave. The **PROVINCIAL MUSEUM OF ALBERTA ❽** is on t
right. Continue on 102 Ave, crossing over Groat Rd, then right to 1
St to follow Jasper Ave left to Downtown Edmonton and the Visi
Information Centre.

Also worth exploring

Drive 45km east of Edmonton on the Yellowhead Highway (Hwy 1
to Elk Island National Park. A popular day trip from Edmonton, t
Elk Island was established as Canada's first animal sanctuary in 19€
home to prairie elk, plains bison, and the larger yet rarer wood bis
The **South Gate Visitor Centre**, *tel: (780) 922-5833*, is open da
May–Oct. Three kilometres farther east on Hwy 16 is the **Ukraini**
Cultural Heritage Village, *tel: (780) 662-3640. Open May–A*
1000–1800, Sept–Oct 1000–1600.

Gateway to the North

Edmonton is frequently called the 'Gateway to the North' because of its
northerly location. Occupying the same latitude as Liverpool, Edmonton
was first settled by the Hudson's Bay Company and North West Co. in
1795 as Fort Edmonton, yet it was more than a century before Edmonton
was incorporated as a city in 1904.

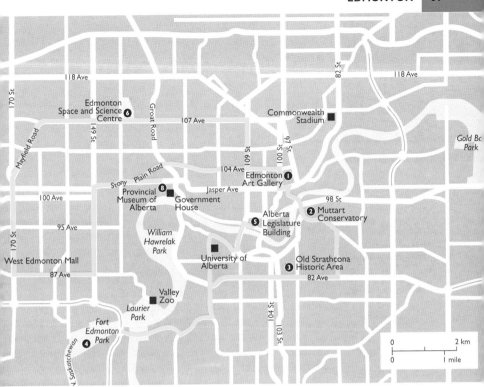

Edmonton takes flight

Edmonton has had a long association with aviation. Dating from 1910 when Hugh Robinson flew a Curtis Flyer to the Edmonton Exhibition, the legendary Wilfred 'Wop' May gets credit for ushering in the era when he introduced mail delivery service and flying passengers in 1919. Wop and his brother Court formed May Airplanes Ltd, which led to Canadian Pacific Airlines. Edmonton became a vibrant centre of aviation and earned its nickname 'Gateway to the North' when bush pilots such as C H 'Punch' Dickins, Grant McConachie and 'Wop' May flew prospectors, mail and supplies into the far north. As traffic increased, a larger airfield was needed so the municipal airport site (now City Centre Airport) was established in 1926. During the Second World War, the 'Muni' was a crucial link in the war effort, chosen for the No 2 Air Observer School (British Commonwealth Air Training Plan). As Edmonton grew, there was considerable controversy about whether to save the airport or move all flights to the Edmonton International Airport south of the city. With the creation of the privatised Edmonton Airports Authority, the City Centre Airport became the hub for regional flights.

Calgary–Edmonton Trail

Ratings

Children	●●●●●
History	●●●●●
Museums	●●●●●
Towns	●●●●●
Food and drink	●●●●○
Outdoor activities	●●●●○
Parks	●●●●○
Historical sights	●●●○○

Linking Alberta's major cities, the Calgary–Edmonton Trail is an easy morning drive across broad plains, over rolling hills and through the verdant city of Red Deer. A vital transportation route since the 19th century, the Calgary–Edmonton Trail was surveyed after the Canadian Pacific Railway reached Calgary. At first little more than a worn pathway used by wagons and Red River carts which connected the North West Mounted Police post in Calgary and the fur trading centre of Edmonton, many motorists now refer to the busy highway as Alberta's autobahn. A stopover point for Scottish settlers, Red Deer is the midway point and beginning of the David Thompson Highway, a less travelled yet no less picturesque route to the Rocky Mountains at the southern end of Jasper National Park. A side trip to Devon describes Leduc No 1, which ushered in Alberta's oil industry and age of prosperity.

ALBERTA HERITAGE EXPOSITION PARK❖❖

Alberta Heritage Exposition Park $
5km west of Leduc on Hwy 39; tel: (780) 986-4037. Open year round, summer 1000–1700. Appointments recommended off-season.

The 32ha site contains restored historic buildings which house artefacts and private collections. The 400-member Leduc West Antique Society began as an antique tractor club, and has expanded to include collectables and antiques associated with Western Canada.

CANADIAN PETROLEUM INTERPRETIVE CENTRE❖❖

Canadian Petroleum Interpretive Centre $
12km west of Hwy 2 on Hwy 19, 2km south of Devon; tel: (780) 987-4323. Open May–Sept, daily 1000–1800.

Situated on the site of the well which ushered in Alberta's oil era, the Canadian Petroleum Interpretive Centre salutes the spirit, resolve and success of the Alberta oil patch. Owned and operated by the Leduc/Devon Oil Field Historical Society, the towering 53m conventional oil derrick adjacent to the Interpretive Centre is a replica of the original that tapped into the huge Leduc oilfield (*see page 69*).

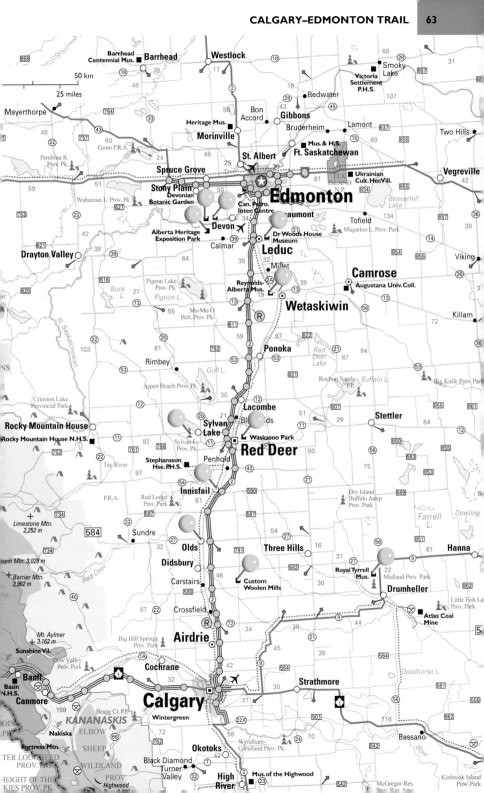

Other outside displays include oilfield equipment, a field battery, four types of full-scale drilling rigs. Videos, guides and drilling equipment tell the story of the oil industry.

Right
Canadian Petroleum
Interpretive Centre

Opposite
Horseshoe Canyon

CUSTOM WOOLEN MILLS LTD**

Custom Woolen Mills Ltd
20km northeast of Carstairs on Hwy 791; tel: (403) 337-2221. Open Mon–Fri 0800–1700.

Demonstrations give visitors an opportunity to see early w processing. The Wool Shoppe sells finished yarns, knitting and w craft supplies. Carding machinery in use was made between 1860 1910, the spinning mule dates from 1910 and the knotting machin circa 1917.

DEVONIAN BOTANIC GARDEN***

Devonian Botanic Garden $ *12km west of Hwy 2 on Hwy 19, 5km north of Devon on Hwy 60; tel: (780) 987-3054. Open year round: Apr–Sept 1000–1900, Sept–Oct 1000–1600, Oct–Apr weekends only 1100–1600.*

A tropical garden in the prairies, Devonian Botanic Garden is hom a collection of exotic orchids, free-flying butterflies and a succu greenhouse. The Kurimoto Japanese garden is set in a pictures landscape and peaceful atmosphere. Operated by the University Alberta, the Garden is home to their microfungus collection, sec largest in Canada. Spread over a 77ha site, the Garden is a deligh setting for picnics and bird watching. There is a berry patch wl visitors may pick and taste the fruit, and a gift shop and restaurant.

R GEORGE HOUSE PROVINCIAL HISTORIC SITE❖

Dr George House Provincial Historic ❧ $ 5713 51 Ave, ·fail; tel: (403) 227- ʼ. Open late May–Aug, ⅰ–Fri 1000–1630.

Built in 1893 by Innisfail's original physician, the red brick house combines a natural history museum and offices. Though Dr Henry George and his wife, an artist who designed the Alberta provincial crest, later moved to Red Deer, the doctor was a collector and had established the first museum in the then Northwest Territories.

R WOODS HOUSE MUSEUM❖❖

Dr Woods House Museum $ 4801 49 Leduc; tel: (780) 986- 7. Open year round: —Aug 1100–1700; ⅰr Tue, Thu, Sun 0–1600.

The home of pioneer physician Dr Robert Woods and his family, the Craftsman bungalow contains his medical wing and attached garage as it was in the 1920s. There is a collection of photographs, textiles and archival material. A registered historic site, the attached garage contains a tea room.

INNISFAIL HISTORICAL VILLAGE MUSEUM*

Innisfail Historical Village Museum $
52 Ave and 42 St, Innisfail; tel: (403) 227-2906. Open mid-May–Labour Day, Tue–Sun 1100–1730 and holiday Mons.

Hudson's Bay Company scout, Anthony Henday, with Cree gui spotted the Rockies from nearby Mud Creek in 1754. The 1886 Spru log building, the only extant Stopping House between Calgary Edmonton, is one of the 13 historic buildings encompassed by Innisfail Historical Village Museum.

OLDS COLLEGE**

Olds College Hwy 2A and Hwy 27, Olds; tel: (403) 556-8330. Open year round, Mon–Fri 0900–1700. Farm buildings off-limits without permission.

Known for innovative agricultural development, Olds College beautiful flower beds and botanical gardens along with fruit trees specimens of trees grown in Alberta. The 700ha campus and farm has greenhouses, a natural fibre centre and an alpaca farm, offerin limited number of sweaters and blankets for sale.

REYNOLDS–ALBERTA MUSEUM***

Reynolds–Alberta Museum $ 2km west of Wetaskawin on Hwy 13; tel: (780) 361-1351. Open year round: Victoria Day–30 June, daily 0900–1700; 1July–Labour Day 0900–1900; Labour Day–Victoria Day, Tue–Sun 0900–1700; open holiday Mons; closed Christmas Day and Easter Sunday.

The Reynolds–Alberta Museum contains some 60 vintage aircraft, restored vehicles, and 1000 pieces of ageing agricultural and indust equipment. Cruise the grounds in a pristine 1935 Chevrolet or soa a glorious open cockpit biplane. The Exhibition Hall conta artefacts, audio-visual presentations and guided tours. Self-guided interpreter-led tours.

RCMP POLICE DOG SERVICE TRAINING CENTRE**

RCMP Police Dog Service Training Centre 4km south of Innisfail on Hwy 2; tel: (403) 227-3346. Open year round, phone ahead for tours; demonstrations late May–Labour Day, Wed 1330.

The national dog training centre for the Royal Canadian Moun Police, the centre conducts tours and demonstrations, though sho be booked in advance. About 20 German Shepherd and Labra retriever dogs and their masters at any one time are undergo training at the centre. Most of the dogs are now imported fr Europe.

OYAL TYRRELL MUSEUM OF PALAEONTOLOGY✦✦✦

Royal Tyrrell Museum of aeontology *6km hwest of downtown rnheller; tel: (403) 823- 7. Open daily, Victoria –Labour Day 0–2100, Labour –Thanksgiving 0–1700; mid-Oct–mid- Tue–Sun 1000–1700.*

ιw al Tyrrell Museum of eontology dino

A world-class exhibition, museum and research facility, the Royal Tyrrell Museum of Palaeontology is the only museum in Canada dedicated to the study and display of prehistoric life. Some 800 fossil specimens and over 50 dramatically exhibited dinosaur skeletons take visitors through 4.5 billion years of the earth's history. At least three hours are recommended for a visit. If you are a die-hard Lost World explorer, spend a week working in the field with palaeontologists during the summer in the richest dinosaur burial grounds in the world. Situated in the barren badlands of Midland Provincial Park, the lunar-like region was a marshland with a semi-tropical climate similar to the Florida Everglades when dinosaurs roamed the valley of the Red Deer River.

LVAN LAKE PROVINCIAL PARK✦✦✦

Sylvan Lake Provincial Park $ *m west of Red Deer; tel: 3) 340-5142. Townsite n year round, park ʋities May–Oct.*

One of Alberta's favourite summer resorts, Sylvan Lake Provincial Park is busy on weekends when the sun shines, the throngs of visitors attracted to the golf course, golden beaches and the enormous Wild Rapids Water Slide. Home of the only functioning lighthouse between Winnipeg and the West Coast, water activities include fishing, boating and windsurfing.

WASKASOO PARK✦✦✦

Waskasoo Park
entrance at Heritage
Ranch, Red Deer; tel: (403)
342-8259; web:
www.city.red-deer.ab.ca
Open year round.

**Kerry Wood Nature
Centre**
6300 45th Ave, Red Deer;
tel: (403) 346-2010. Open
year round.

**Fort Normandeau
Historic Site and
Interpretive Centre $**
west of Hwy 2 on 32nd St,
Red Deer. Open May–Sept.

Spanning 11km along the Red Deer River through the centre of
city of Red Deer, the expansive park was made to preserve a
enhance the natural open space while incorporating develop
facilities. Among the attractions are Heritage Ranch, the **Kerry Wo
Nature Centre,**✦✦ Gaetz Lakes Sanctuary, the Victorian-style Cronqu
House and **Fort Normandeau Interpretive Centre,**✦✦ a reconstruct
of a North West Mounted Police fort. The park provides some 80km
bicycle, pedestrian and equestrian trails.

Accommodation and food

Most of the motels, hotels and B&Bs are moderately priced, reflect
their modest furnishings. Prices are generally are higher in summ
and on weekdays. Book in advance for accommodations in Red Dee
convention and conference centre.

Donkey's Den B&B $$ 2km northwest of Red Deer. Open Apr–Oct;
(403) 347-3577. A log cabin that sleeps up to four and raises donk
on the large acreage.

Red Deer Lodge $$ 4311 49 Ave, Red Deer; tel: (403) 346-8841. Larg
motel in the city; on the edge of downtown.

Rosebud Country Inn $$ 320 north Railway Ave east, Rosebud; tel: (4
823-6495. A cosy inn near Rosebud Theatre, about a 20-minute dr
southwest of Drumheller.

Aladdin Motor Inn $ 7444 Gaetz Ave, Red Deer; tel: (403) 343-2711.
North Hill; has a lounge and the China Bens Restaurant in the plaza

Golden Rod B&B $ 14km west of Airdrie; tel: (403) 948-5341. A work
cattle ranch.

Graham's Beachfront Resort $ 4505 Lakeshore Dr., Sylvan Lake;
(403) 887-2407. Has an outdoor hot tub.

Karriage House B&B $ 5215 47 St, Wetaskawin; tel: (780) 352-5996.
early 19th-century house with adjacent cottage, decorated in per
furnishings.

Voyageur Inn $ Hwy 11, Rocky Mountain House; tel: (403) 845-33
Kitchenettes with microwaves and coffee makers.

Shauney's $$ 4909 48 St, Red Deer; tel: (403) 342-2404. A comforta
dining room which features such exotic fare as bison and ostrich.

Stavros Family Fare $$ 1102A Hwy 9, Drumheller; tel: (403) 823-63
A wide range of Greek, Italian and Canadian fare.

Joey's Only and Tennessee Jack's $ *4 5220 Lakeshore Dr., Sylvan Lake; tel: (403) 887-2788.* Has great ribs and a patio with a view of the lake.

MacEachern Tea House $ *4719 50 Ave, Wetaskawin; tel: (780) 352-8308; open 0930–1630.* Has outstanding cheesecake.

Wildflower Bistro $ *1927 Gaetz Ave, Red Deer; tel: (403) 341-5400.* Has fast-food Chinese, Italian and Greek cuisine.

Dr Joseph Burr Tyrrell

A geologist with the Geological Survey of Canada 1881–98, Joseph Burr Tyrrell is widely recognised as the dean of Canadian mining. After exploring the Northwest Territories, Tyrrell discovered the extensive coal beds at Fernie in BC and at Drumheller. But it was a 70 million-year-old fossilised dinosaur skull, christened Albertosaurus, that attracted world-wide interest. Found in 1884 in the rich dinosaur beds of the Drumheller Valley, the cousin of the fierce, meat-eating T-Rex was the first of hundreds of complete dinosaur skeletons removed from the Badlands. A cartographer, explorer, geologist and mining consultant, Tyrrell later took over a faltering gold mine at Kirkland Lake, Ontario, which kept producing well after his death in 1957. Namesake of the Tyrrell Museum of Palaeontology which opened in 1985; Queen Elizabeth II granted the 'Royal' appellation in 1990.

Leduc No 1

After drilling 133 dry holes in Alberta and Saskatchewan, Imperial Oil was about to give up but decided to drill another line of wildcat wells across Alberta. The first of the wells was on a farm 15km west of Leduc and 50km south of Edmonton. Three months after drilling 1544m, the company was confident that the hole would be a gusher. On a cold winter day on 13 February 1947, Imperial Oil invited businessmen, dignitaries and government officials to the site. As luck would have it, equipment failures the night before delayed the ceremony for hours. Sure enough, drillers hit paydirt at 1600 hours as the drilling mud blew out of the hole, the guests treated to a spectacular sight of towering columns of smoke and fire flaring across the darkening sky. While the oil industry had long been established in the Turner Valley south of Calgary, Leduc No 1 was the big one that ushered in Alberta's booming oil industry.

Suggested tour

Total distance: 300km.

Time: 3 hours to drive, 2–3 days to explore.

Links: The Yellowhead Highway (Hwy 16) links with Edmonton *(see page 50)*, the TransCanada Highway (Hwy 1) with Calgary *(see page 38)*, the David Thompson Highway (Hwy 11) connects with Red Deer, and Hwys 72 and 9 continue east to Drumheller.

Route: From Calgary, take the Deerfoot Trail (Hwy 2) north. The divided highway bypasses Calgary International Airport on the right and continues through barren rangeland to Airdrie, a one-time railway depot and now a booming dormitory community for Calgary. Continue north and take the Hwy 581 exit to the right, then left on Hwy 791 to **CUSTOM WOOLEN MILLS ❶** where workers demonstrate wool processing with ancient machines and sell finished yarns, knitting and wool craft supplies.

Return to Hwy 2 and head north to Olds on the west side on Hwy 2A, predecessor to the original Calgary–Edmonton Trail. **OLDS COLLEGE ❷** trains some 1 300 students in innovative agricultural development, and provides a delightful setting for a leisurely stroll through the flower beds, gardens and greenhouse. Return to Hwy 2 and continue north to the **RCMP POLICE DOG SERVICE TRAINING CENTRE ❸**, 4km south of Innisfail, where dogs imported from Europe are trained with their masters for active duty across Canada.

Back on Hwy 2, the highway angles right toward **Red Deer ❹** and the midway point. Founded in 1882 by Scottish settlers as a stopover point for travellers, Red Deer is the commercial hub for the rolling parkland district of central Alberta. It is also the junction of the David Thompson Highway, a less travelled though no less scenic route to the Rocky Mountains. Hwy 11A is an access road to one of Alberta's most popular summer resorts, **SYLVAN LAKE ❺**, which also connects with Hwy 11 to Rocky Mountain House and Saskatchewan River Crossing.

Hwy 2 continues in a northerly direction through rolling parkland, the divided highway bypassing several small communities such as Lacombe, named after the famous priest and diplomat Father Albert Lacombe, and Ponoka, which means 'elk' in the Blackfoot language. Turn right at the junction of Hwy 13 to Wetaskawin, home of the **REYNOLDS–ALBERTA MUSEUM ❻**, a provincial heritage collection of machinery, aircraft and transportation-related gadgets from the 1890–1950 era. Continue north on Hwy 2A to the city of Leduc, home of the **DR WOODS HOUSE MUSEUM ❼**, the pioneer living quarters and doctor's office in a Craftsman bungalow.

Above
Riding the C&E Trail

Return to Hwy 2 and continue north past Edmonton Internatio
Airport on the left, then exit onto the Hwy 19 turnoff and head w
to the town of Devon, home of the **DEVONIAN BOTANIC GARD**
❽ , **CANADIAN PETROLEUM INTERPRETIVE CENTRE ❾** a
ALBERTA HERITAGE EXPOSITION PARK ❿ . Return to Hwy 2, a
continue on into the city of Edmonton *(see pages, 50–61)*.

Also worth exploring

Some 800 fossil specimens and over 50 dramatically exhibi
dinosaur skeletons take a visitor through 4.5 billion years of
earth's history at the Royal Tyrrell Museum of Palaeontology
Drumheller *(see pages 67 and 69)*. The research centre studies all for
of ancient life, including the Burgess Shale exhibit which provide
3-D look at the unusual creatures that swam in prehistoric waters. T
museum's theme, 'A Celebration of Life', explores the origin of life
the 11,200 sq m facility which also contains an auditorium, cafete
gift shop and bookstore.

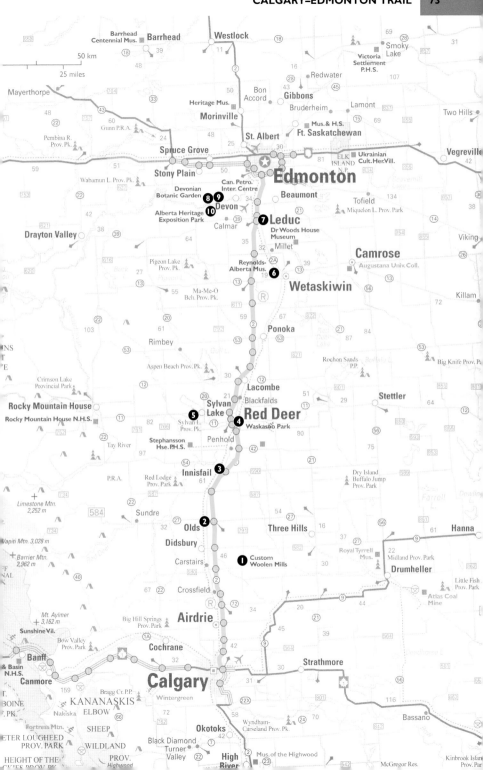

Cowboy Trail

Ratings

Foothills	●●●●●
History	●●●●●
Scenery	●●●●●
Walking	●●●●●
Wildlife	●●●●●
Children	●●●●○
Towns	●●●●○
Food and drink	●●○○○

A lberta's historic Cowboy Trail links the fur-trading p of Rocky Mountain House, the rolling prairie of t foothills and the icy peaks of the Waterton Lakes Natio Park. This north–south highway is home to sprawli ranches, spectacular vistas and friendly towns whe cowboys resplendent in high heels and magnificent sil belt buckles tip their ten-gallon hats and greet strangers w a smile. Along the way you will see the gentlemen of t range herding cattle, graceful quarter horses running f and native dancers performing at a colourful powwo Wildlife is abundant and it is not uncommon to see bea wolves, cougars, elk, moose and deer roaming freely in th natural habitat. The Cowboy Trail crosses cold mounta rivers and streams where fly fishermen test their skills, a leads to country inns, rustic lodges and stunning scenery favourite setting for many Hollywood movies.

BRAGG CREEK❖❖

A funky village full of artisans, Bragg Creek is a pleasant commur for a picnic, hiking and horseback riding as well as shopping Western arts and crafts, sampling cowboy cuisine and taking i native dinner theatre. A dormitory community with many you residents, Bragg Creek dates from 1914 when the first post off opened, the mail carried on horseback along the Stoney Trail. Wh the first settlers arrived in 1885, Bragg Creek was an open meadow contrast to the heavy forests of aspen, fir, poplar and spruce. Seve ranches are tended by descendants of the early settlers yet most w live on the acreages now are young, recent arrivals who work Calgary but prefer to live in these picturesque foothills.

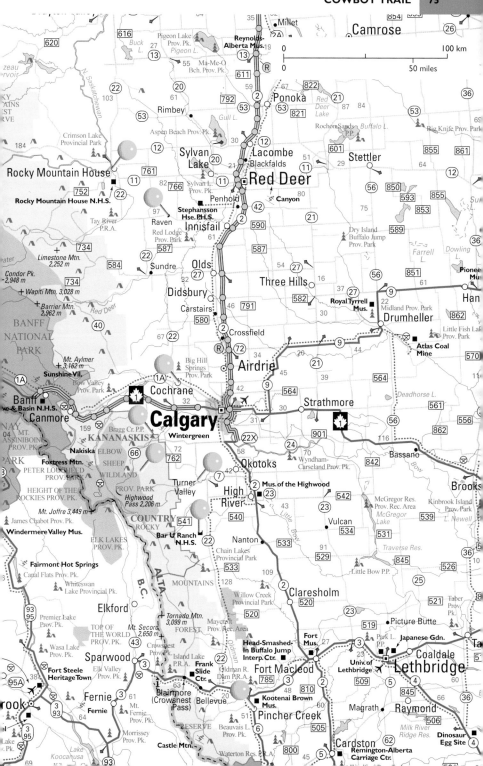

BAR U RANCH NATIONAL HISTORIC SITE✧✧

🏛 Bar U Ranch National Historic Site $
13km south of Longview on Hwy 22; tel: (403) 395-2212, tollfree (800) 568-4996. Open mid-May–mid-Oct, daily 1000–1800.

Once one of the leading ranches in Canada, the Bar U Ranch ⩗ named after its brand by the North West Cattle Co. syndicate. Dat from 1882, the ranch earned international repute as a centre breeding excellence for cattle and purebred Percheron draft hor The Bar U remained one of the largest ranches in the country u⩗ 1950, when land was sold to other ranchers from the estate of millionaire meatpacker Patrick Burns, one of the 'Big Four' ⩗ helped launch the Calgary Stampede. The Bar U's buildings spr⩗ over rangeland near Pekisco Creek, a riparian area favoured by wa⩗ (elk), moose and beavers. The Rocky Mountains provide a dram⩗ backdrop due west. Costumed interpreters lead guided tours thro⩗ the 35 ranch buildings. The Visitor Centre has ranching exhibits an⩗ video of Bar U history. The Roadhouse Restaurant serves ranch-st⩗ food, while the General Store sells local arts and crafts.

KANANASKIS COUNTRY✧✧✧

ℹ Barrier Lake Information Centre
26km southeast of Canmore on Kananaskis Trail (Hwy 40); tel: (403) 673-3985. Open Thur–Sun 0900–1600. Southern section of Hwy 40 closed Dec–mid-June.

🏛 Kananaskis Country Course $$
in season, tel: (403) 591-7272. Has two 18-hole golf courses.

Named by explorer John Palliser after a legendary Indian who surviv⩗ a stunning axe blow to the head, Kananaskis, a Blackfoot word ⩗ 'Meeting of the Waters', is a year-round recreational area contain⩗ superb golf courses and magnificent areas for hiking, biking, fish⩗ skiing and camping. Some 500km of equestrian riding trails prov⩗ unique camping facilities in the valleys of the Elbow, Highwood ⩗ Sheep. A full-service dining, lodging and golf resort, Kananas⩗ Village was purpose-built for the 1988 Winter Olympics. Adjoin⩗ Peter Lougheed Provincial Park, changed from Kananaskis Provin⩗ Park when Alberta's Premier 1971–85 stepped down, comprises so⩗ 500 sq km of beautiful lakes and valleys.

Accommodation and food in Kananaskis Country

Hotel and Lodge at Kananaskis $$$ *Kananaskis Village; tel: (403) 5⩗ 7711, tollfree (800) 268-1133.* The best address in the foothills.

Kananaskis Mountain Lodge $$ *Hwy 40, 28km south of Hwy 1; (403) 591-7500.* Built for the 1988 Winter Olympics, the resort has pillars and a homey redwood exterior.

William Watson Lodge $ *30km south of Kananaskis Village; tel: (4⩗ 591-7229.* A resort for the disabled. Non-Alberta residents sho⩗ reserve 60 days in advance.

L'Escapade $$$ *The Hotel and Lodge at Kananaskis; tel: (403) 591-77⩗* Has an élite ambience with creative Canadian dishes, served to ⩗ sounds of an easy-going dance band.

Opposite
Bar U Ranch sculpture

MEDICINE RIVER WILDLIFE REHABILITATION CENTRE✧✧

ⓘ Medicine River Wildlife Rehabilitation Centre $
5.5km south of Raven; tel: (403) 346-9453. Open daily 1000–1600.

Injured and orphaned wildlife, which can range from hummingbi to grizzly bears, are provided for at the Medicine River Wild Rehabilitation Centre before returning them to the wild. The anim can be viewed in the reception area and education wing, while b can be viewed at an outdoor observation tower. The centre also educational and interactive displays.

OPEN FLAIR PITS✧

ⓘ Open Flair Pits
Turner Valley Info Centre, 223 Main St, Turner Valley; tel: (403) 933-4944. Open mid-May–Aug, Mon–Fri 1000–1600; pits open daily year round.

Natural gas burns around the clock at the Open Flair Pits in the br Turner Valley. The unusual sight of ground burning is caused by gas which seeps through the hillside soil. Site of the first major oil gas find in Alberta in 1914, the oil was depleted by the time Leduc 1 blew in 1947.

PINCHER CREEK HUTTERITE COLONY✧✧✧

ⓘ Pincher Creek Hutterite Colony $
3km west of Pincher Creek; tel: (403) 627-4021; phone ahead for tour. Open year round, daily 0900–1500.

Retaining the dress, customs and simple lifestyle of their 16th-cent ancestors, the Pincher Creek Hutterite Colony welcomes visitors y round at their extensive mixed farming operation. Some 90 m women and children live communally on the self-contained farm t covers some 2000ha. Visitors are shown a variety of anim including sheep, poultry and dairy cattle, though the enclosed operation is off-limits to prevent the possibility of infection. colony contains a kitchen, church and school.

ROCKY MOUNTAIN HOUSE NATIONAL HISTORIC SITE✧

ⓘ Rocky Mountain House National Historic Site $
82km west of Red Deer on Hwy 11 and 5km west of Rocky Mountain House on Hwy 52A; tel: (403) 845-2412. Open late May–Sept.

The site commemorates a series of fur trade posts built 1799–1864 the Hudson's Bay Company and its rival, the North West Co., near junction of the Clearwater and Saskatchewan rivers. An interpretat centre describes the posts and Rocky Mountain House, the centre sporadic trade with the Blackfoot, who kept the post in operat until 1875. Canada's greatest geographer, David Thompson, u Rocky Mountain House as a base while he explored, surveyed a established trading posts in present-day British Columb Washington, Oregon, Idaho and Montana.

˙UDIO WEST BRONZE FOUNDRY AND GALLERY**

Studio West Bronze Foundry Gallery $$ *205 2nd southeast, Cochrane; tel: ˙) 932-2611. Open year d, Mon–Fri 0800–1730, Sun 0900–1630.*

Skilled artisans perform the age-old art of bronze casting at Studio West Bronze Foundry and Gallery. Owned and operated by Don and Shirley Beggs, Studio West specialises in lifesize bronze casts of bison and horses. See artisans at work in the studio and foundry as they work with clay and wax, making miniature to monumental sculptures at the largest sculpture foundry in Western Canada.

˙ve ˙erite Colony, Pincher k

TURNER VALLEY*

Named after the first settlers in the area, James and Robert Turner,
town was the first cornerstone of the Alberta petroleum industry.
was apparent for years through seepage but it was not until 1914 t
Dingman No 1 came in, heralding the first major oil and gas discov
in Alberta. The oil ran out by the time Leduc No 1 blew in in 1947.

Accommodation and food

Accommodation is moderate to budget along the Cowboy Trail. **
bet are the B&Bs, many on working cattle ranches.

Silver Willow Lodge $$$ *3km west of Bragg Creek on Hwy 66; tel: (4*
949-3108. A B&B offering a full breakfast, situated on acreage al
the Elbow River.

Bloomin' Inn Guest Ranch $$ *5km east of Pincher Creek on Tower*
tel: (403) 627-5829. A working cattle ranch that provides a :
breakfast.

Georgetown Inn $$ *1101 Bow Valley Trail, Canmore; tel: (403) 6*
3439. A family owned lodge with an English country inn atmosphe

Highwood River Inn and Nature Bound Tours $$ *23km wes*
Longview on Hwy 541; tel: (403) 558-2456. On the Highwood Rive
the gorgeous rolling foothills, has a video theatre and licensed din
room.

Homestead B&B $$ *30km northeast of Rocky Mountain House on ▮*
761; tel: (403) 729-2635. A hearty full breakfast on their bis
reindeer and whitetail deer farm.

Lazy M Ranch $$ *Off Hwy 761, Caroline; tel: (403) 722-3053; open ▮*
May–mid-Oct. Overnight accommodation or a week-long package
riding, fly fishing and horse training.

Turner Valley Hotel $ *112 Kennedy Dr. Turner Valley; tel: (403) ↋*
7878. Has live entertainment Fri–Sat nights and jam sessions
afternoon.

Voyageur Motel $ *Hwy 11, Rocky Mountain House; tel: (403) 845-3.*
Has kitchenettes with microwaves and coffee makers.

Burger Baron $ *Hwy 11, Rocky Mountain House; tel: (403) 845-6(*
Known for its fine pizza.

Suggested tour

Total distance: 450km. Detour to Kananaskis Country: 70km southwest of Cochrane.

Time: 6–7 hours to drive, 3–5 days to explore.

Links: The Cowboy Trail (Hwy 22) begins at Rocky Mountain House, which links on the west with Hwy 11 from the northern end of Banff National Park, and Red Deer to the east. Hwy 22 connects with numerous secondary roads along its north–south route and crosses over the TransCanada Highway (Hwy 1) west of Calgary.

Route: From **ROCKY MOUNTAIN HOUSE** ❶, take Hwy 22 south 25km, turn left and pass through the ranching town of Caroline. Continue east on Hwy 54 to Raven and turn right 5.5km to the **MEDICINE RIVER WILDLIFE REHABILITATION CENTRE** ❷. Return to Raven, turn left and just before Caroline turn left on Hwy 22 through the town of Sundre. Turn right just after Sundre and pass by the villages of Elkton, Cremona and Bottrel before the junction of Hwy 1A, which leads through Cochrane, named after Sen M H Cochrane who founded the historic Cochrane Ranch in 1881; Cochrane became a shipping point for cattle and a dormitory town for Calgary. Hwy 1A continues east to Calgary, or west to Canmore and Banff.

Continue south over the TransCanada Highway (Hwy 1) past the trendy estate village of Redwood Meadows, then follow the highway in a southwesterly direction toward **BRAGG CREEK** ❸, a Calgary dormitory community and home to interesting gift shops. Travel east

on Hwy 22 for 20km and turn right through the village of Millarv
home to a great farmers' market on Sundays during sumn
Continue south to **TURNER VALLEY ❹**, centre of the first major
strike in Alberta, and the neighbouring community of Black Diamo
Travel south to Longview, film location for Clint Eastwoc
Unforgiven, and 13km south on the west (right) side of the road, p
by the historic **BAR U RANCH ❺**, once the largest ranch in Canad.

The scenery may start to look familiar as many Hollywood mo
have been made in this area. Drive through Chain Lakes Provin
Park, a favourite summer home for ducks, pelicans and Canada ge
The scenic countryside is dotted with lodges, country inns and B&
Hwy 22 continues through the rolling foothills to the junction
Crowsnest Pass Highway (Hwy 3). Turn left, and pass through
villages of Lundbreck and Cowley before the junction with Hwy
turn right to the town of **PINCHER CREEK ❻**.

Detour: to KANANASKIS COUNTRY. From Cochrane travel south
Hwy 22, then right onto the TransCanada Highway (Hwy 1). Fol
the signs, turn onto Hwy 40 and travel through rolling foothills
Kananaskis Village, 50km from the highway. Return to Cochrane
continue south to Highwood Pass and Highwood House, which
closed Dec–mid-June to protect and manage animal species along
44.5km-long Highwood Road Corridor Wildlife Sanctuary. The r
meets Hwy 22 just above Longview.

Bar U Ranch

After gold rushes in BC and the arrival of the railway, ranching reached into
the sheltered, well-watered foothills of southern Alberta. Nurtured by
Englishmen wooed by the glamour of cattle ranching, the newly minted
cowboys made time for polo and afternoon tea breaks. One of the great
cattle companies developed over the years was the Bar U Ranch, owned
over time by Fred Stinson, George Lane and Patrick Burns, who helped
underwrite the first Calgary Stampede. From 1882 to 1950, the Bar U (the
brand of the North West Cattle Co.) earned an international reputation as
a centre of breeding excellence. One of the largest ranches in Canada,
there were 10 million cattle grazing in the early 1900s, and later some 9 000
Percheron draft horses. The ranch was so large that Pat Burns boasted he
could drive from Calgary to the US border (244km) without stepping foot
off his property. The Bar U is now a thumbnail of its original size but the
cattle, horses and chickens, along with the guides in period dress, give a
good image of the rugged life of the cowboy on the range.

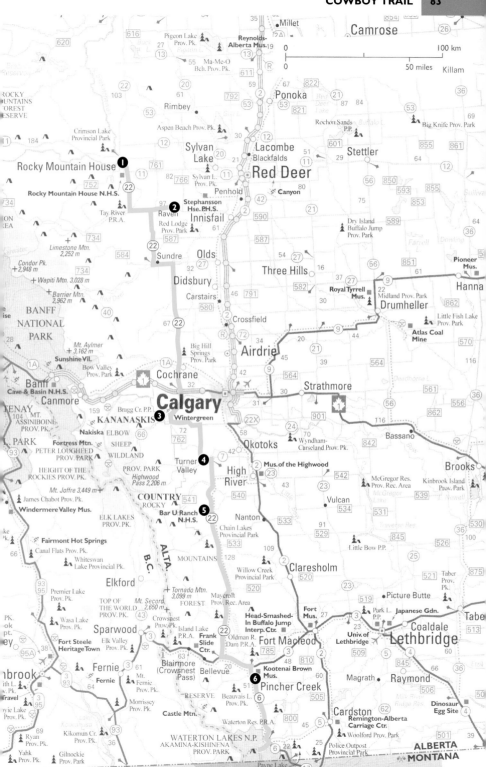

UNESCO Trail North

Ratings

Children	●●●●●
Mountains	●●●●●
National parks	●●●●●
Nature	●●●●●
Outdoor activities	●●●●●
Scenery	●●●●●
Walking	●●●●●
Wildlife	●●●●●

Full of extravagant natural wonders, UNESCO Trail No is one of the most spectacular drives imaginab Covering the largest body of mountain parkland in t world, the adjoining national parks of Banff, Jasp Kootenay and Yoho, together with the provincial parks Mount Assiniboine, Mount Robson and Hamber, make the Rocky Mountain National Parks World Heritage Site 20,238 sq km wilderness area straddling the Continen Divide. The Rockies of painting, postcard and song are endless procession of ragged peaks, sweeping valleys a spectacular mountain passes. Most visitors stop just lc enough to shop in Banff, stroll around Banff Springs Hc and Chateau Lake Louise, and drive along the Icefie Parkway, a rugged alpine wonderland that tests t vocabulary. Watch elk wander through the town of Ba and bighorn sheep graze along the roadway, while otl wildlife keep their distance in the forests and alpi meadows.

BANFF NATIONAL PARK✦✦✦

Rocky Mountain National Parks Canada provides a free tabloid-size newspaper with a page of highlights from each of the six parks: Banff, Glacier, Jasper, Kootenay, Mount Revelstoke and Yoho. The same summaries can be found online: *www.worldweb.com/ ParksCanada-Banff/Guide*

Canada's oldest national park, the Banff Hot Springs Reserve, created on 4ha of land in 1885 to preserve the sulphur hot springs public use. It became the Rocky Mountain Parks Reserve shortly af and was then renamed Banff National Park. Stretching 240km al the eastern slope of the Continental Divide, Banff National Park blend of towering peaks, flowery meadows and cold, aquamarine la and rivers. The hub of most activities in the Rocky Mountains, town of Banff, founded in 1883 as 'Siding 29', was renamed by L Strathcona and Mount Royal (financier and fur trader Dom Alexander Smith) after his home town in Scotland.

Banff Park Museum.✦✦ A taxidermy collection of park wild dating back to 1860 is housed in this Victorian-style railway muse A National Historic Site, the 'museum of a museum' contains a lib on natural history; the interior is lined with Douglas fir and balco set around an atrium. **Banff Springs Hotel.**✦✦ Dating from 1888

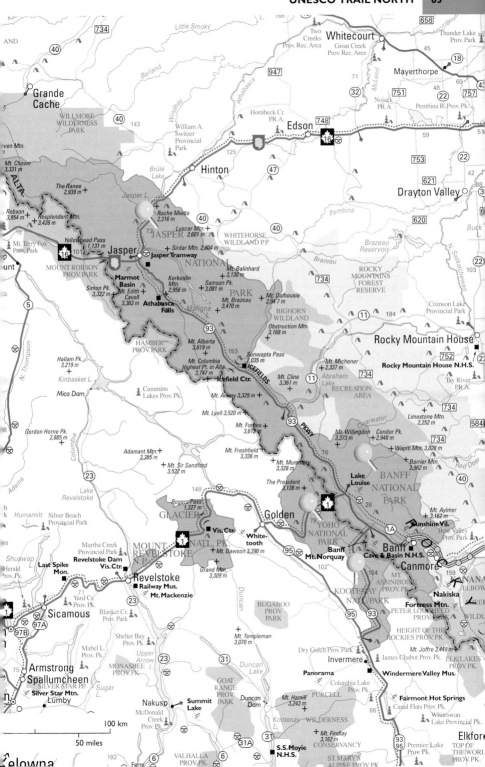

ⓘ Banff National Park Visitor Centre *224 Banff Ave; tel: (403) 762-1550; web: www.parkscanada.pch.gc.ca/ banff Open late May–June and Sept 0800–1800; mid-June–early Sept 0800–2000; late Sept–mid-May 0900–1700.*

Lake Louise Visitor Centre *Samson Mall; tel: (403) 522-3833. Open late May–mid-June and Sept 0800-1800; mid-June–early Sept 0800–1800; late Sept–mid-May 0900–1600.*

Banff Book and Art Den $ *94 Banff Ave; tel: (403) 762-3919. Has a good selection of books on the Canadian Rockies.*

ⓜ Banff Park Museum National Historic Site $ *Banff Ave by Bow River Bridge; tel: (403) 762-1588. Open mid-May–mid-Oct, 1000–1800; mid-Sept–mid-May 1300–1700.*

Cave and Basin National Historic Site $ *311 Cave Ave; tel: (403) 762-1566. Open mid-June–mid-Sept, 1000–1800; mid-Sept–mid-June, variable hours depending on day of week.*

Snocoach Tours on Athabasca Glacier $ *Brewster Transport; tel (Banff): (403) 762-6735; tel (Calgary): (403) 221-8242; tel (Jasper): (780) 852-3332; web: www.brewster.ca Weather-dependent Snocoach tours run mid-Apr–mid-Oct.*

rebuilt after a fire, the landmark hotel was designed to resembl Scottish baronial castle. The hotel caters to large groups and can b circus during busy periods, but the luxurious spa can wipe away stress, for a price. **Cave and Basin National Historic Site.**✦✦ Site of sulphuric hot springs found by railway workers in 1883 that led to creation of Banff. Hands-on displays describe the wildlife and hist of the park, while interpretive trails provide an insight into geology and plant life.

Lake Louise.✦✦✦ Known as the 'Mona Lisa of the Mountain' for calm, aquamarine waters, and 'Lake of the Little Fishes' by lc aboriginal people. Chateau Lake Louise overlooks the lake a stunning Mount Victoria and the Victoria Glacier. Hikers take **Lake Agnes Trail**✦✦ in summer to a tea house or follow the 1.5 return **Lakeshore Trail/Plain of the Six Glaciers Trail.**✦✦✦ Beloved canoeists and photographers, **Moraine Lake**✦✦✦ rivals Lake Louise beauty and fame. Set below the 'Valley of Ten Peaks', Moraine L was named after the moraine boulders (rock pushed along by a glac which dammed the valley and created the lake.

Accommodation and food in Banff National Park

Banff Rocky Mountain Resort $$$ *Banff Ave and Tunnel Mountain tel: (403) 762-5531, tollfree (800) 661-9563. A chalet-style building w fireplaces and kitchens.*

⏴st sighting

⏴e first European known
⏴have seen the Rocky
⏴untains was the
⏴lorer Anthony
⏴day. Viewed near
⏴sent-day Innisfail, Alta
⏴7 Oct 1754, he called
⏴m the 'Shining
⏴untains', a description
⏴origines gave the
⏴ged vista. Yet it was
⏴: until 1793 that
⏴xander Mackenzie
⏴de the first crossing of
⏴ Rockies, and 1885
⏴'ore the CPR
⏴npleted 'The National
⏴eam'.

Banff Springs Hotel $$$ *405 Spray Ave; tel: (403) 762-2211, tollfree (800) 661-1367.* An enormous castle-like hotel that caters to tour groups; a big draw is its world-class spa.

Chateau Lake Louise $$$ *111 Lake Louise Dr. tel: (403) 522-3511, tollfree (800) 441-1414.* Caters to tour groups so individuals may get neglected, though all can enjoy the stunning view of the glacier and aquamarine lake.

Post Hotel $$$ *200 Pipestone Rd, Lake Louise; tel: (403) 522-3989.* An elegant pine and stone lodge alongside a river, best known for its outstanding dining room.

Rimrock Resort Hotel $$$ *Mountain Ave, Banff; tel: (403) 762-3356.* Perched on a mountain side with stunning views of the Bow Valley.

Storm Mountain Lodge $$$ *5km west of TransCanada Highway (Hwy 1) on Hwy 93; tel: (403) 762-4155; open June–Sept.* A log cabin-style lodge built by the CPR.

Edelweiss Dining Room $$$ *Chateau Lake Louise; tel: (403) 522-3511.* Has a dress code for the elegant eatery.

Le Beaujolais $$$ *212 Buffalo St at Banff Ave; tel: (403) 762-2712.* A French gourmet restaurant with an extensive wine selection, frequently rated one of the best in Canada.

Post Hotel $$$ *200 Pipestone Rd, Lake Louise; tel: (403) 522-3989.* A superb reputation for its fine European cuisine blended with a lighter, California flare.

Bumper's The Beef House $$ *603 Banff Ave, Banff; tel: (403) 762-2622.* Features Alberta beef and all-you-can-eat salad bar.

Caboose $$ *Railway Depot, Elk and Lynx Sts, Banff; tel: (403) 762-3622.* Has railway mementoes and serves basic yet good Continental dishes.

The Station $$ *200 Sentinel Rd, Lake Louise; tel: (403) 522-2600.* In the restored CPR station along with early rail cars and period furnishings.

Joe Btfsplk's Diner $ *221 Banff Ave, Banff; tel: (403) 762-5529.* Named after an Al Capp cartoon character, an informal 1950s-style diner that has tasty burgers, cookies and muffins.

⏴posite
⏴wntown Banff

JASPER NATIONAL PARK✦✦✦

The largest and most northerly of the adjoining national parks, Jasper Park Reserve was created in 1907. Originally called Fitzhugh, the town was named after Jasper House, a nearby North West Co. post which was established a century earlier. Yet nomadic people have lived in the valleys of the park for some 10,000 years, about the time the big

Above
Columbia Icefield, Jasper
National Park

**ⓘ Jasper National
Park Info Centre**
*409 Patricia St; tel: (780)
852-3858; web:
www.parkscanada.pch.gc.ca/
jasper
Open daily.*

glaciers receded. When the park was established, Aborigines and Mé
were called squatters on Crown land, and were paid off and ordered
leave the park. Tourists began arriving in 1915, and the first hotel, t
Athabasca, opened in 1921, followed by the landmark Jasper P.
Lodge.

Columbia Icefield.*** A mass of ice on the boundary of Banff a
Jasper national parks, Columbia Icefield lies at the hyrdographic ap
of North America. Astride the Continental Divide, the 325 sq km
ice is called the 'mother of rivers', feeding the Athabasca, Columb
Fraser and Saskatchewan river systems. Meltwater flows into th
oceans: west to the Pacific, east to the Atlantic via Hudson Bay, a
north to the Arctic. **Icefields Parkway.***** The 230km drive along H
93 between Jasper and Lake Louise offers glaciers, waterfalls, wildl
and awesome vistas for several hours' drive by car or narrated
Brewster Coach Tours.

Jasper Tourism and Commerce
Patricia St; tel: (780) -3858; web: v.jaspercanadianrockies.

n daily.

Icefield Info Centre
Icefields Parkway; tel:) 852-6288. Open daily –mid-Oct.

it
cia Lake, Jasper National

Accommodation and food in Jasper National Park

Columbia Icefield Chalet $$$ *100km south of Jasper and 130km north of Lake Louise on Icefields Parkway (Hwy 93); tel: (403) 762-6700, tollfree (877) 423-7433. Open May–Oct.* Has spectacular views of the glaciers.

Jasper Park Lodge $$$ *4km northeast of Jasper off Hwy 16; tel: (780) 852-7038, tollfree (800) 441-1414.* Caters to large groups, though the heated year-round outdoor pool is a hit with everyone.

Alpine Village $$ *2km south of Jasper on Hwy 93A; tel: (780) 852-3285.* Has sun decks that overlook Athabasca River and Mount Edith Cavell.

Becker's Gourmet Restaurant (L'Auberge) $$$ *8km south of Jasper on Hwy 93; tel: (780) 852-3535.* A French restaurant with panoramic views of the Athabasca River.

Le Beauvallon $$$ *96 Giekie St, Chateau Jasper, Jasper; tel: (780) 852-5644.* An elegant restaurant best known for its lamb and venison, served to the strains of a harpist.

ow
vntown Jasper

Kootenay National Park***

ⓘ Vermilion Crossing Visitor Centre
63km northeast of Radium; no phone. Open daily Apr–late May; late May–Sept 1000–1830; early Oct Fri–Sun; public holidays 1100–1800.

🅟 Kootenay National Park
1km north of Hwy 93/95 junction at Radium; tel: (250) 347-9615 or (403) 522-3833; web: www.parkscanada.pch.gc.ca/kootenay Open late May–late June and Labour Day–3rd Fri/Sun of Sept 0930–1630; late June–early Sept 0900–1900; late Sept–late May tel: (250) 347-9615 or 94030 522-3833 for information.

Radium Hot Springs Pools $
3km east of Radium; tel: (250) 347-9301, tollfree (800) 767-1611. Open mid-May–mid-Oct 0900–2300; mid-Oct–mid-May 1200–2100.

On the west slope of Continental Divide, Koote was a travel route during golden age of explorati Ancient pictographs Radium Hot Springs indic it was a meeting point plains and mountain India who enjoyed the sooth waters for centuries. Kootenay (pronounced 'c teh-knee': 'people fr beyond the hills'), settled the area, and made tr across the mountains to hunt for bison on the prairies. Banff–Windermere Parkway, built over nearly a decade starting 1912, is one of the most stunning drives in the Rocky Mountai Most of the park's 1.2 million annual visitors make a pilgrimage soak, swim or absorb the atmosphere in the hot mineral waters **Radium Hot Springs Pools**** in the village of Radium, which more hotel rooms, coffee shops and flower-filled pots than resident

Accommodation and food in Kootenay National Park

Radium Hot Springs Resort $$$ *8100 Golf Course Rd, Hwy 93/95; (250) 347-9311, tollfree (800) 667-6444.* All rooms face one of the t golf courses at this pricey, three-storey boutique hotel.

Kootenay Park Lodge $$$ *Hwy 93 at Vermilion Crossing; tel: (403) 7 9196 or (403) 283-7482; web: www.kootenayparklodge.com Open n May–Sept.* CPR built the lodge in 1923. The home-made sandwiches the gift shop are outstanding.

Alpen Motel $$ *5022 Hwy 93, Radium Hot Springs; tel: (250) 347-98* Cheerful with flower boxes and 14 spotless, non-smoking room block from the park portal.

Old Salzburg Restaurant $$ *4943 Hwy 93; tel: (250) 347-65* Matches the style of many nearby alpine-chalet-style motels w Austrian specialities such as schnitzel.

OHO NATIONAL PARK***

Yoho National Visitor Info Centre nsCanada Hwy 1, Field; (250) 343-6783 or 0) 343-6324; web: w.parkscanada.pch.gc.ca/ 5 en mid-May–late June Sept 0900–1700; late e–Aug 0800–1900; late t–mid-May 0900–1600. ig attraction is the gess Shale Fossil ibit; the bookshop has ood selection of titles.

With 28 towering peaks, Yoho National Park is appropriately named after the Cree words expressing 'awe and wonder'. Bordered by Banff and Kootenay national parks on the western side of the Rockies in BC, the park contains some of the most outstanding scenery in the Rocky Mountains. Waterfalls, emerald lakes, crashing rivers, hanging glaciers, distinctive rock escarpments, and sheer ranges of mountains are divided by the TransCanada Highway (Hwy 1). **Emerald Lake.*** Greener than green, the glassy, glacier-formed, 28m-deep lake is perfect for canoeing. Walk clockwise from the wooden car bridge near the parking area for the best views of the President Range northward.

Accommodation and food in Yoho National Park

Cathedral Mountain Lodge and Chalets $$$ *Yoho Valley Rd; tel: (250) 343-6442 or (403) 762-0514; web: www.cathedralmountain.com Open mid-May–mid-Sept.* Log cabins with fireplaces along the pale blue Kicking Horse River and stunning views of the mountains. A grocery store is good for provisioning before Takakkaw Falls.

Emerald Lake Lodge $$$ *9km north of Field at Emerald Lake; tel: (250) 343-6321, tollfree (800) 663-6336.* Chalets surround the lodge-cum-resort, often booked out by executive conferences. Cilantro's $$ restaurant serves meals and drinks on an umbrella-decked terrace.

Kicking Horse Lodge and Café $$ *Hwy 1, across from Info Centre at Field.* Sells sandwiches, Aboriginal-style souvenirs and books, and is the meeting place for the Yoho-Burgess Shale Foundation tours.

Picnic lunches

Evelyn's Coffee Bar $ *201 Banff Ave, Banff; tel: (403) 762-0352.* Has great sandwiches, quiches and home-made soups.

Loggan's Mountain Bakery and Deli $ *Samson Mall, Lake Louise; tel: (403) 522-2017.* Makes great sandwiches from sweet poppy-seed breads.

Truffles and Trout $ *Jasper Marketplace, corner of Patricia St and Hazel Ave, Jasper; tel: (780) 852-9676.* Specialises in light gourmet meals and boxed lunches.

Mount Eisenhower

Dwight D Eisenhower, Supreme Allied Commander in the Second World War, was honoured in 1946 when Canadian Premier Mackenzie King named a mountain in Banff National Park after the man who was later to become US President. The decision to name a Canadian treasure after an American was unpopular and Premier Joe Clark reversed the decision in 1979, returning to the name Castle Mountain, which the 2766m mountain had borne for 99 years. Situated midway between Banff and Lake Louise, its red-brown peak of layered rock is weathered into turrets and towers: the first tower called Eisenhower Peak.

Suggested tour

Total distance: 540km.

Time: One long day to drive; 2–5 days to explore.

Links: The BC Rockies at Castle Junction for Kootenay National Pa at the Hwy 1 fork to Yoho National Park and Hwy 16 west from Jas to Mount Robson National Park.

Route: TransCanada Highway (Hwy 1) runs from **BANFF NATION** **PARK ❶** east gate by Banff townsite to just north of the Lake Lou exit. Veer left at Castle Mountain junction to take t Banff–Windermere Highway (Hwy 93) through **KOOTEN** **NATIONAL PARK ❷** for 105km to **RADIUM HOT SPRINGS ❸**.

Detour along Bow Valley Parkway: Hwy 1A between Banff and L Louise parallels the TransCanada Highway for 55km but is conside the more scenic, if slower (60kph) route. Pick up the Bow Val Parkway 5.5km west of Banff townsite.

Leaving Radium Hot Springs, turn right onto Hwy 95 and tra 120km through a superb wildlife habitat. Continue on to the sce mountain setting of Golden *(see page 125)*. Turn right onto t TransCanada Highway (Hwy 1) and 25km away is the weste boundary of **YOHO NATIONAL PARK ❹**. A Cree word express 'awe', Yoho is just 45km from west to east yet has some 400km hiking trails, from short walks to day hikes.

Continue on the TransCanada to Lake Louise Village. Another 4.5 up a winding road is **LAKE LOUISE ❺**, the 'Mona Lisa of t Mountain', the most famous landmark of the Rockies. Chateau L Louise overlooks the calm waters, which change from aquamarine emerald green. Rivalling Lake Louise in fame and beauty is Mora Lake, 3km up an access road then 12km on Moraine Lake Road.

Return to the TransCanada, turn left and follow signs to t **ICEFIELDS PARKWAY ❻** (Hwy 93), a spectacular drive followin natural corridor through an unspoiled wilderness, 230km to Jasp The route could be driven in about 3 hours; however, in the pe summer tourist season, the parkway is busy with vehicles, cyclists a pedestrians criss-crossing the roadway to view the scenery a wildlife.

Sunwapta Pass at 2035m marks the southern end of **JASP** **NATIONAL PARK ❼** and the Columbia Icefield. *Wapiti* (elk) wan everywhere around Jasper, a relaxed, tourist-catering town stru along the CN Rail line. Drive out to Jasper Park Lodge for a lov series of water sports recreation lakes, epitomised by the lodge's o Lac Beauvert.

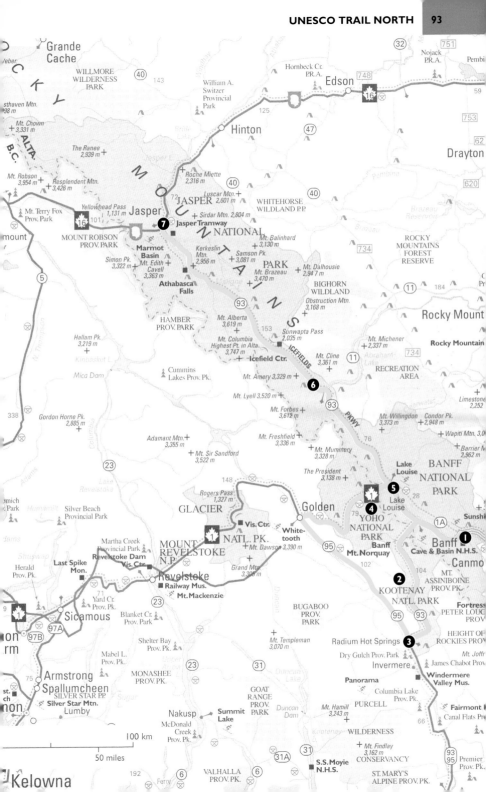

UNESCO Trail South

Ratings

Children	●●●●●
Geology	●●●●●
History	●●●●●
Nature	●●●●●
Walking	●●●●●
Scenery	●●●●○
Towns and villages	●●●●○
Food and Drink	●●○○○

Spanning the earliest syllable of time, the World Herita Sites in UNESCO Trail South preserve a spectacul registry of adventure, heritage and nature. One of the olde inhabited parts of North America, early aboriginal peop settled here up to 28,000 years ago, making camp in what now Waterton Lakes National Park. For some 10,000 yea until as recently as the 19th century, Plains Indians used ingenious system to harvest bison at Head-Smashed-Buffalo Jump. The grandaddy of all treasures is Dinosa Provincial Park, for 79 million years a favourite haunt of t huge reptiles when this barren lunar landscape resembl the lush Florida Everglades. As you drive through t tapestry of southern Alberta, the rolling foothills expa into semi-arid grassland, short-grass prairie and the ee Badlands, once the domain of the dinosaur and now one the richest fossil beds in the world.

BROOKS AQUEDUCT✢

Brooks Aqueduct $
*3km south of Hwy 1,
east of Brooks; tel: (403)
362-4451 (summer); tel:
(403) 653-5139 (winter).
Open mid-May–Labour Day
1000–1800.*

Spanning a 3.2km-wide valley, the elevated Brooks Aqueduct i: National/Provincial Historic Site: a monument to pioneers w developed this bone-dry region. Built by the CPR between 1912 a 1914, the 3186m-long concrete aqueduct was part of a scheme irrigate the region so the railway could sell land to prospecti farmers. Connected to the Bow River 50km away, the aqueduct v discontinued because of costly repairs. A new clay-lined earthen ca now provides farmers with the much-needed moisture to irrigate th crops.

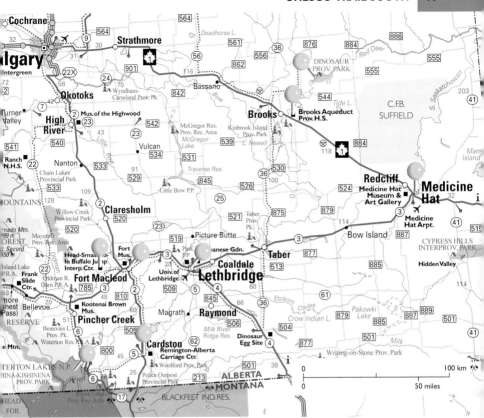

ARDSTON✥✥

Cardston Visitor Information
ntre *490 Main St; tel:* 3) 653-3787. *Open* oria Day ekend–Labour Day 0-2000.

Cardston Alberta Mormon Temple
3rd St west; tel: (403) -1696. *Open May–Sept,* 0900–2100 .

mington–Alberta rriage Centre $
Main St, Cardston; tel: 3) 653-5139. *Open mid-* –mid-Sept 0900–1800; season 1000–1700.

Nestled in the rolling foothills, Cardston was established in 1887 by Mormons to escape anti-polygamy laws in the US. Named after Charles Card, a son-in-law of Brigham Young, work began in 1913 on the towering **Mormon Temple**.✲ Completed ten years later, the Visitor Centre depicts the history of the marble temple and the pioneers who arrived in one of the last great covered wagon migrations. Visitors are welcome, though only church members may enter the temple. The **Remington–Alberta Carriage Centre**✥✥ contains one of the largest collections of horse-drawn vehicles in North America. Over 200 carriages, sleighs and wagons whisk visitors back in time to the days of horses and buggies.

DINOSAUR PROVINCIAL PARK❖❖❖

🏛 Dinosaur Provincial Park $
*49km northeast of Brooks;
tel: (403) 378-4342
(administration); (403) 378-4344 (tour reservations).
Park is open year round
though many services are
available seasonally.*

Established in 1955 to protect one of the world's richest fossil b
Dinosaur Provincial Park contains 35 dinosaur species, plus thousa
of fossil finds. Chiselled by years of wind, water and ice, the 73 sq
World Heritage Site has numerous trails to explore, though muc
the park is a nature preserve and has limited public access. The
way to visit the World Heritage Site is by bus tour. The Field Sta
contains several dinosaur skeletons and a workshop. The p
recommends two full days for an in-depth experience.

FORT MACLEOD❖❖❖

🏛 Fort Macleod Museum
*219 25th St, Fort Macleod;
tel: (403) 553-4703. Open
Mar–June daily 0900–1700;
July–Aug 0900–2000;
Sept–Dec 0900–1700;
closed 24 Dec–28 Feb.*

The oldest town in southern Alberta, Fort Macleod was founde
1874 when the North West Mounted Police established a police
on an island on the Oldman River. Named after an assist
commissioner, James F Macleod, the fort became a police headqua
that wiped out the illegal whiskey trade. The original site was mo
because of constant flooding, and now the reconstructed Fort Muse
tells the story of the colourful past. Downtown Fort Macleod cont
some 30 buildings of historical significance. Walking tour broch
are available at several locations. A guided walking tour is condu
at the Information Centre next to the Fort Museum.

HEAD-SMASHED-IN BUFFALO JUMP❖❖❖

🏛 Head-Smashed-In Buffalo Jump $
*18km northwest of Fort
Macleod on Hwy 785; tel:
(403) 553-2731. Open
Jan–mid-May 1000–1700;
mid-May–Labour Day
0900–1800; mid-Sept–mid-
May 1000–1700. No shuttle
until mid-May.*

Bison provided Aboriginal people with many of life's needs, includ
food, hides for clothing and shelter, sinew, bone and horns for to
and dung for fires. And Head-Smashed-In Buffalo Jump provided
clever setting to harvest the bison. As the herds stampeded across
Porcupine Hills, up to 500 Plains Indians at a time guided the h
animals over the edge, falling 10m to their death. A World Heri
Site, Head-Smashed-In Buffalo Jump is the biggest, oldest and I
preserved buffalo jump in North America, believed to have been
used 10,000 years ago and continuing until the mid-19th cent
Built into the side of a cliff, the seven-level Interpretive Cer
contains a theatre, cafeteria and audio-visual exhibits. Blackfoot gu
describe the site and the hunting techniques of the Northwest Pl
people, and provide guided tours along 2km of outdoor trails. The
is named after an absent-minded brave whose head was smashed i
he watched a stampede from the base of the cliff.

t
-Smashed-In Buffalo Jump
age Site display

THBRIDGE***

**Chinook Country
Tourist Association**
5 Scenic Dr., Lethbridge;
403) 320-1222.

**Fort Whoop-up
Interpretive**
tre $ Indian Battle
; tel: (403) 329-0444.
n mid-May–Sept
0–1800, Sun
0–1700; Oct–mid-May
-Fri and Sun
0–1600; closed Sat and
.

**ka Yuko Japanese
dens** Henderson Park,
bridge; tel: (403) 328-
I. Open May–mid-Oct
0–1600.

While modern Lethbridge was founded in 1885 with the start of large-scale coal mining, some 500 generations of Blackfoot Indians have inhabited the area since prehistoric times. Located on the steep banks of the coulee-scarred Oldman River, the city was named after William Lethbridge, president of the North Western Coal and Navigation Co. Set into the side of a coulee are the impressive buildings of the University of Lethbridge, facing the spindle leg High Level Railway Bridge, 1.5km long and 96m high. **Nikka Yuko Japanese Gardens***** is a symbol of Japanese–Canadian friendship, a memorial to the forced and humiliating evacuation of Japanese Canadians during the Second World War. Situated along the man-made Henderson Lake, the lovely 1.6ha oasis features elements of five traditional Japanese gardens, joined by a meandering path which combines ponds, shrubs, pebbled beaches, moon-shaped bridges, pagoda, bell tower and a Cultural Centre representing a Tea Room and Japanese house styles. Built in Japan and reassembled as a Canadian Centennial project in 1967, the Nikka Yuko Japanese Gardens is an elegant setting of peace and

Below
Nikka Yuko Japanese Gardens, Lethbridge

tranquillity. **Fort Whoop-up**✚✚ is a replica of a notorious 19th-cen fort built by American whiskey traders on Canadian territory further their illicit and often deadly business. Guided and self-gui trails lead through the coulees and river flood plain.

MEDICINE HAT✚✚✚

ⓘ **Tourism Medicine Hat**
413 6th Ave, Medicine Hat; tel: (403) 527-6422. Open mid-May–Labour, Day Mon–Fri 0800–2100; Sat–Sun 0800–1800; Labour Day–Victoria Day, Mon–Sat 0900–1700.

Straddling the winding South Saskatchewan River Valley, the cit: Medicine Hat is the natural gas capital of Canada. Standing guard c the city and adjacent to the TransCanada Highway is the Saa Tepee, a 20-storey structure which towered above the 1988 Wi Olympics in Calgary. Below the tepee is Seven Persons Coulee, on the most important archaeological sites of the northern plain native camp and buffalo jump spanning over 6000 years. Blackfoot word for eagle tail feather headdress, saamis was a hat w by the Medicine Man, or simply, medicine hat, after which the was named. Founded in 1883 with the arrival of the CPR, abundant supply of natural gas and clay led to the manufacturing bricks, pottery and tiles. **Clay Products Interpretive Centr**

Clay Products Interpretive ﹏tre
Wood St southeast, ﹏icine Hat; tel: (403) -1070. Self-guided tours ﹏May–Oct 1000–1700. shop open year round ﹍–1730.

describes the industry, and the nearby Great Wall of China✦✦ contains a large exhibition of china, ceramics and pottery. Self-guided downtown walking tours feature the early 20th-century houses, churches and businesses. Charming copper gaslights imported from Shugg, England add a touch of class and a reminder of Medicine Hat's source of prosperity. Another memorial is the glass-sided City Hall✦ on the banks of the river, which received a Canadian Architectural Award after it opened in 1985.

﹏ATERTON LAKES NATIONAL PARK✦✦✦

Waterton Lakes National Park $
﹏n year round; tel: (403) ﹍-2224. Administration ﹍e open Mon–Fri ﹍0–1600; Information ﹏re mid-May–early Oct; ﹏open mid-May–Labour

Officially known as Waterton–Glacier International Peace Park, Waterton Lakes National Park graces the Canada–US border. The world's first international peace park, Waterton was established in 1932, uniting Alberta's Waterton Lakes National Park and Montana's Glacier National Park. Embracing prairie and mountain, the World Heritage Site contains a variety of plants and animals such as coyotes roaming the grasslands, and bighorn sheep and grizzly bears on the Trail of the Grizzly Bear, the Yellowstone–Yukon corridor where bears are active day and night. Discovered by European fur traders in the mid-19th century, the area was once a Blackfoot stronghold. Horseback riding, lake cruises, sightseeing and shopping are favourite activities, though the Prince of Wales Hotel✦✦, open mid-May–mid-Oct, is the centre of attention. Perched high on a windy bluff overlooking Lake Waterton, the pricey 87-room hotel, named after the popular Prince Edward when the Great Northern Railway opened the chalet-style lodge in 1927, provides a dramatic backdrop to the lake and mountains.

﹏t
﹍e of Wales Hotel, ﹏erton Lakes National Park

Prince of Wales Hotel

The first recorded white man to visit the area, Thomas Blakiston of the Palliser Expedition, named the region of rolling prairie, icy peaks and deep lakes after English naturalist Charles Waterton. Designated a World Heritage Site, the centre of attraction is the Prince of Wales Hotel, named after Prince Edward, son of Queen Mary and King George V. Opened in 1927 as a chain of chalets and hotels by the Great Northern Railway, the chalet-style lodge with steep, gabled roofs over a butter-yellow façade, is a romantic landmark that dominates the story-book setting. Now owned by Parks Canada and managed by Glacier Park Inc., the baronial, dark-panelled interior projects the air of a Scottish hunting lodge. Enjoy afternoon tea in Valerie's Tea Room or sample traditional English entrées in the Royal Stewart Dining Room.

Accommodation and food

Medicine Hat Lodge $$$ *1051 Ross Glen Dr. southeast, Medicine H tel: (403) 529-2222.* Has rooms that face an indoor pool, steam ro and a huge waterslide.

Prince of Wales Hotel $$$ *Waterton Park; year round reservations (4 859-2231. Open mid-May–mid-Oct.* Has creaky floors and rattles in wind, yet this historic hotel is a Canadian favourite.

Bettor Inn $$ *111 Waterton Ave, Waterton; tel: (403) 859-2211. O Apr–mid-Oct.* A two-storey, motel-style inn with rooms that h balconies with views of the lake and mountains.

Bloomin' Inn Guest Ranch $$ *5km east of Pincher Creek on Tower tel: 403-627-5829. Open year round.* The working ranch serves hor cooked meals.

Cloverleaf Motel $$ *7773 8th St southwest, Medicine Hat; tel: (403) 5 5955.* Has an indoor swimming pool.

Kilmorey Lodge $$ *117 Evergreen Ave, Waterton Park; tel: (403) 8 2334.* Has a log-cabin façade with antique furnishings, situated on edge of Waterton National Park.

Pepper Tree Inn $$ *1142 Mayor Magrath Dr. south, Lethbridge; tel: (4 328-4436.* Located near Henderson Park and Nikka Yuko Japan Gardens.

Plains Motel $$ *1004 2nd St West, Brooks; tel: (403) 362-3367.* Has indoor pool and sauna.

Aspen Village Inn $ *111 Wildflower Ave, Waterton; tel: (403) 859-2255. H* a variety of accommodations from de luxe to family cottages.

Tir Na Nog Irish Musical B&B $$$ *2502 20th Ave south, Lethbridge; (403) 328-3696.* Named after the ancient name for Ireland. Ser gourmet dinners.

Valerie's Tea Room $$$ *Prince of Wales Hotel, Waterton; tel: (403) 8 2231. Open mid-May-mid-Oct.* Serves breakfast buffet, English a Continental cuisine, and afternoon tea.

Atrium Dining Room $$ *Medicine Hat Lodge, 1051 Ross Glen southeast, Medicine Hat; tel: (403) 529-2222.* A popular spot for f Continental dining.

Café Martinique $$ *526 Mayor Magrath Dr., Lethbridge; tel: (403) 3 5701.* The Travelodge Hotel is noted for its tender Alberta steaks; Rancho coffee shop has lighter fare.

Sven Eriksen's Family Restaurant $$ *1715 Mayor Magrath Dr., Lethbridge; tel: 403-328-7756.* A colonial-style restaurant that specialises in chicken and prime rib.

Country Bakery $ *303 Windflower Ave, Bayshore Inn, Waterton; tel: (403) 859-2181.* Has fresh breads and a great Kootenai Burger.

Suggested tour

Total distance: 265km. Detour: 165km from Lethbridge to Medicine Hat; 145km Medicine Hat–Dinosaur Provincial Park.

Time: 3 hours to drive; 2–3 days to explore; 2 hours to drive Lethbridge–Medicine Hat; 2 hours to drive Medicine Hat–Dinosaur Provincial Park.

Links: Hwy 2 connects Calgary and Fort Macleod, then Hwy 3 (Crowsnest Pass Highway) to Lethbridge and continues on to Medicine Hat. Hwy 3 connects with Hwy 36 to Brooks and the TransCanada Highway (Hwy 1), and Hwy 36 north of Brooks.

Route: From LETHBRIDGE ❶, travel south on Hwy 5, which angles in a southwesterly direction toward the town of CARDSTON ❷, founded by Mormons who travelled by covered wagon in the late 1800s from Utah. Main attractions are the grandiose Mormon Temple and the Alberta Carriage Centre Museum, which houses a handsome collection of buggies and sleighs. Hwy 5 continues in a westerly direction to WATERTON LAKES NATIONAL PARK ❸, a UNESCO World Heritage Site on the Alberta–Montana border. Dry rolling hills of the prairies soar to icy peaks nearly 3000m high. Hwy 6, which originates a few kilometres south at the US border, skirts the eastern side of the park, continues north to the town of PINCHER CREEK ❹. North of the town, the highway meets the Crowsnest Pass Highway (Hwy 3), which runs in an east–west direction. Turn right on Hwy 3, then left onto Hwy 2, then left again onto Hwy 785, a secondary road which leads to HEAD-SMASHED-IN BUFFALO JUMP ❺, a World Heritage Site. Return to Hwy 3 to the town of FORT MACLEOD ❻, the oldest community in southern Alberta, established to crack the illicit and frequently poisonous whiskey trading. Return to Hwy 3 and continue on to the city of Lethbridge, the largest centre in southern Alberta.

Detour: to Medicine Hat and Dinosaur Provincial Park. From Lethbridge, take the Crowsnest Pass Highway (Hwy 3) east to Taber, passing through several small communities and the lush irrigated farmlands of sweetcorn and sugar beets and on to the natural gas city of MEDICINE HAT ❼ on the TransCanada Highway (Hwy 1). Continue on the TransCanada Highway and watch for signs, turning

Below
Dinosaur Provincial Park

right onto Hwy 876, a good gravel road which turns to pavement, a on to **DINOSAUR PROVINCIAL PARK ❽** . Return to the TransCan. Highway and watch for signs for the **BROOKS AQUEDUCT ❾** so of the highway on the east side of Brooks.

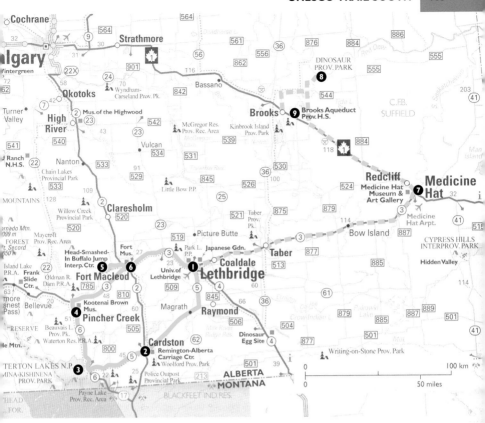

Dinosaurs

Dinosaur life ended abruptly and for an unexplained reason 66.4 million years ago. The huge reptiles were especially common in southern Alberta, their domain a tropical swamp similar to what is now the Everglades in Florida. With changing weather patterns, the region became a barren outback of sandstone and mudstone after rain, drought and wind-driven sand eroded the region, burying the dinosaur remains and preserving them for all time. The desert-like badlands of the Red Deer River valley, which include Dinosaur Provincial Park, contain one of the most diverse collections of dinosaur specimens in the world. Reconstructed dinosaur skeletons are exhibited some 170km northwest at the highly acclaimed Royal Tyrrell Museum of Palaeontology (see page 67) at Drumheller.

Crowsnest Highway

Ratings

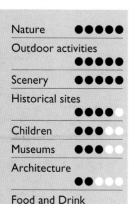

Nature	●●●●●
Outdoor activities	●●●●●
Scenery	●●●●●
Historical sites	●●●●○
Children	●●●○○
Museums	●●●○○
Architecture	●●○○○
Food and Drink	●●○○○

Skirting the US border, the Crowsnest Highway is the m
southerly of the highway passes crossing the Continer
Divide. Originating in Medicine Hat and ending just east
Vancouver at Hope, the highway probably takes its na
from Crow Indians who 'nested' after a fight with noma
Cree; for centuries the 1357m Crowsnest Pass was an acc
to hunt bison in the Alberta foothills. Zigzagging west a
south for several hundred kilometres, the 'Crow Highw
links Aboriginal, gold mining, lumbering and railw
history, and the tragic coal-mining past with sce
recreation lakes, a magnificent waterfall and an alp
village, famous for accordions and alpenhorns. Some c
Fernie the Aspen of BC, and few dispute the world's larg
operating cuckoo clock in Kimberley, though its homesp
Bavarian alpine theme is somewhat of a curiosity. The sce
alps in winter transform into a wonderland, with major
resorts at Kimberley and Fernie.

BLAIRMORE***

Frank Slide Interpretive Centre $

1.5km north of Hwy 3, Blairmore; tel: (403) 562-7388. Open daily: mid-May–mid-Sept 0900–1800; mid-Sept–mid-May 1000–1700; closed Christmas Eve, Christmas Day, New Year's Day, Easter Sunday.

The bustling coal mining town of Frank was devastated in 1903 wl
unstable limestone crashed from the east slope of Turtle Mount
and buried a section of the sleeping town. Called 'The Mountain t
Walks' by aboriginals, it is monitored daily for movement, though
only activity now is wandering sheep.

Accommodation and food in Blairmore

Cosmopolitan Hotel $ *13001 20th Ave; tel: (403) 562-7321*
moderate hotel, providing a base for exploring the mining areas.

Inn on the Border $ *Hwy 3, Crowsnest Pass; tel: (250) 425-015*
moderate B&B in a scenic spot.

Michel Country Inn $ *Michel, 4km north of Sparwood; tel: (250) 4
0110.* A hotel, pub and restaurant in this ghost town.

RANBROOK*

Cranbrook and District Chamber f Commerce Info entre 2279 Cranbrook St rth; tel: (250) 426-5914, llfree (800) 222-6174. pen mid-May–Labour Day on–Fri 0830–1700; at–Sun 0900–1700.

lizabeth Lake anctuary Wildlife rea and Info Centre 101 1st Ave south. Open ne–Labour Day 900–1700.

Canadian Museum of Rail Travel $$ an Horne St north at Baker : (Hwy 3/95); tel: (250) 89-3918; web: ww.crowsnest.bc.ca/cmrt pen July–Aug, daily 800–1800; Easter–June nd Sept–Thanksgiving, daily 000–1800; hanksgiving–Easter ue–Sat 1200–1700.

imsmith Lake rovincial Park $ km west of Cranbrook on m Smith Lake Rd; web: ww.elp.gov.bc.ca/bcparks/ xplore/parkpgs/jimsmith. tm pen May–Oct.

A major city in the Rocky Mountains, Cranbrook was a Ktunaxa camp and pasture before the 1870s known as Joseph's Prairie. Despite local protest, Col James Baker, member of the Legislature 1886–1900, bought the land and named it Cranbrook Farm after his birthplace in England. Located at the apex of three valleys, the city became a divisional point on the CPR and new capital of the region, serving the forestry and coal mining industries. **Canadian Museum of Rail Travel.** Train buffs are in their glory touring through the nine original cars from the TransCanada Limited, a CPR luxury service between Vancouver and Montreal. Built in 1929 and designed as a nine-car travelling hotel, the cars are the last of their type made in Canada. The *Argyle* dining car serves tea and light snacks in a stunning restored carriage.

Elizabeth Lake Sanctuary Wildlife Area. A 113ha section of the Rocky Mountain Trench on the south side of Cranbrook is preserved for birds on their annual migration. Watch mallards, songbirds and Canada geese from a viewing hide as they share the marsh with moose, painted turtles and white-tailed deer. **Jimsmith Lake Provincial Park.** Join the locals swimming, canoeing, picnicking and camping. You can cross-country ski to the lake in winter and lace up the skates to enjoy the ice.

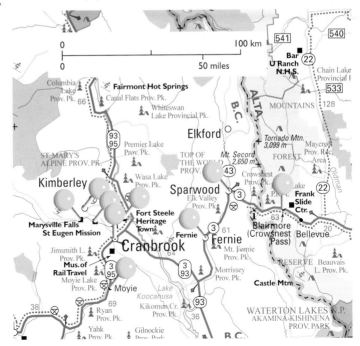

Accommodation and food in Cranbrook

Prestige Rocky Mountain Resort $$$ *209 Van Horne St south;* *(250) 417-0444, tollfree (877) 737-8443.* A modern, de luxe railw theme hotel has 108 rooms adjacent to the railway museum.

Heritage Inn $$ *803 Cranbrook St; tel: (250) 489-4301, tollfree (8* *663-2708.* This motor inn has 101 rooms and a central location.

Super 8 $ *2370 Cranbrook St north; tel: (250) 489-8028, tollfree (8* *800-8000.* Clean and comfortable at the north end of town, the h is across from the Info Centre.

Bavarian Chalet $$ *617 Cranbrook St at 9th Ave; tel: (250) 489-33* On Thur–Sat have the prime rib, otherwise it's a mixture of Germ specialities and all-Canadian. Closed Sun.

City Café $$ *1015 Baker St; tel: (250) 489-5413.* German schnitzel good choice but the sandwiches served on crusty French bread very popular.

Kootenay Cattle Co. $$ *40 Van Horne St north; tel: (250) 489-58* One of a chain of regional restaurants, this eatery's shabby exter belies the juicy steaks on the menu and its popularity with lo people.

FERNIE❖❖

ⓘ Fernie Chamber of Commerce Info Centre *Hwy 3 at Dicken Rd (look for the oil derrick); web: www.fernie.net and the delightful humour of www.city.fernie.bc.ca Open summer 0900–1900, shorter hours in winter.*

ⓖ Fernie Alpine Resort $$ *Ski Area Rd; tel: (250) 423-4655; web: www.skifernie.com For snow information tel: (250) 423-3555 or (888) 754-7325. Ski season: open late Nov–mid-Apr daily 0900–1600.*

With its mountain setting and fine heritage buildings, Fernie could called the Aspen of BC. Skiing in winter and fly-fishing in summer the big draws to this former coal mining town, once a base for Ktunaxa. **Fernie Alpine Resort.**❖❖ Lizard Range forms an impress drop, and with 9m annual snowfall the resort is a paradise for alpi and Nordic skiers. Mountain bike, ride a horse, kayak, raft, hike, fish or take a chairlift ride to scenic views in summer.

Accommodation and food in Fernie

Canadian Spruce B&B $$ *661 4th Ave; tel: (250) 423-6445 or (8* *605-8013.* A 1908 multi-storey heritage house with fireplaces, a sitti porch and central location.

Little Witch Log Inn $$ *Hwy 3 at Dicken Rd, next to the Info Centre;* *(250) 423-4696 or (888) 423-9772; web: littlewitch.com* Radiant fl heating completes the cosy feeling of this log cabin, chalet-style lod

Wolf's Den Mountain Lodge $$ *Ski Area Rd, Fernie Alpine Ski Resort; tel: (250) 423-9202, tollfree (800) 258-7669; web: www.skifernie.com /accom/wdfsden/index.asp* Open all year, the 42-room lodge offers ski-in, ski-out slope access.

Jamochas Coffee House and Bagel Co. $ *851 7th Ave (Hwy 3); tel: (250) 423-6977 Open 0800–2200.* Cribbage, bread, coffee and atmosphere are welcome after a drive.

)RT STEELE HERITAGE TOWN✢✢✢

Fort Steele Heritage Town $$ *93, 8km north of Hwy 3 junction; tel: (250) -3351. Open daily ise–dusk.* Actors and ans in period costume ummer.

Named after North West Mounted Police Supt Sam Steele who brought law and order during the 1864 Kootenay Gold Rush, Fort Steele boomed until the CPR bypassed the town for Cranbrook. At the confluence of the Kootenay and St Mary rivers, the *de facto* capital of the East Kootenay's rich mining economy declined when BC legislator Col James Baker persuaded the CPR to build its divisional point on his Cranbrook holdings. The restoration of Fort Steele contains some 50 buildings, including several from the original NWMP post. Guides and artisans in period costume bring history to life, providing a well-rounded introduction to Fort Steele's golden years, as a steam train and a Clydesdale-drawn wagon offer rides through the complex.

ht
: Steele Heritage Town
er at work

KIMBERLEY✥✥

ℹ Kimberley Visitor Info Centre
350 Ross St; tel: (250) 427-3666; web:
www.cyberlink.bc.ca/
~kimbchamber

🚂 Bavarian City Mining Railway and Cominco Powerhouse Mining Tours $
Open late June–Labour Day, in conjunction with the Railway ride. The Power House tour is a stop en route on the railway.

Cominco Gardens $
306 3rd Ave. Open May–Sept dawn to dusk. Tea room open daily in summer 1000–1800.

Happy Hans
Located at the Kimberley Visitor Info Centre.

Platzl
T-shaped pedestrian street encircled by Wallinger Ave, Howard St, Kimberley Ave and Ross St.

Named after her South African namesake, BC's highest city (111? was dedicated to silver, zinc and lead mining production at Cominco (Sullivan Mine). Happy Hans, the world's largest operat cuckoo clock, Bavarian kitsch and a ski resort at North Star Mount have replaced the mining industry. Salvaged railway cars at **Bavarian City Mining Railway✥** show off the countryside on 11km ride through the scenic countryside. The mining comp wanted to promote fertiliser in 1927. The resultant **Comin Gardens✥** boast 48,000 blooms annually, with dedicated rose, pra and Victorian gazebo areas. In the **Platzl✥** Bavarian architect restaurants, shops, wandering accordion players and depictions of Happy Hans town mascot reflect the transition the town economy made from mining lead to mining tourists. The beer-stein-wav **Happy Hans✥** statue in *lederhosen* is hard to miss.

Accommodation and food in Kimberley

Wild Rose Ranch and Resort $$$ *east of Wasa Lake, north 8km Wolf Creek Rd; tel: (250) 422-3403, tollfree (800) 324-6188.* A fam owned tourist ranch purpose-built for horse riders and fly fishers i stunning mountain-view setting. Join in as the family drives ca once a month May–Nov.

Old Bauernhaus $$$ *280 Norton St, up the ski hill; tel: (250) 427-1 Open Thur–Mon 1700–2230.* Bavaria was never so authentic as in 350 plus year-old building, dismantled and reassembled here.

Right
Platzl, downtown Kimberley

ve
y Hans, town mascot, Kimberley

Chef Bernard's $$ *170 Spokane St, on the Platzl; tel: (250) 427-4820, tollfree (800) 905-8338 Open daily 0800–2200, 0700–2200 in summer.* The chef is well known and locally beloved in this Bavarian schnitzelhaus which serves excellent pasta dishes.

Snowdrift Café $ *on the Platzl; tel: (250) 427-2002 Open Mon–Sat 1000–2200, Sun 1200–1800.* Big, rich cups of *latte* and home-grown spinach salad with gorgonzola cheese, walnuts, mushrooms, carrots and whole wheat bread reflect the quality of the menu at this superb vegetarian restaurant.

ARYSVILLE FALLS✦✦✦

Marysville Falls $
7km south of
berley.

An easy 10-minute afternoon walk along rocky Mark Creek to a spectacularly crashing 30m cascade is worth a brief stop.

OYIE✦ AND MOYIE LAKE PROVINCIAL PARK✦✦

Moyie and Moyie Lake Provincial k $
n south of Cranbrook,
3; web:
.elp.gov.bc.ca/bcparks/
ore/parkpgs/moyie.htm
n Apr–Oct.

Nestled within the Purcell Mountains, bears roam around the popular windsurfing and swimming lake. Explorer David Thompson's party was almost swept away by Moyie River spring floods in 1808. Today's 200 Moyie residents point with pride to lovely buildings and a well-preserved fire hall which served when the St Eugene Mine flourished in the late-19th century, one of the richest lead–silver mines in the province.

EUGENE MISSION✦✦

St Eugene Mission $ 7468 Mission Rd,
brook; tel: (250) 489-
2. Stop by nearby
naxa Tribal Office for
rmation and to go
e church.

A restored 1897 Gothic-style mission church has hand-painted Italian stained and leaded glass and interior supports resembling a barn. Across Old Airport Road is the former Kootenay Indian Residential School, now a destination resort.

SPARWOOD✥✥

① Sparwood and District Visitor Info Centre Hwy 3 and Aspen Dr., Sparwood; tel: (250) 425-2423. Information on accommodations, dining, Titan truck and coal mine tours.

The town that replaced the blackened, bulldozed coal-mining to of Natal and Michel, Sparwood lays claim to the world's largest du truck, a 9m-high green Terex Titan with 3m-high wheels, at the Centre.

Suggested tour

Total distance: 270km Blairmore to Cranbrook, including the circ route to Kimberley and Fort Steele and back to Cranbrook. Det 90km south to Moyie.

Time: An easy day to drive. 2–3 days to explore, including detour.

Links: The Columbia River (*see page 122*) lies north of Wasa. Conti south on Hwy 3, the Crowsnest Highway, to Creston and Kootenays (*see page 114*). North of Fernie, Hwy 3 runs east to Crowsnest Pass and enters Alberta, and continues on to Blairmore.

Route: The Crowsnest Highway (Hwy 3) goes through **BLAIRMO ①**, where a tragic slide on Turtle Mountain killed 70 people in th sleep in 1903. The Frank Slide Interpretive Centre explains avalanche, mining and living conditions in the mine's heyday.

Hwy 3 continues west over the Crowsnest Pass (1396m) on BC–Alberta boundary to the town of **SPARWOOD ②**, home of world's largest dump truck. The route follows a southerly direction the town of **FERNIE ③**. Coal mining boomed around 1900 from valley into Alberta, and Fernie and area became rich, though plag by a legendary curse on the mines, claiming many lives. Fernie Alp Resort buzzes with winter activity in a stunning range of mountain.

The Elk Valley traverses the Elk River, named after the numer wapiti (elk) spotted by settlers. Hwy 3 continues through Elko, th joins up with Hwy 93, turning in a northwesterly direction to a junction. Turn right and follow the signs to **FORT STEELE HERIT TOWN ④** for time travel through one of BC's best and most authen historic site restorations. Continue along Hwy 93/95 to Wasa L Provincial Park for swimming in the Kootenay's warmest l (May–Oct). Turn left onto Hwy 95A past Ta Ta Creek to **KIMBERLEY**

① British Columbia Provincial Parks–Kootenay District Wasa Lake Dr., Wasa; tel: (250) 422-4200. Information on all Crowsnest area provincial parks.

Kimberley's heart is the Platzl, the Bavarian chalet-style pedestr plaza, with a cuckoo clock that claims to be the world's larges chimes on the hour, revealing the ubiquitous Happy Hans yodelli Catch the Bavarian City Mining Railway excursion train at the Pl A short drive up the hill provides vistas over the Kootenay R Valley. Before leaving town, take in the thousands of bloom Cominco Gardens.

Take Hwy 95A south in the direction of Marysville, stop at the bridge and hike down Mark Creek for a view of the magnificent **MARYSVILLE FALLS** ❻. Continue toward Cranbrook, then left on to Old Airport Road to **ST EUGENE MISSION** ❼ in the bucolic midst of the tribal headquarters for the Ktunaxa/Kinbasket First Nation St Mary's Reserve. The restored historic church is lovely. Ask at the tribal centre to have the church unlocked. Continue on to Hwy 95A and **CRANBROOK** ❽.

The main city in the area, Cranbrook's big attraction is the Canadian Museum of Rail Travel and the red wooden railway Water Tower nearby, situated along the CPR line where rolling stock provides a realistic background for the historic railway carriages. A graceful reconstructed red-brick Rotary Clock Tower (Baker and Cranbrook Sts) is the focal point for a Chamber of Commerce Heritage Tour brochure at Cranbrook's downtown and Baker Hill residential area buildings. Elizabeth Lake Sanctuary Wildlife Area is a peaceful spot for picnicking and walking the lakeside trail accompanied by birdsong. Follow signs when crossing Hwy 3 to Jimsmith Lake Provincial Park for swimming, fishing and canoeing.

Detour: to Moyie. Take Hwy 3/95 south of Cranbrook to **MOYIE** ❾, a village set on a scenic hillside. **MOYIE LAKE PROVINCIAL PARK** has watersports and sailing.

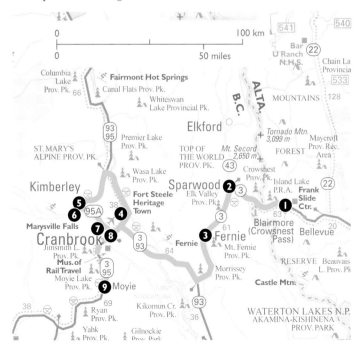

The Kootenays

Ratings

History	●●●●●
Mountains	●●●●●
Nature	●●●●●
Scenery	●●●●●
Children	●●●●○
Outdoor activities	●●●●○
Parks	●●●●○
Food and drink	●●○○○

Dominated by the sinuous and raucous waterways of Kootenay River and Kootenay Lake, and the soari peaks of the Purcell and Selkirk mountains, the region heaven for lovers of rugged mountains and lakes. Followi a dirt track carved open from Hope to Fort Steele, the o highway linking southern BC is more vertical th horizontal. What little flat space exists between mounta ranges is more often filled with water. Ghost towns abou in the Upper and Lower Kootenay (named after a sm Aboriginal band), no surprise in a region best known rushes in search of gold, copper, silver and lead, as smelter ruins, decaying mine shafts and abandon cemeteries. The future is as bright as the past. Urb professionals from across Canada have transformed one-ti backwaters into modern enclaves surrounding gold opportunities for boating, hiking, fishing and skiing.

AINSWORTH HOT SPRINGS❖❖

Ainsworth Hot Springs $$
Hwy 31, 13km north of Balfour; tel: (250) 229-4212.

The hot springs flow from a steam bath with stalactites, an abando horseshoe-shaped mine shaft. Spa aficionados swear by the wa which has the highest mineral content of any natural springs Canada. Everyone else swears by the stunning views across Koote Lake from the 45°C (113°F) outdoor baths.

BOUNDARY CREEK PROVINCIAL PARK❖❖

Boundary Creek Provincial Park $
Hwy 3, west of Greenwood; tel: (250) 494-6500. Open May–Oct.

A slag heap and crumbling chimney are all that remain of the larg copper processor in North America before the First World War, serv up to 20 mines in the surrounding hills. The park also has pleas camping and picnicking spots along Boundary Creek.

ASTLEGAR ❖❖

Castlegar Info Centre 1995 6th Ave; 250) 365-6313; web: /.castlegar.com

Brilliant Suspension Bridge ise of Airport Hill. Park e south end of the tenay River Bridge and 500m down the old way.

tlegar Museum $ 13th Ave; tel: (250) -6440. Open July–Aug –Sat 1000–1700.

khobor Historical ge $ Across from egar Airport; tel: (250) -6622. Open daily –Sept.

gh Keenleyside Dam m north of town; tel:) 365-5299. Open daily.

kerberg Island dge $ 9th St and 7th tel: (250) 365-5511. n May–Aug.

Perched dramatically on benchlands west of the Columbia River and opposite the junction of the Kootenay River, Castlegar began as a railway and timber town. Odorous fumes still blow from a pulp mill just below **Hugh Keenleyside Dam,**❖ which backs the Columbia into Arrow Lakes, stretching 230km north of Revelstoke (see page 126). Doukhobor farms added an important agricultural element to the economy. When local authorities ignored requests for a bridge across the Kootenay River, the Doukhobors (see page 120) designed and built their own span in 1913, which carried Hwy 3 traffic for decades. It forms part of the **Brilliant Suspension Bridge,**❖❖❖ a National Heritage Site.

Castlegar Museum,❖ an old CPR station, concentrates on area history from the early stages of the 20th century. **Doukhobor Historical Village**❖❖❖ is a reproduction of a typical village and includes the communal main house, cottages and workrooms. The furnishings, photographs and artworks are authentic, as are the costumed guides who explain traditional Doukhobor life and beliefs. The small river island which forms **Zuckerberg Island Heritage Park**❖❖❖ was named after a local Russian teacher who built an onion-dome home in the forest. Reached by the 91m pedestrian-only suspension bridge, Zuckerberg's home has been restored as a museum and tea room.

Accommodation and food in Castlegar

Fireside Inn $$ 1810 8th Ave; tel: (250) 365-2128. Convenient and central.

Flamingo Motel $ 1660 Columbia Ave; tel: (250) 365-7978. Has a park-like setting.

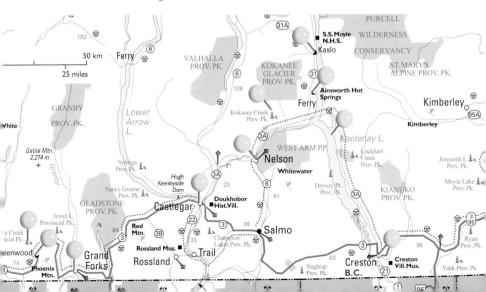

CRESTON**

ⓘ **Creston and District Chamber of Commerce**
1711 Canyon St (Hwy 3); tel: (250) 428-4342. Open July–Aug, daily 0900–1700; Sept–June Mon–Fri.

ⓜ **Creston Valley Museum and Archives** *$ 219 Devon St; tel: (250) 428-9262. Open May–Oct, daily 1000–1530. Tours any time of year by appointment.*

Creston Valley Wildlife Management Area and Centre *$ Hwy 3, 10km northwest of Creston; tel: (250) 428-3259. web: www. cwildlife.bc.ca/index.html. Open Victoria Day–Labour Day, daily 0800–1800; trails open 24 hours.*

A small farming town overlooks a plain where the Kootenay Ri once sprawled between the Purcell and Selkirk mountains in 'Valley of the Swans'. The river has been diked and channell creating fertile grain fields. Creston's rural past appears on mural: the town centre. Highlight of the **Creston Valley Museum a Archives*** is a replica of a traditional Kootenay canoe, a 'sturge nosed' craft with ends pointing down into the water. **Creston Val Wildlife Centre,*** the interpretation centre for the 6800ha Cres Valley Wildlife Management Area, offers guided canoe tours of on BC's richest wetland areas, also walking trails and educatio displays. The area has the largest concentration of nesting osprey: North America as well as massive bird migrations spring and autu (fall).

Accommodation and food in Creston

Downtowner Motor Inn *$$ 1218 Canyon St; tel: (250) 428-22* Central and good value.

Café Miladro *$ 129 north 10th Ave; tel: (250) 428-7252.* The I choice for carnivores in the Kootenays.

Rendezvous Restaurant *$$ 1230 Canyon St; tel: (250) 428-9554.* the best steaks.

GRAND FORKS***

ⓘ **Grand Forks Visitor Info Centre**
7362 5th St; tel: (250) 442-2833. Open May–Sept, daily 0830–1700; Sept–May Mon–Fri 0830–1615; web: www.boundary.bc.ca

ⓜ **Boundary Museum** *$ Hwy 3 and 5th St; tel: (250) 442-3737. Open May–Sept, daily 0930 –1630; Oct–Apr Mon–Fri.*

Mountain View Doukhobor Museum *$ 3655 Hardy Mountain Rd, north of Hwy 3; tel: (250) 442-8855. Open June–Oct daily.*

Named after its proximity to the convergence of the Granby a Kettle rivers, the attractive valley town boomed with the Gran Smelter, once the largest copper smelter in the British Empire. Russ is taught in schools, thanks to the large Doukhobor population w also influence menus of voreniki, galooptsi and borscht. **Bound Museum**** houses artefacts from aboriginals to Doukhobors, mir and railways. See the overview, then take a self-guided tour of som the 300-plus heritage buildings from the mining and railway era w a free museum map. **Mountain View Doukhobor Museum,*** i 1912 Doukhobor communal home, overflows with period artefa and records. Many other Doukhobor buildings are visible along Ha Mountain Road as it twists back to Hwy 3. The **Phoenix Interpre Forest,*** a 22km, self-guided back-road route between Grand Fo and Greenwood, passes many of the former mines, towns and railw that made the Boundary rich in the early-20th century.

Accommodation and food in Grand Forks

Grand Forks Motor Inn $$ *2729 Hwy 3; tel: (250) 442-2127.* Is central and good value.

Aromas Espresso Café and Bakery $ *7229 5th St; tel: (250) 442-0119.* A good stop for budget breakfast, lunch or picnic supplies.

Chef's Garden Restaurant $$ *4415 Hwy 3, 5 km south, near Hardy Mountain Rd; tel: (250) 442-0257.* The best Doukhobor restaurant in BC, serving vegetarian Russian cuisine.

Grand Forks Hotel and Restaurant $$ *7382 2nd St; tel: (250) 442-5944.* Runs a close second to Chef's Garden and also has non-vegetarian choices.

REENWOOD**

*enix Interpretive
est $*
*Sagemore Rd, 19.5km
of Grand Forks; self-
ng map at museums
-and Forks and
-nwood; tel: (250)
-5411. Drivable year
d.*

**Greenwood
Museum $**
*south Copper St; tel:
) 445-6355. Open mid-
-mid-Oct, daily
0–1600.*

*zkar Park $
3, northwest side of
.*

*-w
-ric buildings, Greenwood*

The smallest city in BC (pop. 800), Greenwood was a service centre for dozens of mines in the early-20th century, a wild town with noisy pianos and midnight gambling parties. When mining collapsed after the First World War, Greenwood became a ghost town. Japanese-Canadians were interned in the empty buildings during the Second World War and many stayed on. Many historic buildings have been restored. **Greenwood Museum**** is small but speaks with emotion of the stories of grief and joy and the Japanese community. At **Lotzkar Park,**** the best-preserved smelter ruins in North America rise above a barren ridge of black smelter slag that once glowed red hot, even at noon. Locals call it a 'corner of hell gone mad'.

KASLO***

ⓘ Kaslo Lake Historical Society
324 Front St; tel: (250) 353-2525. Open May–Oct.

ⓘ SS Moyie National Historic Site $
Front St; tel: (250) 353-2525. Open May–Oct for self-guiding tours.

The 'Little Switzerland of the Americas', Kaslo was a lumber to before lead and silver strikes brought miners flooding onto Kootenays. Tourism is number one today, thanks to the resto Victorian-era homes, commercial buildings and heritage sites, an departure point for boating, fishing and mountaineering. meticulously restored 49m SS *Moyie*, beached at the **SS *Moyie* Natio Historic Site,***** sailed Kootenay Lake until 1957, the last sternwhe in regular passenger service in Canada.

KOKANEE CREEK PROVINCIAL PARK***

ⓘ Kokanee Creek Provincial Park $
4750 Hwy 3A, 20km northeast of Nelson; tel: (250) 825-3500; web: www.elp.gov.bc.ca/bcparks/ explore/parkpgs/kokanee.htm Open Apr–Oct.

Built on a site of a former lakeside estate, the park offers hiki boating, camping, fishing and Redfish Creek spawning channel, artificial spawning channel for kokanee salmon. Best time to see bright-red fish is mid-Aug–mid-Sept. The park also shelters a m osprey population.

KOOTENAY LAKE***

ⓘ Crawford Bay
Hwy 3A, 78km north of Creston.

Glass House $
Hwy 3A, 25km north of Creston; tel: (250) 223-8372. Open May–Oct.

Kokanee Springs Golf Resort $$ *Crawford Bay; tel: (250) 227-9226. Open mid-Apr–Thanksgiving.*

Kootenay Lake $ *north of Creston, west to Nelson.*

Lockhart Beach Provincial Park $ *Hwy 3A, north of Creston; tel: (250) 422-4200.*

This long (100km), narrow (2–6km wide) lake between the Purcell Selkirk mountains was a major navigation route long before it beca a prime recreation area. Facilities lie along Hwy 3A, north fr Creston to Kootenay Bay. There you can link to Balfour by BC Ferr with more facilities along Hwy 3A west into Nelson. **Crawford Bay** a collection of artisans producing woven brooms and metalwork traditional blacksmith shop. There is also an 18-hole champions golf course, **Kokanee Springs Golf Resort.*** Mortician David Br built the **Glass House,**** a scenic lakeside house, from half a mill embalming fluid bottles in the 1950s, as he explained, 'to indul whim of a peculiar nature'. There is excellent camping and hiking **Lockhart Beach Provincial Park.**** Farther west is the larger undeveloped Kianuko Provincial Park which protects the headwa of Kianuko Creek.

NELSON✦✦✦

ⓘ Nelson and District Chamber of Commerce 225
Hall St; tel: (250) 352-3433; web: www.city.nelson.bc.ca Open year round.

Ⓜ Chamber of Mines Eastern BC Museum $
215 Hall St; tel: (250) 352-5242.

Lakeside Park $
foot of the Nelson Bridge.

Nelson Museum $
corner of Nelson Ave and Anderson St; tel: (250) 352-9813. Open afternoons year round.

Streetcar No 23 $
downtown to Lakeside Park.

Set on the slopes of the Selkirk Mountains overlooking Kootenay La Nelson's steep streets and hundreds of handsome heritage buildi provided the scene for the 1986 Steve Martin film *Roxanne*. Lc painters have enshrined the movie star on a mural at the end Vernon Street. Film publicity helped Nelson reinforce its incarnat as a rural refuge for urban professionals who expect high-sp Internet connections and the perfect *latte* after a tough day at computer. The impressive Court House✦✦✦ and City Hall✦✦✦ w designed by Francis Rattenbury, the architect who designed Empress Hotel and Legislature Building in Victoria. Guides in per costumes from the Chamber of Commerce lead walking and driv tours of the town's 355 heritage buildings in summer, or follow s guiding maps in any season. A dozen galleries stage monthly shows 75 local artists. Maps of Artwalk are available at the Info Centre. **Chamber of Mines Eastern BC Museum,**✦ run by the provin mining association with a strictly local collection, emphasi steamboats and mines. **Streetcar No 23**✦✦✦ is BC's only operat historic streetcar, making regular runs the length of the town al the lakeshore.

Right
Street barbecue, Nelson

Accommodation and food in Nelson

Prestige Lakeside Resort $$$ *701 Lakeside Dr.; tel: (250) 352-7222.* Nelson's most luxurious hotel.

Garden Inn $$ *408 Victoria St; tel: (250) 352-3226.* A pleasant B&B in a historic home.

Heritage Inn $$ *422 Vernon St; tel: (250) 352-5331.* Has been Nelson's landmark hotel since the 1890s.

All Seasons Café $$ *620 Herridge Lane; tel: (250) 352-0101.* Offers outstanding Northwest cuisine and an outstanding wine list.

Main Street Diner $$ *616 Baker St; tel: (250) 354-4848.* Offers solid Greek meals.

Max and Irma's Kitchen $$ *515A Kootenay St; tel: (250) 352-2332.* Serves Nelson's best pizza and Italian dishes.

Suggested tour

Total distance: 300km.

Time: Greenwood to Creston can be driven in one day, however 2–3 days allows time to enjoy and explore.

Links: Hwy 3 leads to the Crowsnest (*see page 104*). To the west of Greenwood on Hwy 3 are the Cascade Mountains and the Okanagan Valley (*see page 198*).

Route: Only east–west road in the southern BC interior, Hwy 3 passes through the smallest city in BC, **GREENWOOD ❶**, a one-time mine boom town. Continue over Eholt Summit, named after an abandoned mining town, to **GRAND FORKS ❷**, the commercial hub of Boundary Country, an agricultural town that boomed with mineral strikes in nearby hills.

Hwy 3 continues eastbound through Boundary Country, a transition zone between the drier, fertile Okanagan Valley to the west and the high Kootenay peaks, while Hwy 395 near the lake leads south into Washington.

Hwy 3 goes along Christina Lake, then leaves Boundary Country and descends into the Kootenays, over Bonanza Pass and on the downhill leg to **CASTLEGAR ❸**. Take Hwy 3A and cross over the Kinnaird Bridge. A layaway 2.5km northeast of Castlegar overlooks the disused Brilliant Suspension Bridge and Brilliant Dam. The highway passes Bonnington Falls and four hydroelectric dams along the Kootenay River, built to take advantage of the 200m fall from Kootenay Lake at **NELSON ❹** to the Columbia River at Castlegar.

After exploring the pretty town of Nelson, return to the junction Hwys 3A and 6, turn south on Hwy 6, cross over the bright ora Nelson Bridge and skirt the Selkirk Mountains in the direction Salmo, the Latin word for salmon. At Burnt Flat Junction, turn east Hwy 3 and continue over the 'The Skyway', at 1774m one of highest paved roads in Canada, past the Creston Valley Wild Centre and on into **CRESTON** ❼.

Scenic alternative: The more interesting 150km route to Crest follows Hwy 3A east of Nelson to Balfour. The 30-minute crossing free but the line-up can take most of the day, especially in summ Hwy 3A follows along the shores of **KOOTENAY LAKE**, pass Crawford Bay, Lockhart Beach Provincial Park and Glass House.

Detour: From Balfour, turn north on Hwy 31 to **AINSWORTH H SPRINGS** ❺ and Cody Caves Provincial Park on the way to **KAS** ❻. The charming village has more than 60 heritage buildin including the dry-docked SS *Moyie*, a sternwheeler that once carr passengers on the lake. Return to Balfour.

The Doukhobors

A sect of radical Russian dissenters, persecuted in the 18th century for their heresy and pacifism, was called Doukhobors or 'wrestlers against the Holy Spirit' by an Orthodox archbishop. Assisted by British and American Quakers, over 7000 emigrated to Canada in 1898–9 in what was to become southeastern Saskatchewan. Exiled spiritual leader Peter (Lordly) Verigin joined the group, and in 1908 led the Doukhobors to southern BC after their homesteads were cancelled when they refused to swear an oath of allegiance demanded by the new minister of the interior. They settled on flat land across the Columbia River from Castlegar, and built many of the earliest bridges when authorities refused their request, including the graceful Brilliant Suspension Bridge over the Kootenay River.

The new immigrants planted orchards, grain and vegetables while building sawmills, jam factories, pipe works and similar enterprises. Their communal living arrangements, outspoken pacifism and vocal opposition to meat, tobacco and alcohol won few friends locally. Many were imprisoned for nude protest parades. Communal villages have disappeared but thousands of Doukhobors still live in Boundary Country from Castlegar to Grand Forks. Many of their distinctive farm buildings are still visible along country roads, and Russian restaurants – invariably Doukhobor – are local institutions, though the 'no meat, no booze, no smoking' slogan is a distant memory.

...ht
...efacts at Doukhobor
...torical Village

Columbia River

Ratings

Mountains	●●●●●
Nature	●●●●●
Outdoor activities	●●●●●
Parks	●●●●●
Scenery	●●●●●
Wildlife	●●●●●
Geology	●●●●○
Food and drink	●●●○○

Cutting deep gorges along its 2 044km course, t powerful Columbia River was named by Bost explorer-trader Robert Gray after his ship the *Columbia* a after which British Columbia is named. The Colu](l begins its much dammed and serpentine route to the Paci Ocean near Portland, Oregon from Columbia Lake. Bi migration along the Columbia Valley is breathtaking spring and autumn (fall). Migration of humans over one the world's snowiest mountain areas at Rogers Pass is alm as awe-inspiring because of the technical expertise it takes keep the route open against avalanches. This is railw country, from the hub at Golden at the north end of t Columbia Valley, to Revelstoke west of the Selki Mountains along the Columbia River, west of Golden o Rogers Pass. Glaciers, old-growth cedars and wild-flow meadows lie in-between the towns, each claiming t distinction as Gateway to the Columbia.

BUGABOO PROVINCIAL PARK✦✦✦

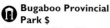 **Bugaboo Provincial Park $**
45km west of Hwy 95 at Brisco; tel: (250) 422-4200. Commercial heli-skiing lodge near park entrance.

An alpine wilderness, Bugaboo Provincial Park is a rugg(breathtaking landscape that attracts serious mountain climbers a heli-skiers from around the world. The park can be reached by a go gravel logging road, 45km west of Hwy 95 at Brisco. The 13,64(park is home to a variety of wildlife such as pikas, marmots, grou squirrels and mountain goats. There are 20 wilderness campsites h no services.

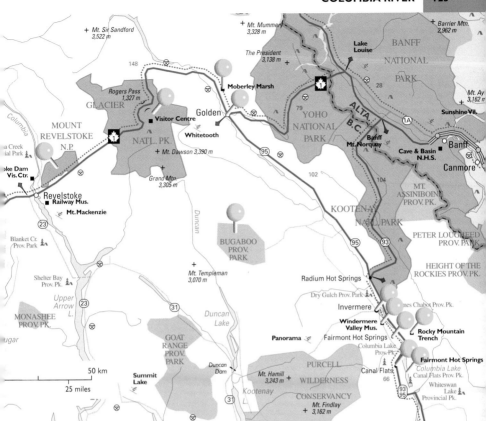

ANAL FLATS*

Canal Flats
Historic Point, Hwy 95 at south end of Columbia Lake.

Sitting on a 2km strip of land that separates the southward-flowing Kootenay River and the northward Columbia River, Canal Flats originates from an 1889 canal built to divert the Kootenay away from valley farms. Too narrow locks were the canal's downfall. The *North Star*, only the second vessel to pass through, wrecked the locks and system in 1902. Look for skeleton sculptures on the east side of Hwy 95 at Canal Flats. Doug 'Up' Bonz is a skilled bone and fossil finder with a gift for humour and sculpture. The bones of birds and small animals become skeletons of impossible creatures, shown off around the property and in the trailer that is his workshop and sales gallery.

COLUMBIA LAKE✧

Columbia Lake
*south of Fairmont Hot
Springs on the east side of
Hwy 93/95.*

A sign at a lay-by on the east side of Hwy 93/95 states 'Columbia L
– Source of Columbia River which empties into Pacific Ocean
Astoria – Oregon', that is, 2 044km southwest of the headwaters. Sp
golden hoodoos (eroded columns of rock) rise sheer above Du
Creek at the lake's north end.

Right
Columbia River

FAIRMONT HOT SPRINGS✧✧✧

**Fairmont Hot
Springs Resort $$**
*midway between Canal Flats
and Invermere on Hwy
93/95; tel: (250) 345-6311,
tollfree (800) 663-4979;
web:
fairmonthotspringsresort.com
Open year round with a
Ski Hill $$*

Hot Pools $
open daily 0800–2200.

**Mountainside Golf
Course $$$** *tel: (250)
345-6314, tollfree (800)
663-4979. One of two 18-
hole courses, offering
magnificent views over the
Columbia River Valley.*

Soak in the 43–48°C (109.4–118.4°F) hot springs, Canada's larg
odourless natural hot pools which have been long used by Ktuna
(Kootenay) people. From several vantage points, including t
Mountainside Golf Course, the forest-bound resort looks westward
the craggy line of the Purcell Mountain Range. Hiking, biking, ho
riding and winter skiing supplement the pools' attraction for the loc
guests and another 750,000 visitors who make an annual pilgrima
to the resort.

LACIER NATIONAL PARK✧✧

Rogers Pass
*69km east of
elstoke, 72km west of
len, on Hwy 1 in Glacier
ional Park.*

**Glacier National
Park $**
*int Revelstoke and
ier national parks HQ,
St and Campbell Ave,
elstoke; tel: (250) 837-
0; web:
v.parkscan.harbour.com/
ier*

gers Pass Centre
*ers Pass; tel: (250) 814-
3 or (250) 837-7500.
n May–mid-June and
Sept–Oct, daily
0–1700; mid-June–mid-
: 0800–2030; Nov
r–Mon 0900–1700;
–Mar 0700–1700.*

The northern Selkirk Mountain Range, the birthplace of North American technical climbing (mountaineering) in 1888, is a land of snow and over 400 active glaciers and icefields, including Illecillewaet Glacier, visible from the TransCanada Highway on a clear day. Waterfalls and wild flowers are abundant in season. If travelling east, you will see the 14.5km Mount Macdonald Tunnel, North America's longest railway tunnel, built after hundreds died between 1885 and 1911 trying to keep Rogers Pass open. **Rogers Pass.**✧✧✧ Many peaks poke the sky at 3700m, catching shrouds of snow which slide dangerously below. **Rogers Pass Centre**✧✧ offers excellent explanations of the Snow Wars waged by the CPR and more currently by Parks Canada and the Royal Canadian Horse Artillery to keep the TransCanada Highway open. Abandoned Rails Trail follows Hwy 1 past side-paths and snowsheds 1.3km to the Rogers Pass Monument,✧ which commemorates completion of the TransCanada Highway in 1962, the first alternative to rail travel over the pass.

Accommodation and food in Glacier National Park

Best Western Glacier Park Lodge $$$ *Rogers Pass; tel: (250) 837-2126, tollfree (800) 528-1234.* The only non-camping accommodation in the park provides 50 rooms next to the Rogers Pass Centre, with a restaurant, 24-hour cafeteria and petrol station.

OLDEN✧

**Golden and
District Chamber
Commerce Info
ntre**
* north 10th Ave; tel:
0) 344-7125, tollfree
0) 622-4653; web:
v.rockies.net/columbia-
ey
n May–Sept Mon–Fri
0–1700.

Trains, lorries, rivers, an active sawmill, tourists and outdoor enthusiasts (hang gliders, rock climbers, whitewater kayakers and rafters, mountain bikers, hikers and anglers) all use Golden as a convenient valley-floor base. Here is the confluence of the Columbia and Kicking Horse rivers and access to Yoho National Park (*see page 91*) or Glacier National Park. Mountains rise along both sides of the valley, causing spectacular sunsets over the Purcells.

Accommodation and food in Golden

Golden Rim Motor Inn $$ *1416 Golden View Rd; tel: (250) 344-2216.* Has views of the Columbia River Valley.

Sportsman Motel $ *1200 12th St north; tel: (250) 344-2915.* Quiet and away from the highway.

Legendz $ *1405 west TransCanada Hwy; tel: (250) 344-5059.* Serves delicious steaks and creamy eggs, with other Marilyn Munroe and James Dean-era specialities.

INVERMERE*

ⓘ Invermere Columbia Valley Chamber of Commerce Visitor Info Centre *651 Hwy 93/95 Crossroads, Windermere; tel: (250) 342-2844 or (250) 342-6316; web: www.adventurevalley.com/ chamberofcommerce Open May–Labour Day Mon–Fri 0900–1700.*

🏛 James Chabot Provincial Park $ *North end of Windermere Lake; web: www.elp.gov.bc.ca/bcparks/ explore/parkpgs/james.htm*

At the northwest corner of Windermere Lake, the area's commerc centre south of Golden boasts Sept–Oct kokanee salmon spawning its end of the 15km lake and lakeside **James Chabot Provincial Par** with a swimming beach and watersports.

MOBERLY MARSH/BURGES AND JAMES GADSEN PROVINCIAL PARK*

Most drivers do not stop in the rush to and from Golden, b migratory waterfowl do along this stretch of marsh between t TransCanada Highway and the Columbia River. Spot muskrats a ospreys from a 3.5km riverbank Dyke Trail.

MOUNT REVELSTOKE NATIONAL PARK***

ⓘ Revelstoke Info Centre *junction of TransCanada Highway (Hwy 1) and Hwy 233. Open summer.*

Revelstoke Chamber of Commerce *204 Campbell Ave; tel: (250) 837-5345, tollfree (800) 487-1493; web: www.revelstokecc.bc.ca Open Mon–Fri 0830–1200, 1300–1630; summer open through lunch. For snow sports, web: www.revelstokecc. bc.ca/snow/start.htm*

Unlike the Rocky Mountain National Parks, which were spurred on the CPR and the need for an all-weather automobile route (Kootena this park was a result of City of Revelstoke citizens building a trail the mountain's summit and lobbying for a road. That road, Meado in the Sky Parkway, draws thousands of mid-summer visitors to t rich displays of wild flowers.

Giant Cedars Trail.* Rainforest in the interior of BC? Eig hundred-year-old Western red cedars along a half kilometre boardw tell the tale. The damp, mossy streambed is dim but vibrant w many hues of green. **Meadows in the Sky.*** Stop at the elabor archway Welcome Station entrance to the 26km Meadows in the S Parkway for information. Depending on the severity of the p winter, the parkway may be closed part of the way up, even thou the route is normally open early July–late Sept. Enjoy the winding,

**Mount Revelstoke
National Park $**
nt Revelstoke and
ier national parks HQ,
St and Campbell Ave,
Istoke; tel: (250) 837-
0 or (250) 837-6867;

.parkscan.harbour.com/
ev
dens at Meadows in
Sky Parkway have park
rmation.

nt Cedars Trail $
west of east boundary
lount Revelstoke
onal Park.

**adows in the Sky
rkway) $** 3km east of
Istoke in Mount
Istoke National Park.
ers are prohibited
ond the parkway trailer
ting area 0.5km from
1.

elstoke Dam $
north of Revelstoke; tel:
) 837-6515. Open
–mid-June, daily
0–1700; mid-June–mid-
0800–2000; mid-
–Thanksgiving
0–1700.

**elstoke Railway
eum $** Victoria Rd,
Istoke; tel: (250) 837-
0, tollfree (877) 837-
0; web:
.railwaymuseum.com
n July–Aug, daily
0–2000; May–June and
0900–1700; Apr and
Mon–Sat 0900–1700;
Mon–Fri 0900–1700;
–Mar Mon–Fri
0–1700.

ve
rative window,
Istoke

osite
house near the Columbia

switchback drive past fine views of Revelstoke and the Columbia River. Park at Balsam Lake and take the Summit Shuttle to the wildflower meadows or hike the colourful carpet by way of the 1km Summit Trail to the top.

BC Hydro operates **Revelstoke Dam**◆ and generating station, a must for those fascinated by waterway engineering and the intricacies of changes to the Columbia River. It is not large but the **Revelstoke Railway Museum**◆◆ is a good introduction to the challenges faced by CPR engineers and officials who encountered avalanches, difficult soil, steep grades, harsh winters and labour strife while constructing and maintaining the railway. Prized are the Business Car No 4 and Mikado P-2k class locomotive No 5468, on display in a replica of Victoria's E&N Roundhouse.

Accommodation and food in Revelstoke

Many Revelstoke motels are near the noisy railway tracks at the west end of town.

Canyon Motor Inn $$ 1911 Fraser Dr., off Hwy 1 at Columbia River Bridge; tel: (250) 837-5221, tollfree (800) 382-7763. Has small, very clean rooms in a quiet spot near the river.

Blue Berry Patch $ 212 Mackenzie Ave; tel: (250) 837-5500. Has delicious breakfast blueberry cornmeal and apple rhubarb muffins, and wraps and sandwiches for lunch.

Three Bears' Bistro Sweet Shop $$ 114 Mackenzie Ave, Grizzly Plaza; tel: (250) 837-9575. Has great coffee, salads and home-made soup.

Tony Roma's $$ 306 Mackenzie Ave; tel: (250) 837-4106. Offers huge, tasty portions of Italian specialities.

ROCKY MOUNTAIN TRENCH❖

Astronauts say this depression between mountain ranges wh
extends from Alaska along the western side of the Rocky Mount
into the Central US is one of the most prominent features on ea
The rift valley separates the ancient Columbia Mountains from
craggier, younger Rocky Mountains on the eastern side, with l
wetlands and cultivated farmland in-between. Rocky Mount
Trench, dividing the Rocky and Cascade mountain ranges from Al
to the Central US, has the Columbia River at its bottom in this area

WINDERMERE❖

**St Peter's Anglican
Church $** *Kootenay
St; tel: (250) 342-6644.*

The town and its namesake lake are a resort get-away for locals
people from colder climes. **St Peter's Anglican Church❖** was stoler
1897, removed via a railway flatcar from Donald, 210km north,
residents who wanted a ready-made church when most Don
inhabitants moved to Revelstoke along with the CPR operations.

Suggested tour

Total distance: 310km.

Time: 2 days.

Links: From Revelstoke, continue west on the TransCanada High
(Hwy 1) to the Shuswap Lakes (*see page 160*). At Golden, go eas
Yoho National Park in BC Rockies or at Radium Junction, go eas
Kootenay National Park in the UNESCO Trail North (*see page 8*
South of Canal Flats on Hwy 93/95 to the Crowsnest (*see page 104*).

Route: At **Revelstoke ❶**, the pretty city called 'Home of the Wor
Largest Sculpted Grizzly Bears', visit the Revelstoke Railway Muse
Revelstoke Museum and the amazing collection at Piano Keep Gall
Travel east on the TransCanada Highway and enter **MOU**
REVELSTOKE NATIONAL PARK ❷, and take the park's jewel,
Meadows in the Sky Parkway, a 42km drive to Balsam Lake park
and a 2km shuttle ride or walk to Mount Revelstoke's summ
carpeted with wild flowers in mid-summer. Return to Hwy 1 and s
and take the short 0.5km Giant Cedars Trail for a view of
rainforest; look for bats in summer. In May, walk the 1.2km Sk
Cabbage Trail for views of birds and the odiferous plants flowe
yellow along the Illecillewaet River.

Opposite
Sinclair Canyon, Kootenay
National Park

In **GLACIER NATIONAL PARK** ❸, the Illecillewaet Glacier ('"
Great Glacier') campground and trail head to a series of trails near
glacier, accessible from Hwy 1. Rogers Pass Monument (1382
memorial arch to the 1962 TransCanada Highway completion, is 1
from Rogers Pass Centre with a roaring fire, excellent exhibit and f
depictions of avalanche control and snow management, and a w
stocked book store. Tunnels covering the TransCanada Highway
snowsheds, built to deflect the violent impact of avalanches. Be
leaving the park, Beaver Valley has a lovely picnic spot and v
flowers in summer. Continue past **BURGES and JAMES GADSD**
PROVINCIAL PARK ❹ at Moberley Marsh and Donald, where
CPR line first crossed the Columbia River.

At the junction of the TransCanada Highway in **GOLDEN**
continue south on Hwy 95 along the Columbia River Valley, throu
the Great Blue Heron Rookery, the second largest population
Western Canada. At **Radium** ❻, Hwy 93 splits off east from Hwy
to Radium Hot Springs and Kootenay National Park.

Travel south on Hwy 95 to **INVERMERE** ❼ on the west side w
views of the Purcell Mountains and **WINDERMERE** ❽ on
highway side. Continue along Windermere Lake to **FAIRMONT H**
SPRINGS ❾, an oasis for soaking, swimming, golfing, hiking a
winter skiing. Looming mysteriously to the right are the Dutch Cr
Hoodoos. Travel south on the west side of **COLUMBIA LAKE**
headwaters of the Columbia River. The wetlands that begin here
the most extensive and richest on earth, 26,000ha of protected spa
Continue along the Rocky Mountain Trench and on into **CAN**
FLATS ❿.

Detour: To Panorama Mountain Village. Follow the signs and t
right into the town of Invermere, then turn right again at the s
near the top of the hill. Follow the winding, hilly road for 18km
Panorama Mountain Village, a year-round retreat for golf, hot po
hiking and skiing.

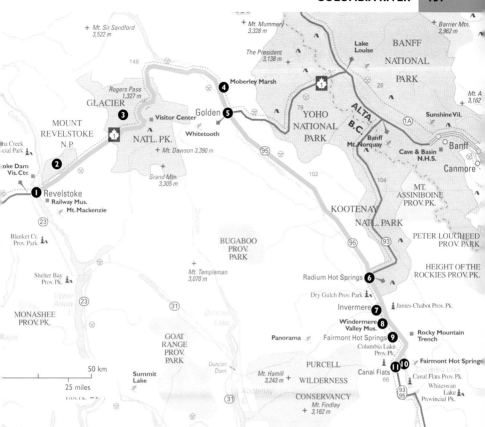

The man behind Rogers Pass

A railway engineer and surveyor, Albert Bowman Rogers is described by Parks Canada as 'short, sharp and rough-tongued'. A native of Massachusetts, Rogers graduated from Yale University and was hired by the CPR to find a southerly route through the rugged Selkirk Mountains, a route that would be closer to the Canada–US border. In 1881, he tried the Pass's west side, and 'many a time I wished myself dead'. He approached from the east the following year and 'felt like a piece of liver' after finding a viable pass through the mountains. The incentives were a $5000 bonus and the naming of the pass after him, yet in his typically stubborn style, Rogers never cashed the cheque.

Cariboo Country

Ratings

Geology	●●●●●
Nature	●●●●●
Outdoor activities	●●●●●
Scenery	●●●●●
Children	●●●●○
History	●●●●○
Mountains	●●●●○
Wildlife	●●●●○

A semi-wilderness of forests, mountains, lakes and prai the Cariboo is a land where towns are small, few and between. What many call the Real West is a land wh cattle outnumber people and dreams grow as big as the is broad. East of the Fraser River lie lakes and de evergreens that stretch to the Cariboo Mountains. West the Chilcotin ('people of the young man's river' Tsilhqot'in), a vast rolling plain rising from the mig Fraser and running to the foothills of the Coast Mounta The region contains vast tracts of protected parkland t are barely mapped. Farther west is the glacial crown of Coast Range, dropping precipitously into deep fiords wh cut inland up to 70km from the Pacific Ocean. This la called Cariboo Country conjures up images of those br early explorers who travelled along the rugged Grease Trai

ALEXIS CREEK✣

 Alexis Creek
112km west of Williams Lake.

With nearly 250 residents, this Chilcotin community has petrol, RCMP detachment, post office, grocery store and a BC Forest Serv office.

Accommodation and food in Alexis Creek

Chilcotin Hotel $ *tel: (250) 394-4214.* The only hotel and restau in town.

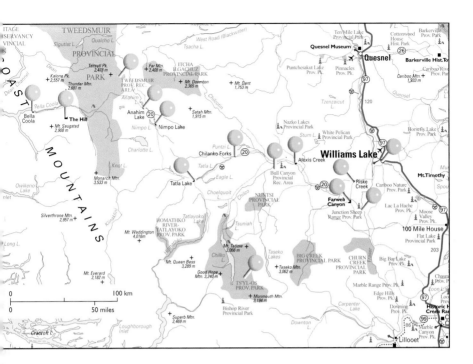

NAHIM LAKE❖❖❖

A C Christensen General Store *(250) 742-3266. The source for area information and supplies.*

Anahim Lake Resort $$ *Hwy 20; (250) 742-3200.*

This aboriginal village is the largest in the West Chilcotin and a centre for fishing the Dean and nearby rivers. Anahim Lake Resort offers fishing, air taxi service, hiking, riding and general relaxation. The locally renowned August Stampede is authentic here, much less commercial than early July's Calgary Stampede.

ELLA COOLA❖❖

Tourism Bella Coola *10 Cliff St; tel: (1) 799-5268 or (888) -1181. Open June–Sept 0–1630. Contact the for information about Bella Coola Valley eum, Mackenzie way.*

British Capt George Vancouver sailed up fiord-like North Bentinck Arm to Bella Coola in 1793, just weeks before Alexander Mackenzie walked down the narrow valley to the Pacific. Norwegian farmers arrived in 1894 to share the valley with Nuxalk (Bella Coola) aboriginal people. Town and fiord are ringed by sheer mountains, providing endless opportunities for fishing, hiking and outdoor adventure.

ⓘ Quesnel Forest Office *322 Johnston Ave, Quesnel; tel: (250) 992-4400.* For information on travelling the Alexander Mackenzie Heritage Trail/Nuxalk –Carrier Grease Trail.

➔ Hagensborg *Hwy 20, 18km east of Bella Coola.*

ⓗ Acwsalcta Nuxalk Nation School $ *4km east off Hwy 20.*

Sir Alexander Mackenzie Provincial Park and Mackenzie Rock $ *60km west on Dean Channel, no land access.* Ask about transport at the museum.

Thorsen Creek Petroglyphs $ *Off Hwy 20, east of Bella Coola.* Ask for directions at the museum.

The **Acwsalcta Nuxalk Nation School**✧✧✧ has some of the fi▮ aboriginal artwork on public display along the coast. Bella C▮ Valley Museum,✧ in a 19th-century schoolhouse and surveyor's ca▮ has Hudson's Bay Company relics and Norwegian goods. Norwe▮ farmers at **Hagensborg**✧ were Bella Coola's first non-aborig▮ residents in modern times. Many of the century-old homes and b▮ show adze marks produced by the original builders. Mackenzie Roc▮ **Sir Alexander Mackenzie Provincial Park**✧✧✧ was the final sto▮ Mackenzie's 1793 trek across Canada. He painted a messag▮ vermilion and bear grease: 'Alexander Mackenzie, from Canada▮ land, the twenty-second of July, one thousand, seven hundred ▮ ninety-three', which was later chiselled into the rock. The **Tho▮ Creek Petroglyphs**✧✧✧ are dozens of carvings lining rocks along creek.

Accommodation and food in Bella Coola

Bella Coola Valley Inn $$ *Corner of Dean and Mackenzie St; tel: (▮ 799-5316.* The best motel in town and the closest to the BC Fe▮ dock.

Tallheo Cannery $$ *Across the harbour from Bella Coola; tel: (250) ▮ 2344.*

BULL CANYON PROVINCIAL RECREATION AREA✧✧✧

ⓗ Bull Canyon Provincial Recreation Area $ *Hwy 20, 6km west of Alexis Creek; tel: (250) 398-4414; web: www.elp.gov.bc.ca/bcparks/ explore/parkpgs/bullcan.htm*

This pleasant picnic and camping stop along the grey-green Chilc▮ River was a cattle roundup point and the site of a decisive ba▮ between Tsilhqot'in and Secwepemc bands.

Right
Cariboo Country's rolling plains

HILANKO FORKS***

Chilanko Forks
62km west of Alexis
k.

Chilanko Forks is a traditional Chilcotin town with a general store and petrol station. A marsh by the airport access road is good for beaver and muskrat spotting.

RWELL CANYON***

Farwell Canyon
19km south of Hwy 20
Riske Creek.

The Chilcotin River has cut a deep canyon through soft golden cliffs, creating flat-topped hoodoos (columns of rock formed by erosion) capped by sand dunes that shift with the wind.

HE HILL***

The Hill
Hwy 20, east of Bella
a.

The final barrier to land travel between Bella Coola and the rest of BC was finally breached in 1953 by local bulldozer operators who were tired of government highway engineers saying a road down the sheer western face of the Coast Range was impossible. Views from the single-track gravel road are stupendous but there are no verges or lay-bys.

NCTION SHEEP RANGE PROVINCIAL PARK***

**Junction Sheep
Range Provincial**
k $ 15km south of Hwy
el: (250) 398-4414;

.elp.gov.bc.ca/bcparks/
ore/parkpgs/junction.htm

This isolated park protects the world's largest herd of California bighorn sheep, as well as some 40 or so species of butterfly.

t
orn sheep

NIMPO LAKE❖❖❖

Dean River Resort
tel: (250) 742-3331.

This 12km lake claims to be BC's float plane capital for the many charter flights to remote rivers and lakes. **Dean River Resort**❖❖❖ is most comfortable of several lake-front fishing resorts.

RISKE CREEK❖

Riske Creek
46km west of Williams Lake.

The tiny farming town of Riske Creek is named after a 19th-cent Polish farmer, an early settler in the area.

Accommodation and food in Riske Creek

Chilcotin Lodge $$ *Riske Creek; tel: (250) 659-5646.* A former hunt lodge turned B&B, restaurant and campground.

TATLA LAKE❖❖❖

Tatla Lake $
109km from Alexis Creek.

Lake and town are the half-way point between Williams Lake Bella Coola. Nordic skiing is a popular winter activity, rivalling diving in summer.

TS'YL-OS PROVINCIAL PARK❖❖❖

Ts'yl-Os Provincial Park $
100km south of Hwy 20 from Lees Corner; tel: (250) 398-4414; web: www.elp.gov.bc.ca/bcparks/ explore/parkpgs/ts.htm

Lakes and streams in this undeveloped wilderness produce one-qua of the entire Fraser River salmon run. Apart from two gravel roads Hwy 20, the only access is by air, boat, horse or foot.

TWEEDSMUIR PROVINCIAL PARK❖❖❖

Tweedsmuir Provincial Park $
HQ on Hwy 20 east of Bella Coola; tel: (250) 398-4414; web: www.elp.gov.bc.ca/bcparks /explore/parkpgs/tweed.htm

Tweedsmuir is 980,000ha of wilderness outside a narrow corri along Hwy 20. The best easy walks are on the Bella Coola side al the Atnarko River Spawning Channels, where grizzlies and black b have the right of way.

WILLIAMS LAKE*

● **Cariboo Chilcotin Coast Tourism** sociation *118A 1st Ave th, Williams Lake; tel: 0) 392-2226.*

Iliams Lake and trict Chamber of mmerce *1148 South adway (Hwy 97, south * of city); tel: (250) 392- 25; web: www.lake.com en June–Aug, daily 00–1700; Sept–June n–Fri 0900–1600.*

● **Scout Island Nature Centre $** *t end of city, off Hwy 97, t of city centre; tel: (250) 3-8532. Open Apr–Sept, y 0800–1600.*

ationhouse Gallery $ *orth Mackenzie Ave in BC Rail Station; tel: (250) 2-6113. Open Mon–Sat 00–1700.*

illiams Lake Museum *13 north 4th Ave; tel: 0) 392-7404. Open e–Sept Mon–Sat 00–1600; Oct–May e–Sat 1100–1600.*

This is the only real town between Hope and Quesnel, a cowboy city that has expanded into forestry, mining, agriculture and tourism. Williams Lake's public gallery, the **Stationhouse Gallery,**✦✦✦ concentrates on BC artists, while **Williams Lake Museum**✦✦✦ focuses on the ranching, rodeo and cowboy history of the Cariboo region. Scout Island Nature Centre,✦✦✦ a small marsh, has lakeside walking paths, wildlife watching and a summer nature centre.

Accommodation and food in Williams Lake

Fraser Inn $$ *285 Donald Rd; tel: (250) 398-7055; web: www.fraserinn.com* The largest hotel in town.

Overlander Hotel $$ *1118 Lakeview Cres.; tel: (250) 392-3321, tollfree (800) 663-6898.* A busy, moderate hotel with a good restaurant.

Rowat's Waterside B&B $$ *1397 Borland Rd; tel: (250) 392-7395.* A short walk from Scout Island.

Great Cariboo Steak Company $$ *Fraser Inn, 285 Donald Rd; tel: (250) 398-7395.* Known for oversized steaks.

Hearth Restaurant $$ *99 3rd Ave; tel: (250) 398-6831.* In the Cariboo Friendship Society, has open-beam aboriginal decor.

Suggested tour

Total distance: 465km.

Time: Allow 10–12 hours to drive; 2–5 days to explore.

Links: From Williams Lake, Hwy 97, the Gold Rush Trail (*see page 140*) leads north toward Prince George or south toward Hope (*see page 223*). From Bella Coola, BC Ferries Discovery Coast route (*see page 182–4*) leads south to Port Hardy and North Vancouver Island (*see page 226*).

Route: From **BELLA COOLA** ❶, sitting at the head of the North Bentinck Arm and mouth of the Bella Coola River, travel east on Hwy 20 which runs gently uphill through the Bella Coola Valley. Continue on to Hagensborg which still has many of the square-cut, hand-hewn buildings left by early Norwegian settlers from Minnesota a century ago. The highway runs through dense forest along the Atnarko and Bella Coola rivers.

Use low gear to creep up (or down) the steep 18 per cent grade as the pavement ends. There are no verges, no guard-rails and no lay-bys to enjoy the spectacular views along the 9km of single-track, hairpin turns that climb 1300m from the Bella Coola Valley to the Heckman

Alexander Mackenzie–Grease Trail

The 450km trail, stretching from the junction of the Blackwater and Fraser rivers near Quesnel to the Dean Channel north of Bella Coola, was a main trade route of the Bella Coola, Carrier and Chilcotin bands, a corridor used by aboriginal people for 6 000 years. The name given the road, 'Grease', was taken from the processed oil of the oolichan (a small smelt-like fish that was dried or rendered into fat), a major trading commodity of the Bella Coola band.

Alexander Mackenzie, an explorer and fur trader with the North West Co., was advised by Indians to travel overland on his expedition to reach the Pacific. He was guided along the rugged Grease Trail, the first European to journey across North America. A national historic trail, the foot and horse track is made up of highways, forest access roads, local wagon roads, rivers and coastal waters.

Pass east of the top of **THE HILL ❷**, surveyed and built by lo volunteers when government engineers said it was impossible.

The 1 524m Heckman Pass is the east entrance to **TWEEDSMU PROVINCIAL PARK ❸**. There are good views of the multicolou Rainbow Mountains from the Tsulko River east of Heckman Pa Local aboriginal bands mined obsidian from the Rainbows, a string ancient volcanoes stained red, yellow and purple by mineral deposit

The paved highway begins west of **ANAHIM LAKE ❹**, a sm Tsilhqot'in community named after a prominent leader in the 186 Gravel roads lead north along the Dean River, but check locally conditions before setting out. Beyond the last tyre tracks lies t Nuxalk–Carrier Grease Trail east to the Fraser and west to Bella Cool

Hwy 20 crosses the Dean River east of Anahim Lake. A histori marker commemorates the 1864 Chilcotin War when Tsilhqot warriors, fearing a smallpox epidemic, clashed with men attempting build a road across the Chilcotin to the Cariboo gold fields provincial inquiry in 1993 granted five posthumous pardons an memorial was erected.

The pavement ends again at Nimpo Lake. The well-maintained gra highway winds southward through Coast Range foothills. Tatla La western edge of the Chilcotin Plateau, is the midway point Williams Lake. The gently rolling grasslands, also called the Fra Plateau, stretch east to the Fraser River. It is a pleasant drive summer but the weather is deceptively gentle. Winter temperatu can feel like -50°C (-58°F) with winds driving blinding blizzar Pollywog Marsh is a pleasant lakeside rest stop. Best view of the ent Tatla Lake valley is from a lay-by 22km beyond the lake.

Pavement begins again 15km east, just west of **CHILANKO FORKS** The highway east is dotted with stunning views to the Coast Range.

BULL CANYON PROVINCIAL PARK ❻ is a pleasant picnic a camping spot in an aspen forest along the grey-green Chilcotin Riv The canyon was the site of an epic battle between the Tsilhqot'in a Secwepemc bands, and a cattle roundup point. **ALEXIS CREEK ❼** the main settlement in the eastern Chilcotin.

The road continues south and west to **TS'YL-OS PROVINCIAL PA ❽**, created to protect traditional Aboriginal lands from logging.

One of the best views of the Chilcotin is from a rest area at the top a long grade 12km east of Lee's Corner, named after an ill-fat attempt to drive 200 head of cattle 2 500km through the mountains the Klondike gold fields in 1896. The town of Riske Creek, named af an early rancher, is 1.5km east at the log cabins painted bright yell on the north side of Hwy 20.

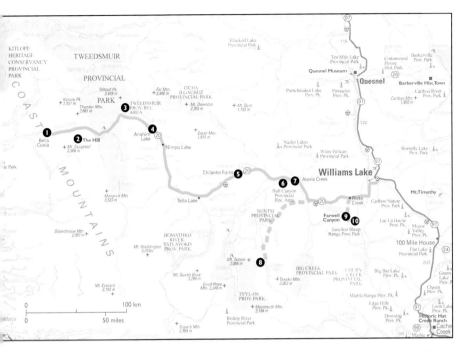

Detour: Follow the gravel road along the rolling curves of the almost treeless plain to **FARWELL CANYON ❾** and a wooden bridge over the Chilcotin River. There are early aboriginal rock paintings on the overhang at the south end of the bridge. Local Tsilhqot'in fishers net salmon from the river in summer and autumn (fall), drying their catch on racks nearby. The road loops 50km back to Hwy 20 at Lee's Corner.

The enormous antennae rising from the prairie form part of the Loran-C navigation system. A good gravel road 9.5km west leads 16km east to the fairy tale hoodoos of Farwell Canyon and **JUNCTION SHEEP RANGE PROVINCIAL PARK ❿**, a reserve for California bighorn sheep.

Continue east across Becher's Prairie, rolling grassland strewn with boulders deposited by retreating glaciers. Nesting boxes on fenceposts attract bluebirds and tree swallows that feast on the mosquitoes that can plague the small lakes and ponds dotting the Chilcotin. The eastern edge of the plateau is the immense Fraser River trench. Watch slow-moving logging trucks on the steep grades at both ends of the Sheep Creek Bridge over the river. The mouth of the Fraser River is 500km south. Continue 25km east into **WILLIAMS LAKE**.

Cariboo Gold Rush Trai

Ratings

History	●●●●●
Nature	●●●●●
Outdoor activities	●●●●●
Scenery	●●●●●
Walking	●●●●●
Museums	●●●●○
Children	●●●○○
Food and drink	●●○○○

The Cariboo Gold Rush of the 1860s transformed BC fr a distant source of furs into a major presence on t world stage. Nearly every product, place and attitude that part of BC today has its roots in the Gold Rush. Most of t province's major highways exist because they once fill Gold Rush needs. Even timber, largest of BC's tradition industries, owes much to the insatiable Gold Rush dema for wooden buildings, railway sleepers and fuel. Who fi discovered gold and where may never be known. Aborigin traders brought small amounts to the Hudson's B Company for years but the fur-trading giant hid its secr fearing that an influx of gold seekers would disrupt profitable monopoly. When gold was discovered in t Cariboo Mountain region, the company began to relinqui its colonial responsibilities and controlling interest fell the International Financial Society.

ASHCROFT MANOR❖❖

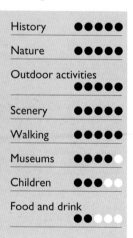

Ashcroft Manor $
*10km south of Cache
Creek on Hwy 1; tel: (250)
453-9983. Open daily
0900–1700.*

Built in 1862 as a roadhouse for the Cariboo Waggon Road, Ashcr grew into a prosperous farm, ranch, mill and social centre in t sagebrush and cactus desert south of Kamloops. The manor also serv as one of BC's earliest court houses. Most of the complex burn down in 1943, but a church and roadhouse, now a museum a tearoom, survived.

BARKERVILLE HISTORIC TOWN❖❖❖

For most of the 1860s, Barkerville was the biggest town north of S Francisco and west of Chicago. More than 100,000 hopeful min and hangers-on travelled the Cariboo Waggon Road to Barkervi between 1862 and 1870. They turned what had been a shanty to

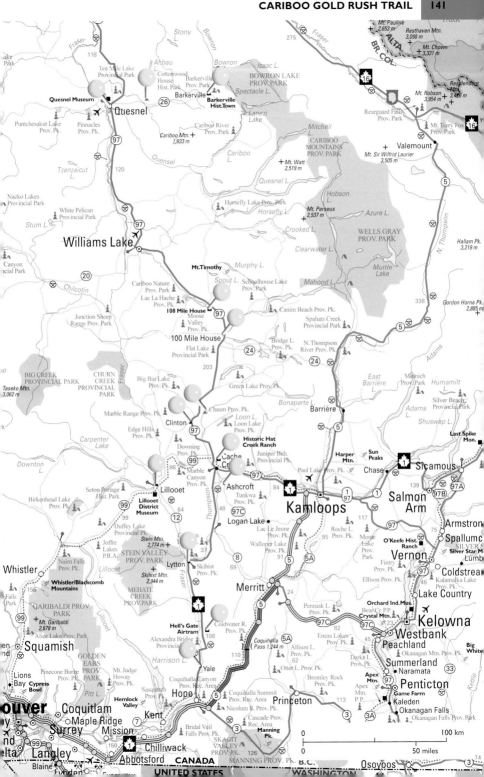

Barkerville Historic Town $
Hwy 26, 8km east of Wells; tel: (250) 994-3302; web: www.heritage.gov.bc.ca/bark/ bark.htm Open daily 0800–2000 year-round; costumed interpreters and full services mid-May–mid-Sept.

into a city so rich and so confident that it nearly outdid Victoria i bid to become the capital of BC.

The gold along Williams Creek ran out in little more than a dec but the town survived to become a thriving heritage site. More th 125 buildings remain, most of them original, if heavily restored. bordellos and dance halls never reopened, but restaurants, theat churches, stores, bakeries, photographers and a Chinese grocery back in business during the summer months. In winter, the o residents are ground squirrels and park wardens.

For a better sense of just how far Barkerville lies from the rest of walk (or ski in winter) that last 1.6km of the old wagon road west Richfield with *A Walk to Richfield*, a self-guiding map keyed to historic sites. The map is available at the Barkerville Visitor Cen Most visitor facilities are in Wells.

CHASM PROVINCIAL PARK✦✦✦

Chasm Provincial Park $ *Hwy 97, 16km northeast of Clinton; tel: (250) 398-4414. Open June–Sept.*

The Painted Chasm is an enormous river-carved gash through 12 and 15 million years of lava atop the Fraser Plateau. The 1.5km g shows multiple layers of reds and yellows that are especially brill in late afternoon sun.

CLINTON✦

Clinton and District Chamber of Commerce
1522 Cariboo Hwy; tel: (250) 459-2640; web: www.village.clinton.bc.ca Open daily in summer, Mon–Fri in winter.

South Cariboo Historical Museum $ *1419 Cariboo Hwy. Open Tue–Sun 1100–1600.*

Straddling the junction of two wagon roads, Clinton was origina called Junction, a name discarded when Queen Victoria decided Colonial Secretary needed a town named in his honour. Little changed in the years since. Clinton remains a quintessential cowt town where everyone knows everyone, and if you have to directions, you most definitely do not belong. Most of the horseb. trail riding, hiking, rafting and other outdoor activities take place guest ranches scattered in the hills and valleys to the west. Sou Cariboo Historical Museum,✦✦✦ set in an 1890s school hou chronicles the transition from Gold Rush to cowboy country.

Accommodation in Clinton

Many area ranches have discovered that guests are more profita (and less laborious) than huge cattle herds. The self-proclaimed Gu Ranch Capital of BC has facilities ranging from rustic to ritzy.

Big Bar Guest Ranch $$ *tel: (250) 459-2333; web: www.bigbarra .com* One of the first and still among the best for families: horseb.

riding, hiking, river rafting, backcountry camping trips, Nordic skiing and similar activities are geared for beginners.

Moondance Guest Ranch $$$ *tel: (250) 459-7775; web: www.moondanceguestranch.com* A luxury ranch with private cabins, gourmet meals and wood-fired saunas.

OTTONWOOD HOUSE HISTORIC SITE❖❖

Cottonwood House Historic Site $
26, 28km east of Hwy
tel: (250) 994-3332;

.heritage.gov.bc.ca/cott/
htm
n May–Sept
0–1700.

Another of the roadhouses *en route* to Barkerville, Cottonwood was a family residence 1874–1951. Period buildings include the main house, root cellar and a double barn, all explained by costumed interpreters.

AT CREEK RANCH❖❖❖

Hat Creek Ranch $
Hwys 97 and 99; tel:
) 457-9722; web:
.heritage.gov.bc.ca/hat/
tm
n daily 1000-1800;
ces and costumed
preters May–Sept.

Still a working ranch, Hat Creek is the last intact roadhouse on the Cariboo Waggon Road. The 20 heritage buildings include one of the largest barns in BC. Stagecoaches and wagon trains used ranch facilities until automobiles began using the road in 1916. Facilities include trail rides, ranching demonstrations, museum displays and a summer aboriginal village.

w
Creek Ranch

HELL'S GATE✦✦✦

Hell's Gate $$
*TransCanada Highway
(Hwy 1), 10.5km from
Alexandra Bridge Provincial
Park; tel: (604) 867-9277;
web: www.hellsgate.bc.ca
Open Apr–Oct 0900–1700.*

An average of 850,000 cu metres of water blasts through a space ab
the width of a city street every second. River rafters run the rap
daily in summer but only one steamboat, the *Skuzzy*, ever mad
upstream, winching through the raging narrows with bolts driven i
the rock. The rapids are more fearsome now. In 1913, a care
Canadian National Railway construction crew touched off a landsl
that choked the river and blocked the salmon run for years. F
ladders built 1945–6 helped, but modern salmon runs are less th
one-third the pre-1913 volume, even in the best of years.

For the best view of the rapids, ride the Airtram✦✦✦ 152m down
across the canyon to a museum, restaurant, gift shop and view
platform. A suspension bridge crosses the river just downstream, a
railway trains pass every half-hour.

Below
Hell's Gate cable car

LILLOOET✦✦

**Lillooet and
District Chamber
of Commerce** *790 Main
St; tel: (250) 256-4308.
Open July–Aug, daily
0900–1700; Sept–June
Mon–Sat 1100–1500.*

Lillooet Museum $
*790 Main St; tel: (250)
256-4308. Open May–Oct,
daily.*

Mile-0-Motel $$
*616 Main St; tel: (250)
256-7511. Central and
comfortable.*

The main streets of Lillooet are extraordinarily wide to allow the
team ox wagons that worked the Cariboo Waggon Road to t
around. The Mile Zero Cairn✦✦✦ opposite the Visitor Info Centre is M
0 for the roadhouses and supply points north. **Lillooet Museum**
shares a former Anglican church with the Visitor Info Centre an
trove of mining and pioneer artefacts. A self-guiding museum r
lists 15 historical sites on Main Street alone.

'TTON*

Lytton and District Chamber of nmerce *400 Fraser St; 250) 455-2523. Open -Sept, daily; Oct–May -Fri.*

Lytton Museum $ *next to the Info Centre. ꞁ daily in summer.*

Lytton lives by logging and river rafting. Companies based here put in up and down the Fraser and North Thompson rivers for trips that last a few hours to a few days. Five kilometres of riverfront have also been set aside as a Gold Panning Recreational Reserve with hand-panning only. Ask for information and pans at the **Lytton Museum**,** which is devoted to the Cariboo Waggon Road and mining history.

)0 MILE HOUSE*

South Cariboo Visitor Info Centre *Cariboo Hwy 97; tel: ꞁ) 395-5353. Open daily ꞁ–1630 in summer; –Fri rest of year.*

This small town is the service centre for the Central Cariboo and a major Nordic skiing area in winter. It began as a Cariboo Road stage stop in the 1860s. Seventy years later, Lord Martin Cecil, Marquis of Exeter, began and headquartered his Emissaries of Divine Light here.

)8 MILE HOUSE***

Best Western 108 Resort $$$ *5 Telqua Drive, 108 House; tel: (250) 791- ꞁ, tollfree (800) 667- ꞁ. Borders on riding ꞁ, two lakes and a ꞁA golf course.*

barn $ *Hwy 97, 13km ꞁ of 100 Mile House; tel: ꞁ) 791-5288. Open -Sept, daily ꞁ–1700.*

Hills Health and Guest Ranch $$$ *ꞁn north of 100 Mile ꞁe off Hwy 97; tel: (250) ꞁ5225. A ranch with a -class spa resort.*

The one-time roadhouse has become a museum with a collection of heritage buildings moved to the site, including one of the largest **log barns*** in Canada.

t ꞁMile House ranch

QUESNEL✦✦✦

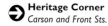

ⓘ Quesnel and District Information Centre
Le Bourdais Park, 705 Carson Ave; tel: (250) 992-8716. Open July–Aug, daily 0800–1800; May–June and Sept 0900–1600; Oct–Apr Mon–Fri 0900–1600.

➔ Heritage Corner
Carson and Front Sts.

ⓜ Quesnel and District Museum and Archives $
705 Carson Ave; tel: (250) 992-9580; web: www.sd28.bc.ca/museum Open May–Sept daily; Oct–Apr Mon–Fri.

Sitting at the confluence of the Fraser and Quesnel rivers, Quesnel the last river town before the final overland trek to the gold field Barkerville. There is still enough gold in the rivers to keep prospect busy. Much of the river has been staked or claimed, but there is pu panning at the river junction. **Heritage Corner**✦✦✦ is the centre town, marked by massive steamboat and mining machinery in the riverfront park and a scenic 1929 bridge across the Fraser River. Highlight of the **Quesnel and District Museum and Archives**✦✦✦ is an extraordinary collection of area photographs from 1865 onward.

YALE✦✦✦

ⓜ Historic Yale Museum $
21179 Douglas St; tel: (640) 863-2324; web: www.heritage.gov.bc.ca/yale/yale.htm Open June–Sept daily; spring and autumn (fall) Wed–Sun.

St John the Divine Church $
next to the museum.

A handful of people still live in this Gold Rush boom town, tho most of the town centre is a pleasant historic district. The interio the 1859 Anglican **St John the Divine Church**✦✦✦ remains alm unchanged since its consecration. The oldest church in BC is fi with period photographs and exhibits concentrating on the two St villages that were once here and Gold Rush memorabilia. Ask ab gold panning at Foreshore Park on the riverfront. Costum interpreters give guided tours in summer, including lantern tour the pioneer cemetery.

Suggested tour

Total distance: 600km.

Time: Allow 2 days to drive from Barkerville to Hope and a wee explore along the way.

Links: From Quesnel, Hwy 97 continues north to Prince George. Cache Creek, the TransCanada Highway (Hwy 1) leads east Kamloops (*see page 191*) and the Shuswap Lakes (*see page 160*). Fi Hope, Hwy 3 runs east through the Lower Fraser River Valley (*see p 218*) to Vancouver (*see page 268*) and west to the Cascades

iams Lake

he prominent mission
e area, Williams Lake
ild have shared in the
boo gold rush
inza of the 1860s. Yet
n Cariboo Road
ractors asked Tom
fee, who owned a
ing roadhouse in the
t of Williams Lake,
short-term loan so
could pay their
kers, Manifee refused.
contractors then re-
ed the road through
Mile House, 14km to
east, where the
house owner was
e than pleased to lend
n money. Manifee got
nore business, and
until the Pacific Great
ern Railway arrived in
d did Williams Lake,
ed after Secwepemc
f William, get on its

Route: From **BARKERVILLE ❶**, head west to **COTTONWOOD HOUSE HISTORIC PARK ❷**, another Gold Rush roadhouse, before arriving at **QUESNEL ❸**, midway point between Prince George and Williams Lake. Hwy 97 continues south through Kersley, past Australian Rest Area to Fort Alexandria Monument that marks the end of Alexander Mackenzie's journey down the Fraser. Continue on to Soda Creek, terminus of the Cariboo Waggon Road.

Williams Lake ❹, home of BC's largest rodeo, is at the junction of Hwy 20 west to Bella Coola (*see page 133*). Continue in an easterly direction toward 150 Mile House, once an important junction where passengers changed stagecoaches going west to the Chilcotin or east to the gold fields. Hwy 97 follows the eastern shoreline of Lac La Hache to **108 MILE HOUSE ❺**, an open-air museum of late 19th-century buildings, including a Watson Clydesdale barn, one of the largest log barns in Canada. The neighbouring town of **100 MILE HOUSE ❻** is a major producer of log houses for North American and Japanese markets.

South is **CHASM PROVINCIAL PARK ❼**, a vast gorge cut through 15 million years of lava eruptions. Just south is **CLINTON ❽**, a centre for cattle and guest ranches, and a point where green hills and conifers are replaced by sagebrush as the road leads to **HAT CREEK RANCH ❾** and the junction of Hwy 97 and Hwy 99.

Alternative route: To Lytton. From Hat Creek Ranch, travel in a westerly direction on Hwy 99 through Marble Canyon Provincial Park and through the hamlet of Pavilion and Pavilion General Store, one of the oldest buildings in BC still on its original site. Hwy 99 corkscrews down rolling semi-desert Fraser Benchlands along the original wagon track road. Head across the Bridge of the 23 Camels, named after the ill-fated freight carriers during the Cariboo Gold Rush, and on into **LILLOOET ❿**. Hwy 12 continues in a southeasterly direction toward **LYTTON ⓫**, a non-stop, exciting 65km drive as the roadway hugs the mountainside, while the yellow-brown waters of the mighty Fraser River rage far below.

From Hat Creek, continue south to Cache Creek, in the heart of desert country, where Hwy 97 ends as it meets the TransCanada Highway. Off the TransCanada Highway turnoff to Ashcroft and **ASHCROFT MANOR ⓬**. Dating from 1862, the manor was a ranch with grist and sawmills that served the Cariboo miners. Goldpan Provincial Park is a river-raft launch, and a popular site for steelhead fishing in autumn (fall). The highway continues along to Lytton, at the confluence of coffee-coloured Fraser and the icy-blue Thompson rivers. By 18 Royal Engineers had blasted the Cariboo Waggon Road through Lytton, opening the interior to miners, loggers and settlers. Hw follows the same route, and usually the same roadbed.

The TransCanada Highway continues along to Siska, one of Nlaka'pamux Nation communities along the Fraser Canyon. Sevo tribal artists are building world-wide reputations carving soapsto from traditional quarries nearby. Siska Art Gallery and Band Muse (*tel: (250) 455-2539*) displays and sells local art as well as CDs by Siska Halaw Singers and Drummers. The highway snakes high ab the Fraser River toward **Boston Bar ⓭** and continues to **HELL'S G⁄** **⓮**, the narrowest spot along an already narrow canyon.

The highway continues south to **YALE ⓯**, past **Emory Cr** **Provincial Park ⓰** to the city of Hope, a Gold Rush boomtown se a dramatic amphitheatre of mountains.

Right
Sunflowers at Williams Lake

Margaret 'Ma' Murray

Threatened with lawsuits and horsewhipping for her biting 'that's fur damshur' editorials on economics, politics and morals, Margaret 'Ma' Murray delighted her readers and infuriated politicians with her acid, earthy wit. She and her husband George published the *Bridge River–Lillooet News* in Lillooet and the *Alaska Highway News* in Fort St John from the 1940s to the 1980s. 'The state of politics in Canada', wrote the feisty pioneer editor, 'is as low as a snake's belly in Arkansas but a snake never goes so low that he didn't have a pit to hiss in.' Quoted across Canada, the legendary editor who 'guaranteed a chuckle every week and a belly laugh once a month or your money back' died in 1982 at the age of 94.

Sea to Sky Highway

Ratings

Children	●●●●●
Mountains	●●●●●
Outdoor activities	●●●●●
Skiing	●●●●●
Entertainment	●●●●○
Food and drink	●●●●○
Nature	●●●●○
Villages	●●●○○

The Sea to Sky Highway, also called the Squami Highway after the Squamish First Nations, is spectacular drive. Yet by any name it is not a relaxing dri the roadway curling and twisting along the glacier-car shores of Howe Sound to the base of Whistler Mountain, c of North America's great holiday destinations. Much of t roadway is carved into the sheer cliffs hugging Howe Sou The drive is scenic but the mountain terrain must be trea with care and respect: the frequent 'No Stopping' signs w of rockfall and avalanche hazards. Nonetheless, the lawful stopping spots provide picture-postcard views of Ferries navigating the protected waters of Howe Sou Mountains rise just beyond the highway, some scarred w the remains of enormous mining operations, some ne touched, and all cut by ice-cold streams rushing from the back to the sea.

BRACKENDALE EAGLE RESERVE✦✦✦

Brackendale Eagle Reserve $
Government Rd. Park at the dike and walk to the viewpoint on the river. Best eagle viewing Dec–Feb.

The 600ha Eagle Reserve lies along both banks of the Squamish Ri north of Squamish, providing winter habitat and food for as many 2 000 bald eagles in mid-winter. Eagles flock to the river to feed spawning fish, a feeding frenzy that usually peaks around Christi and tapers into mid-Feb, when the eagles disperse. Eagles can observed from a riverside walk and observation point on the east ba or from the water with rafting and kayaking operators out Squamish.

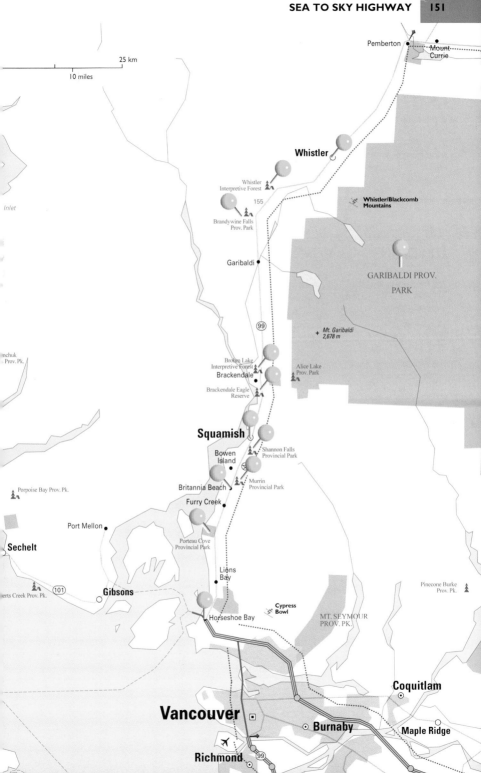

Pemberton
Mount Currie

Whistler

Whistler Interpretive Forest

Whistler/Blackcomb Mountains

155

Brandywine Falls Prov. Park

Inlet

Garibaldi

GARIBALDI PROV. PARK

Mt. Garibaldi 2,678 m

99

Brohm Lake Interpretive Forest

Alice Lake Prov. Park

Brackendale

Brackendale Eagle Reserve

nchuk Prov. Pk.

Squamish

Shannon Falls Provincial Park

Bowen Island

Britannia Beach

Murrin Provincial Park

Furry Creek

Porpoise Bay Prov. Pk.

Port Mellon

Porteau Cove Provincial Park

Sechelt

Lions Bay

erts Creek Prov. Pk.

101

Gibsons

Pinecone Burke Prov. Pk.

Cypress Bowl

MT. SEYMOUR PROV. PK.

Horseshoe Bay

Coquitlam

Vancouver

Burnaby

Maple Ridge

Richmond

99

25 km

10 miles

BRANDYWINE FALLS PROVINCIAL PARK✦✦✦

**Brandywine Falls
Provincial Park $**
Hwy 99, 47km north of
Squamish; tel: (604) 898-
3678; web:
www.elp.gov.bc.ca/bcparks/
explore/parkpgs/brandywi.
htm
Open daily.

Brandywine Falls is the centrepiece of the park, an impressive smo
and wide 66m cataract erupting from atop an ancient lava b
Viewpoint is an easy 10-minute hike through the forest from
highway. The name dates from a brandy versus wine bet over
height of the falls by two early railway surveyors: neither had cash
one bet brandy and the other wine.

BRITANNIA BEACH✦

Britannia Beach
Hwy 99, 33km north of
Horseshoe Bay.

**BC Museum of
Mining $$**
tel: (604) 896-2233. Open
May–Oct, daily; year round
for pre-booked tours.

Once a busy support and supply town for the Britannia Mine,
largest producer of copper in the British Empire 1930–5, the br
spot along Howe Sound is bustling again as a centre for arts and cr
shops, galleries, a general store and an ever-changing list of restaura
and bistros. The car park east of Hwy 99 is also a popular spot
RCMP radar speed traps.

During some 70 years of operation, the massive Britannia M
employed over 60,000 persons who produced some 600 million k
of copper. The facility closed in 1974 and re-emerged as the
Museum of Mining,✦✦✦ with nearly the entire plant battered
intact. A national historic site, the facilities include mining muse
displays in the heritage support buildings just off the highway to
east. Outdoor displays include a 355-tonne 'Super Mine' truck
other massive equipment. Guided tours take visitors inside the m
and tunnels to see slushers, muckers, drills and one of the
surviving gravity-fed ore concentrators in the world. If the site lo
familiar, it probably is. The spooky, rust-stained shop that seems
spill down the mountainside has starred in dozens of movie and
productions over the years.

BROHM LAKE INTERPRETIVE FOREST✦

**Brohm Lake
Interpretive Forest**
$ Hwy 99, 13km north of
Squamish; tel: (604) 898-
2100.

There is fishing in the shallow lake and swimming in the clear w
that seldom warms to more than frigid. Eleven kilometres of trails
through 400ha of forest with spreading views of the Tanta
Mountain Range and one the largest ice fields in North America.

ARIBALDI PROVINCIAL PARK✦✦✦

**Garibaldi
Provincial Park $**
*t of Hwy 99,
amish–Whistler; tel:
4) 898-3678. Highway
*s indicate trail access.
*en daily but weather
y make access difficult.

There is no road access into the wilderness park but well-developed trail systems lead to five of the most popular camping and hiking areas: Black Tusk/Garibaldi Lake, Cheakamus Lake, Diamond Head, Singing Pass and Wedgemount Lake. In summer, look for azure-blue lakes, vast meadows of wild flowers, untouched stands of Douglas fir, yellow and red cedar, mountain hemlock and lodgepole pine, depending on altitude. The entire park gets heavy snow in winter but Diamond Head is particularly popular with experienced Nordic skiers and snow campers. The park is also accessible via trails from Whistler.

ORSESHOE BAY✦✦

**North Vancouver
Info Centre**
*east 2nd St, North
couver; tel: (604) 987-
38. Open daily in summer,
n–Fri autumn
l)–spring.*

BC Ferries
*end of Hwy 1; tel:
0) 386-3431 or (888)
3-3779; web:
w.bcferries.bc.ca*

A terminus for BC Ferries to Nanaimo (*see map page 233*) as well as more local services, Horseshoe Bay lies at the entrance to Howe Sound. A dormitory community for Vancouver, the charming town offers restaurants, pubs, shopping and a pleasant park with views across the harbour from beneath spreading shade trees.

MURRIN PROVINCIAL PARK✦✦✦

**Murrin Provincial
Park $**
*y 99, 3km north of
annia Beach; tel: (604)
3-3678. Open daily.*

Donated by BC Electric Railway and named after its president 1929–6, the park is popular for walking, picnicking, swimming, fishing, sunbathing and novice to intermediate rock climbing up the steep, almost vertical cliffs. More experienced rock climbers head for the granite cliffs of Stawamus Chief, just up the road.

PORTEAU COVE PROVINCIAL PARK✦✦✦

Porteau Cove Provincial Park $
Hwy 99, 25km north of Horseshoe Bay; tel: (604) 689-9025; web: www.elp.gov.bc.ca/bcparks/explore/parkpgs/porteau.htm
Open daily.

On the east shore of Howe Sound, the Cove was once an import: ferry landing but today is better known for beachcombing, fishing a scuba-diving. Several ships have been scuttled just off the beach to † north of the pier for divers to explore. The Cove also has a good po to watch for the *Royal Hudson* steam train *en route* between Squam and North Vancouver in summer (*see page 173*), and is the tu around point for the Pacific Starlight dinner train from Nor Vancouver (*see page 174*). The actual cove is at the more protect south end of the park, beyond the camping area.

SHANNON FALLS PROVINCIAL PARK✦✦✦

Shannon Falls Provincial Park $
Hwy 99, 7km north of Britannia Beach; tel: (604) 898-3678. Open daily.

Six times the elevation of Niagara, the 335m Shannon Falls is the th highest in BC. A 5-minute walk along a pleasant but well-worn for trail, the falls can also be viewed from your car. Best time to visi shortly after noon when the sun highlights the falls dropping fr the cliff high above. Expect crowds in summer, including motor coa tours *en route* to Whistler.

SQUAMISH✦✦

Chamber of Commerce Info Centre *37950 Cleveland Ave; tel: (604) 892-9244. Open daily.*

Soo Coalition for Sustainable Forests $ *tel: (604) 892-9766.*

Squamish Estuary $
west from 3rd Ave beyond Vancouver St, just southwest of town.

West Coast Railway Heritage Park $$
3km north of Hwy 99 to Centennial Way, then 1km west; tel: (604) 898-9336. Open May–Oct, daily.

At the head of a narrow corridor on Howe Sound, 'squamish' mea 'mother of the winds' in the language of the Coast Salish, appropriate description of local weather. Squamish is surrounded sheer rock faces that heat up in the daytime sun, creating afterno updrafts that build into world championship windsurfing gusts.

Squamish is a timber town of two minds. Forestry jobs and incon are slowly declining while hiking, kayaking, cycling, fishing, ro climbing and other outdoor activities are growing in econom importance, and luring outsiders who hate nothing so much as t sight of logging trucks, pulp mills and clearcuts. Outdoor recreatio winning but timber interests are stringing out their measur withdrawal as long and as gracefully as possible. **Soo Coalition f Sustainable Forests,**✦✦✦ the timber industry advocacy group, arran; mill and forest tours.

The **West Coast Railway Heritage Park**✦✦✦ is a must-see for r buffs, with more than four dozen vintage railway carriages a locomotive engines. Highlights include a gleaming 1890 Execut: Business Carriage panelled in hand-rubbed teak, a restored Colon Car that once carried migrants across the prairies on hard benches, t only surviving steam locomotive engine from the Pacific Great Eastern Railway that once served Howe Sound, and a gargantuan orange snowplow. **Squamish Estuary**❖❖❖ has excellent bird-watching, especially during the spring and autumn (fall) migrations.

Accommodation and food in Squamish

Howe Sound Inn and Brewing Company $$ *37801 Cleveland Ave; tel: (604) 892-2603.* The only brewpub on the Sound concentrates on local seafood and seasonal vegetables. Hotel rooms upstairs.

Sunflower Bakery $ *38086 Cleveland Ave; tel: (604) 892-2231.* A good source for light lunches or picnic supplies.

ᴛAWAMUS CHIEF PROVINCIAL PARK❖

Stawamus Chief Provincial Park $
north of Shannon Falls east of Hwy 99; tel: 4) 898-3678; web: w.elp.gov.bc.ca/bcparks/ lore/parkpgs/stawamus.

ɘn daily.

Hikers and rock climbers are drawn to the 652m Chief, the second biggest granite monolith after Gibraltar, sacred to Squamish First Nations. There are some 180 different ascent routes, including a rugged walking trail that gains 550m in just 2.5km. Best spot to watch climbers is from a lay-by on the eastern side of the highway, about 1km north of the park entrance.

ᵀHISTLER❖❖❖

Created in the hope of luring the Winter Olympics to Canada in the 1960s, Whistler developers have not let decades of lukewarm interest from the International Olympic Committee slow things down. North America's most successful mountain development may have started as a ski resort but has become just as successful – and just as busy – in summer.

Two mountains, Blackcomb and Whistler, have been trimmed and groomed for just about every mountain activity known to man or estate developer: skiing, golf, hiking, mountain biking, fishing, kayaking, rafting, canoeing, shopping, eating, drinking, climbing and snowboarding are only the beginning. The ski season extends well into summer, thanks to lifts that access high-altitude glaciers. A few hundred metres below, families with hiking boots and backpacks can watch for deer, marmots, bears and other wildlife amid alpine meadows and open forest.

At the base is Whistler Village, an artificial and hugely successful European-style pedestrian village packed with hotels, restaurants, shops, cafés, clubs, plazas, bridges, creeks, gazebos, musicians a magicians, none of them more than a 10-minute stroll aw Relaxing? No, but Whistler was designed for excitement, glamour . glitz. The original activity centre was Whistler Village, at the foo Whistler Mountain. The Village still has more restaurants, more sh and more variety than the rest of the resort. A short walk across valley is Upper Village, a more expensive, more exclusive and frenetic enclave surrounding Fairmont Chateau Whistler. Sma valleys to the south are filled with condominium developments t rely largely on the Village for services and entertainment.

For activity information in any season, contact the Whistler Re: Association and the Whistler Activity and Information Centre in Whistler Village Conference Centre. Shops near the gondola base Whistler Village hire out bikes, skates and other equipment in sum and skis or snowboards in winter. Summer is Whistler's value seas as well as its most active. At the base, five lakes are strung I turquoise and green beads on a necklace, woven together with 20 of mostly paved trails for easy walking, cycling and roller blading. lakeside parks offer broad lawns, sandy beaches and full picnick facilities with sailing, windsurfing, boating and fishing.

Both Whistler and Blackcomb lifts remain open, except for sh maintenance periods in autumn (fall), with summer skiing Blackcomb and hiking or mountain biking on both mountains. Ot possibilities include golf, climbing, backpacking, hang-gliding, h hiking, jet boating, 'flight-seeing' and hay rides. Winter is Whistl *raison d'être*, with 200-plus named runs and three dozen li Blackcomb has the longest lift-serviced vertical in North Ameri

Below
Whistler

1609m, as well as the longest uninterrupted fall-line skiing on the continent. Whistler comes a close second, with 1530m of vertical served by lifts. Then there is Nordic skiing on valley golf courses and trails, ice-skating, snow shoeing and sleigh rides.

Even if you are spending the day at Whistler, check out Fairmont Chateau Whistler at the base of two mountains. The enormous castle-like resort beneath a copper-green roof still manages to feel comfortable, thanks to touches such as Mennonite hooked rugs and quilts, and First Nations-inspired twig furniture. The Great Hall and Mallard Bar are best for people-watching. Whistler is short on history but the Whistler Museum and Archives makes the best of skiing gear from the 1960s, fishing souvenirs from the 1920s and local logging paraphernalia.

Accommodation and food in Whistler

Most Whistler hotels, inns, condos and other accommodations have their own booking number, but it is easier to book through the *Whistler Resort Association; tel: (604) 664-5625, tollfree: (800) 944-7853.* Expect 2–3-night minimum stays in high season (Jan–Mar), the lowest rates in Apr and Nov–Dec, and mid-range rates during the rest of the year.

Fairmont Chateau Whistler $$$ *4599 Chateau Blvd, Upper Village; tel: (604) 938-8000.* The best address for visitors in town.

Fairmont Pan Pacific Lodge $$$ *4320 Sundial Cres., Whistler Village; tel: (604) 905-2999.* Has full-kitchen suites and a few steps from both Whistler and Blackcomb gondolas.

Executive Inn $$ *4250 Village Drol, Whistler Village; tel: (604) 932-3200.* One of the better mid-range hotels with kitchens and plenty of room for families.

Residence Inn $$ *4899 Tainted Cliff Rd, Upper Village; tel: (604) 905-3400.* Has a prime ski-in, ski-out location midway up the base of Blackcomb Mountain.

Araxi Ristorante $$ *Whistler Village Sq.; tel: (604) 932-4540.* Gets raves for its pasta and wine list.

Caramba $$ *Town Plaza; tel: (604) 938-1879.* The liveliest Italian restaurant in Whistler.

Thai One On $$ *Upper Village; tel: (604) 932-4822.* A calm refuge with Thai dishes as good as any in Vancouver.

Ingrid's Village Café $ *102, 4305 Skiers Approach, Whistler Village; tel: (604) 932-7000.* Worth the out-the-door queues for vegetarian dishes.

Zeuski's Taverna $ *Unit 40, 4314 Main St, Town Plaza; tel: (604) 932-6009.* Cheerful, cheap and always busy.

Whistler Interpretive Forest❖❖

🄷 **Whistler
Interpretive Forest**
$ *Hwy 99, 9km north of
Brandywine Fall Provincial
Park; tel: (604) 932-5535.
Open daily.*

There is an extensive and well-marked network of hiking a mountain biking trails throughout a working forest between Hwy and Garibaldi Provincial Park. Watch for logging trucks and be sure park entirely off the roadway. Almost directly across Hwy 99 Function Junction, a catchy name for a perfectly ordinary service a for Whistler Resort. There are bakeries, hardware stores, a brewe plumbers, electrical supplies and all the other mechanical and serv functions that resorts like to keep out of sight and out of mind.

Suggested tour

Total distance: 120km.

Time: 2–4 hours, depending on traffic.

Links: The Squamish Highway (Hwy 99) connects to Vancouver *page 268*) to the south, or continue north on Hwy 99 to the Gold R Trail (*see page 140*) near Hat Creek Ranch (*see page 143*).

Route: From **WHISTLER** ❶, take Hwy 99, the Sea to Sky Highw south to **BRANDYWINE FALLS PROVINCIAL PARK** ❷ and Da Lake. Continue south toward **SQUAMISH** ❸, a timber town tha turning toward outdoor recreation.

Just south is **SHANNON FALLS PROVINCIAL PARK** ❹ with one the highest waterfalls in BC, a 5-minute walk from the car park, a Stawamus Chief, a massive peak that is a favourite with rock climbe Continue south to **BRITANNIA BEACH** ❺ and the Britannia Mine museum that was once the largest copper producer in the Brit Empire. Eight kilometres south is **PORTEAU COVE** ❻, a one-ti ferry landing for Howe Sound ferry service that has become a popu park for beachcombing, boating, fishing and scuba diving.

The views become spectacular, and can be enjoyed from several l bys which are accessible only from the southbound lanes. The twisti highway is narrow and verges are almost non-existent, hugging hills above Howe Sound. Hwy 1, the TransCanada Highway, runs the ferry line-up at **HORSESHOE BAY** ❼. Follow signs eastbound West Vancouver and over the Lions Gate Bridge, built by the Ir brewing Guinness family in 1938 to link British properties on North Shore to Vancouver.

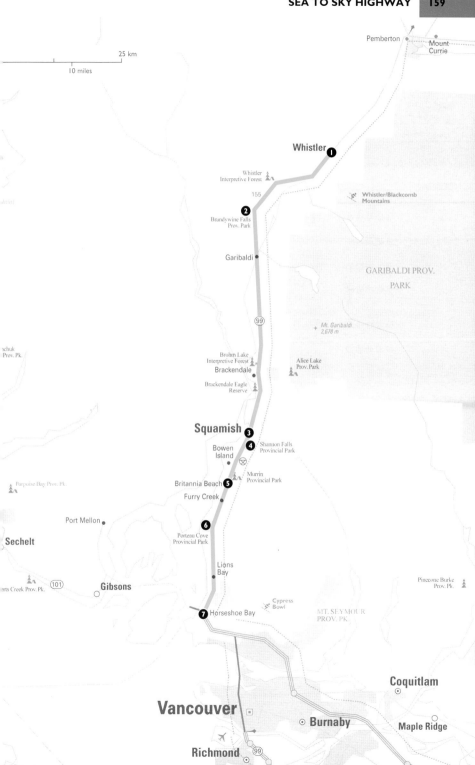

25 km

10 miles

Pemberton

Mount Currie

Whistler **1**

Whistler Interpretive Forest

155

Whistler/Blackcomb Mountains

2

Brandywine Falls Prov. Park

Garibaldi

GARIBALDI PROV. PARK

99

Mt. Garibaldi 2,678 m

chuk Prov. Pk.

Brohm Lake Interpretive Forest

Brackendale

Alice Lake Prov. Park

Brackendale Eagle Reserve

Squamish **3**

4 Shannon Falls Provincial Park

Bowen Island

Murrin Provincial Park

Britannia Beach **5**

Furry Creek

Porpoise Bay Prov. Pk.

6

Porteau Cove Provincial Park

Port Mellon

Sechelt

Lions Bay

Pinecone Burke Prov. Pk.

rts Creek Prov. Pk.

101

Gibsons

Cypress Bowl

MT. SEYMOUR PROV. PK.

7 Horseshoe Bay

Coquitlam

Vancouver

Burnaby

Maple Ridge

Richmond

99

Shuswap Lakes

Ratings

Children	●●●●●
Lakes	●●●●●
Mountains	●●●●●
Nature	●●●●●
Outdoor activities	●●●●●
Scenery	●●●●●
Parks	●●●●○
Food and drink	●●●○○

The scenic Shuswap lakes region contains an oasis of lor narrow lakes, linked to rivers which are home to some the most amazing salmon runs in the world. The lak soaring mountains and sandy beaches are easy to reach fro the TransCanada Highway. The Shuswap, a band of Salish linguistic stock whose origin and meaning is unknow have lived in the region for thousands of years. Some 50 Shuswap now live on reserves in the area, a region mu smaller than their original vast hunting territory. Wild a historic, the Shuswap region is abundant with deer, ospr golden eagles and black bears. Shuswap Lake is the magr for fleets of houseboats which are drawn to the protect waters, and some 20 small marine parks. Highways sk tiny historic towns, and follow rail lines which tra lakeshores and river canyons past rugged peaks and foami waterfalls.

CHASE✷✷✷

ℹ Chase and District Chamber of Commerce
400 Shuswap Ave; tel (250) 679-8432. Open July–Aug, daily; Sept–June Mon, Wed and Fri.

ℹ Chase Museum and Archives $
1042 Shuswap Ave; tel: (250) 679-8432. Open June–Aug, daily.

A carpenter from New York who was lucky enough not to strike g in the Cariboo instead found fortune building a timber and ca town. Chase is better known today for its outdoor recreati opportunities: canoeing down 55km of calm water to Kamloo fishing, house-boating, hiking, swimming, golfing and winter skii The town is surrounded by calm pine forests at the head of Lir Shuswap Lake. The municipal beach is particularly scenic and popu **The Chase Museum and Archives,✷✷** the former Blessed Sacram Church, is filled to the rafters with the town's first physician's off the gleaming mahogany bar from an early hotel, an antique barb chair and everything in-between. **Niskonlith Lake Provincial Park** has camping, magnificent wild-flower displays May–June and go rainbow trout fishing year round.

Niskonlith Lake
Provincial Park $
northwest of Chase on
onlith Lake; tel: (250)
-3000; web:
.elp.gov.bc.ca/bcparks/
ore/parkpgs/niskonli.htm
n Apr–Oct.

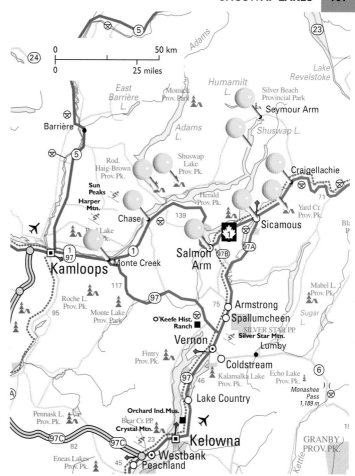

RAIGELLACHIE

Craigellachie $
Hwy 1, east of
nous; tel: (250) 837-
5; web:
.revelstokecc.bc.ca/
tion/lspike.htm
shop open daily in
ner.

A stone cairn, caboose and railway station-type souvenir shop
commemorate the driving of the last spike to complete the Canadian
Pacific Railway in 1885.

LITTLE SHUSWAP LAKE✧✧✧

ⓘ Little Shuswap Lake $
north and east of Chase to Adams River and Little River.

Little Shuswap is the smallest of the Shuswap lakes but has the m accessible beaches from the TransCanada Highway.

MONTE CREEK✧

The hamlet and railway station at Monte Creek are best known as site of an abortive railway robbery in 1906 by the infam 'gentleman bandit', Bill Miner, who netted less than $15. Miner captured, sentenced to life in prison, escaped, and eventually lan in a US prison for later robberies. A romantic Hollywood movie, *Grey Fox*, was filmed in the area.

RODERICK HAIG-BROWN PROVINCIAL PARK✧✧✧

ⓘ Roderick Haig-Brown Provincial Park $
north of Hwy 1 at Squilax; tel: (250) 851-3000; web: www.elp.gov.bc.ca/bcparks/ explore/parkpgs/roderick.htm

The park surrounds and protects 11km of the Adams River betw Adams Lake and Little Shuswap Lake. The river has the largest sock run in North America, well over one million of the bright-red fighting their way up the Fraser and North Thompson rivers to sp every fourth year (2002, 2006). Off-years merely feature a few hunc thousand salmon plus attendant bears, eagles, ravens, mink, gulls other wildlife. Observation decks provide a clear view of spawn with naturalists on hand during the height of the l summer–autumn (fall) salmon runs.

SALMON ARM✧

ⓘ Salmon Arm and District Chamber of Commerce
751 Marine Park Dr. northeast; tel: (250) 832-2230. Open Victoria Day–Labour Day, daily 0900-1700; in winter Mon–Fri 0900–1700.

The commercial centre of the Shuswap lakes region, Salmon Arm born as a fruit and dairy town on the rich floodplain of the Salr River, which enters Shuswap Lake here. The town and the south of Shuswap Lake were named 'salmon' because of the massive run salmon that made their way from the Pacific Ocean each year. salmon disappeared when faulty railway construction blocked Fraser River at Hell's Gate (*see page 144*) in 1912, destroying the run. Even without the salmon, Salmon Arm is a popular port to

R J Haney Heritage Park and Museum
wy 97B, 4km east of non Arm; tel: (250) 832-3. Open June–Aug –Sat 1300–1700, or by ointment.

ary Peace Park and lic Wharf $
ine Park Dr. at the lake.

houseboats (like floating RVs) to explore the far reaches of Shuswap Lake. The **R J Haney Heritage Park and Museum**✦✦✦ includes a historic church, farm buildings and schoolhouse. **Rotary Peace Park** and **Public Wharf**,✦✦✦ a 250m pier and walkway, curves out from the park with excellent views of shorebirds and waterfowl. At least 150 different species of birds nest around the mouth of the Salmon River each spring. Best breeding displays are Apr–June.

Accommodation and food in Salmon Arm

Motels line the TransCanada Highway through the town, or to explore Shuswap Lake by water hire a houseboat.

Salmon Arm Bay Houseboat Vacations $$ *tel: (250) 832-2745.* One of several local operators.

Shuswap Lake Houseboat Association *tel: (250) 836-2450.* Lists houseboat operators around the lake.

w
on Arm golf course

SEYMOUR ARM❖❖❖

Seymour Arm
north end of Seymour Arm, the northern most arm of Shuswap Lake, 47km north of Anglemont by logging road.

A few old buildings still line the streets but the restaurant, p general store and a small hotel are all at the wharf on Bughouse B The town is accessible by road in summer and by ferry from Sicam all year.

SHUSWAP LAKE❖❖❖

Shuswap Lake $
the lake stretches from Sorento, south to Salmon Arm, east to Sicamous and north to Seymour Arm.

The narrow, H-shaped lake is the most popular houseboat destination in BC. The 1000km of shoreline tends to be steep with shoals or reefs. Warm summer weather means few storms and heavy waves. Nineteen species of fish keep anglers busy year round.

SHUSWAP LAKE PROVINCIAL PARK❖❖❖

Shuswap Lake Provincial Park $
272 campsites; tel: (250) 851-3000.

The 149ha park has 272 campsites on the shores of Shuswap Lak huge area with 1000km of shoreline. Depressions of a 3000-year- village, a reconstructed kekuli (pit house) and Copper Island 2 offshore are big attractions. Shuswap Lake Provincial Marine Park 26 campsites on the shores of the lake, many accessible only by wa The sites are very popular with house-boaters.

SICAMOUS❖❖

Sicamous and District Chamber of Commerce
110 Finlayson St (near Government Dock); tel: (250) 836-3313; web: www.sicamouschamber.bc.ca Open daily in summer, winter Mon–Fri.

Shuswap Lakes Ferry Service $$
tel: (250) 836-2200. Services to Seymour Arm all year.

The name comes from a Secwepemc word that means 'narrow 'squeezed in the middle', a good name for the tiny narrows betw Mara and Shuswap lakes. The one-time railway camp has becom resort town that is especially popular with house-boaters: lc operators have more than 300 vessels to rent, no experience requi **D Dutchman Dairy**❖❖❖ has an exotic game farm and 50 flavour what aficionados call BC's best commercial ice cream. Even co tours stop for a cone: highly recommended is the banana and b walnut. For those who do not want to drive their own boats, **Shusv Lakes Ferry Service**❖❖❖ offers regular vehicle and passenger ferry year) and sightseeing (summer only) services between Sicamous Seymour Arm.

D Dutchman Dairy
$ Hwy 1, 1km east of
mous; tel: (250) 836-
4. Open daily
0–1900.

Accommodation and food in Sicamous

Motels and restaurants line the TransCanada Highway and Hwy 97A from Vernon.

Sicamous Inn $$ *tel: (250) 836-4117*. The largest in town, with the best facilities.

ht
utchman Dairy

ow
seboats at Sicamous

YARD CREEK PROVINCIAL PARK ❖❖❖

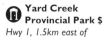 **Yard Creek Provincial Park $**
Hwy 1, 1.5km east of Sicamous; tel: (250) 851-3000; web: www.elp.gov.bc.ca/bcparks/explore/parkpgs/yard.htm Open May–Sept.

This wet, upland forest has excellent bird watching and pleasa hiking trails beneath hemlock and cedars along a sparkling creek, a is a popular camping and picnic spot.

David Thompson

Born into poverty in Westminster, England in 1770, David Thompson apprenticed as a clerk with the Hudson's Bay Company, arriving on the shores of Hudson Bay at the tender age of 14. Thompson studied surveying and mapmaking while recovering from a broken leg, an incident that took most of a year to mend but changed his life. After a frustrating stint with the Hudson's Bay Company, he left to join the rival North West Co. to map their outposts and waterways. Using Rocky Mountain House as a base, Thompson mapped the fur-trading territories east of the Rocky Mountains, the uncharted Columbia River basin, and present-day British Columbia, Washington, Oregon, Idaho and Montana. Over his career, Thompson travelled by foot, horse and canoe an amazing 88,000km. Thompson's precise maps were used well into the 20th century, yet when Canada's greatest geographer died near Montreal at the age of 87, he passed away in poverty and virtual obscurity.

The Last Spike

The carrot to lure BC into Confederation in 1871 was a promise by the government in Ottawa to provide a transcontinental railway linking the British colony with the rest of Canada. After a scandal that brought down the Government, the contract was awarded to the Canadian Pacific Railway. One of the great engineering projects of the day, it was nevertheless an enormous financial burden for a young country of only 3.5 million. Five years later and fifteen impatient years after signing the accord 'The Last Spike' was driven by Lord Strathcona on 7 November 1885 at Craigellachie, 25km east of Sicamous, a tiny village where crews from the east and west met. Craigellachie was named by fur trader and CPR financier Lord Strathcona (Donald Smith) after a rocky crag near his hometown in Morayshire, Scotland.

Opposite Top
Shuswap Lake

Opposite Bottom
The Last Spike cairn, Craigellachie

Suggested tour

Total distance: 160km.

Time: 2 hours to drive; 2–5 days to explore.

Links: Columbia River (*see page 122*) and Revelstoke are just east
the TransCanada Highway (Hwy 1); Kamloops (*see page 191*) is
west.

Route: The TransCanada Highway (Hwy 1) passes
CRAIGELLACHIE ❶, the village where the 'last spike' was driver
1885 for the transcontinental Canadian Pacific Railway. The high
continues on to **YARD CREEK PROVINCIAL PARK** ❷.

Just beyond is **SICAMOUS** ❸, appropriately named by Secwepemc
Shuswap) 'in the middle', straddling the narrow junction of Shus
Lake and Mara Lake, where Hwy 97A stretches southward to Verr
and the Okanagan Valley (*see page 198*). The best place to adm
Shuswap Lake, a vast lake system that extends north, south and w
is the Shuswap Rest Area, a picnic area east of Canoe on the north
of Hwy 1.

Continue along the TransCanada Highway past the junction w
Hwy 97B, another artery which leads south to Vernon and
Okanagan Valley. If the valley seems hazy, blame the lumber mil
Canoe, which still burns sawdust and other waste. Hwy 1 leads
SALMON ARM ❹, a small picturesque town at the end of one
Shuswap Lake's four long arms.

Continue on to Sorrento, named after the romantic Italian tow
tiny community that swells to more than 4 000 in summer wh
motels, resorts, RV parks and campgrounds fill up. Hwy 1 contin
west to Squilax and the turnoff just beyond to **SHUSWAP LA
PROVINCIAL PARK** ❺, a favoured family vacation area. Conti
west across the North Shuswap (Squilax) Bridge over the Little Ri
The 4km river between the two Shuswap lakes was once a thriv
trade centre for Secwepemc. The river is better known today for tr
fishing in Feb, Mar and Oct. Jade Mountain Lookout offers br
views of Little Shuswap Lake.

The TransCanada Highway and South Thompson River descend
CHASE ❻, a ranching and lumber town on the south shore of Li
Shuswap Lake. The earliest known human remains in BC, a n
trapped in a mudflow about 8 000 years ago, were found along G
Creek, near the north end of the bridge at Pritchard.

The high cliffs on the north side of the river have been eroded into
irregular series of columns and buttresses that can take on fanta
shapes in the late afternoon light. Hwy 1 follows the river west
MONTE CREEK ❼.

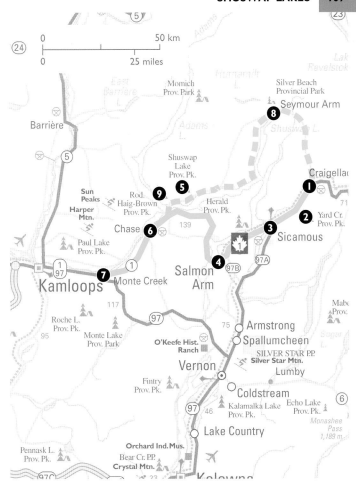

Detour: From Craigellachie, take the gravel logging road north to **SEYMOUR ARM** ❽, a village that was once a boomtown during the 1880s Big Bend Gold Rush; the general store still has a working old glass hand pump for petrol. Continue in a southwesterly direction on the Squilax–Anglemont Road through the hamlets of Anglemont, Magna Bay, Scotch Creek and Lee Creek, and **SHUSWAP LAKE PROVINCIAL PARK** ❺. The road angles northwest to **RODERICK HAIG-BROWN PROVINCIAL PARK** ❾ and the Adams River.

Little Shuswap Lake Road runs to Quaaout Lodge, a resort and outdoor recreation centre owned by the Squilax/Little Shuswap Lake First Nation. The popular resort is jammed mid-July when the Nation hosts the annual Squilax Powwow, drawing attendees from across North America. Continue on to the TransCanada Highway and Squilax.

Train travel

Ratings

Heritage	●●●●●
Mountains	●●●●●
Nature	●●●●●
Railways	●●●●●
Scenery	●●●●●
Children	●●●●○
Food and drink	●●●●○
Entertainment	●●●○○

'**B**onds of steel': railways influenced the development Canada and especially Alberta and BC like no oth industry. When settlers, miners, gold rush prospectors a immigrants raced west to claim land or resources many to the train. Returning by rail to Eastern Canada were the r materials from the land, forest, ocean and rivers, along wi cattle and cultivated crops. BC was lured into Confederati as a province in 1871 with the assurance by the Governme that a transcontinental link would be built within a deca The completion of the Canadian Pacific Railway w formalised with the Last Spike driven in 1885, followed t next year by the first CPR passenger train from Montre which arrived at the Vancouver suburb of Port Mooc Passenger routes today wind leisurely along crag mountain massifs, crawl through river canyons, sk shimmering lakes, and traverse deserts, ranchlands a golden grainfields.

ALBERTA PRAIRIE RAILWAY EXCURSIONS❖❖❖

Alberta Prairie Railway Excursions
$$$ 4611 47th Ave, Stettler ; tel: (403) 742-2811; web: www.nucleus.com/Heartland Open mid-May–mid-Oct. Trips vary in length from 4–8 hours; reservations recommended 30 days in advance.

Route: 67km route from Stettler–Big Valley–Stettler.

Just as the train leaves the station, it comes to a screeching halt wh the dreaded Bolton Gang holds up the train. After Gabriel Dumc arrests the bandits and donates the loot to children's charities, t train continues on to Big Valley, a divisional point for the form Canadian Northern Railway, where passengers enjoy an Alberta ro beef dinner. On the return trip, actors in period costume sing a reminisce about the good ole days.

Opposite
Panorama car, *Whistler Northwind*

CARIBOO PROSPECTOR✧✧✧

Cariboo Prospector $$$
BC Rail Ltd, 1311 west 1st St, North Vancouver; tel: (604) 984-5246, tollfree (800) 663-8238 and (800) 339-8752; web: www.bcrail.com/bcrpass/bcrpsca.htm
Runs three times weekly.

Below
Cariboo Prospector, Anderson Lake

Route: Prince George–Quesnel–Williams Lake–Exeter/100 M House–Lillooet–Whistler–North Vancouver.

A 13.5-hour trip from Prince George to North Vancouver, many for a return summer day trip to Whistler, which includes breakfast dinner at your seat on the train and a Whistler gondola ride. The tr is remarkable for its engineering: lightweight, self-propelled passen cars called Budd Cars. For passengers who venture north of Ho Sound, Squamish and the mountains around Whistler, the tr travels inland along the Fraser River most of the distance to Pri George from its junction with Cayoosh Creek at Lillooet. N Clinton, enter Cariboo Gold Rush and ranching country: roll pastures, barns and cowboys. Ranching's heartland is at Willi Lake. If pausing at Quesnel, do not miss the restored historic G Rush town of Barkerville (see page 140).

E&N 'MALAHAT' RAILINER✧✧

E&N 'Malahat' Railiner $$
VIA Rail Canada, 450 Pondora Ave, Victoria; tel: (250) 383-4324, tollfree (800) 561-8630. Runs daily.

Route: Victoria–Duncan–Nanaimo–Parksville–Courtenay.

There is only one class on the Malahat yet everyone can get on and as many times as they wish and can order stops on request, a fine v to venture leisurely beyond Duncan's totem poles, Nanaimo's Bast near the marina and Parksville's swimming beach. The Chemair murals are worth a stop, a wallside composite history of First Natic first settlers, Chinese merchants, lumberjacks, fishers and the railw Unlimited stopovers are permitted but there is no provision for luggage so travel light.

XPLORER❖❖❖

Explorer $$$
*BCRail Ltd, 1311 west
St, North Vancouver; tel:
(.) 984-5246 or (800)
-8238; web:
v.bcrail.com/bcrpass
s late May–Sept.*

Route: Whistler–Kelly Lake.

This railway journey (formerly called Whistler Explorer) provides a 4-hour out/9-hour back tourist excursion following the Gold Rush Trail from the magnificent mountains around Whistler Resort through the Pemberton Valley to remote Kelly Lake. A 1000m rise in elevation takes the *Explorer* through flower meadows and changing forest. Walk a quick circuit around the lake during the 45-minute stop before reboarding. Lunch is served on the return leg.

UDSON STEAM EXCURSION❖❖❖

**Hudson Steam
Excursion $$**
*Rail Ltd, 1311 west 1st
North Vancouver; tel:
() 984-5246, tollfree
)) 663-8238; web:
v.bcrail.com/bcrpass/bcrh
on.htm
www.mountain-
r.net/~chadwick/hudson/
son.htm
s mid-May–Sept
d–Sun. Can be
bined with MV
annia in one direction
booked through BC
.*

Route: North Vancouver–Squamish.

One of BC's most famous and beloved rail excursions takes just 2 hours and operates only half the week in summer. Pulled by one of the oldest steam locomotives in North America, the 1912-era *Port Coquitlam No 3716* is the backup engine while *The Royal Hudson* steam locomotive *No 2860* is out of service for extensive repair. Built to pull long freight trains over steep grades, the *Port Coquitlam* takes passengers along the spectacular 'Sea to Sky' route. Bunker C Bear, the train mascot, entertains children as parents watch the views. In Parlour Class, enjoy brunch on the way up to Squamish or afternoon high tea while returning to North Vancouver. Rail buffs won't miss a Squamish stopover for West Coast Railway·Heritage Park vintage rolling stock.

ht
Royal Hudson

KETTLE VALLEY STEAM RAILWAY❖❖

**Kettle Valley
Steam Railway $**
*Prairie Valley Station, west
side of Summerland; tel:
(250) 494-8422. Runs
varying days mid-May–early
Oct, departing 1030 and
1330.*

Route: 10km route from Prairie Valley Station to Canyon View Sidi

One of BC's few operational steam trains takes passengers on a
minute journey along a preserved section of the Kettle Valley Railw
Part of the CPR-owned 500km Coast-to-Kootenay line, the KVR cro
the McCulloch Trestle over a canyon 73m above Trout Creek a
chugs along hillsides overlooking beautiful orchards and vineyard
the Okanagan Valley.

OKANAGAN VALLEY WINE TRAIN❖❖

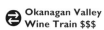
**Okanagan Valley
Wine Train $$$**
*991 Richter St, Kelowna;
tel: (250) 712-9888; tollfree
(888) 674-8725
web:
www.okanaganwinetrain.com
Departing July–Sept Fri–Sat
1630, Sun 1100.*

Board the Okanagan Valley Wine Train in Kelowna for dinner an
leisurely, 5-hour journey along picturesque valleys, lakes, orcha
farms and through the middle of a golf course. At the end of the li
the Las Vegas Follies Revue offers a colourful family show before
return trip to Kelowna. Travel in a day coach, a theme bar car c
sleeping car, the refurbished, long-distance Super Continental Limi
coaches built for the Canadian National Railway.

PACIFIC STARLIGHT DINNER TRAIN❖❖❖

**Pacific Starlight
Dinner Train $$$**
*BC Rail Ltd, 1311 west 1st
St, North Vancouver; tel:
(604) 984-5246, tollfree
(800) 339-8752 or (800)
363-3373; web:
www.bcrail.com/starlight
Runs May–early Oct
Wed–Sun; early
Oct–Thanksgiving Fri–Sat .*

Route: North Vancouver–Porteau Cove–North Vancouver.

Dressed for a fine dining evening, it is light when you board the ni
car train at 1815 in North Vancouver. The train, which also off
Sunday brunch and Murder Mystery evenings, serves supper w
entrées such as beef tenderloin, coho salmon or guinea fowl in eit
Salon or Dome Car seating. Each car has a 1930s or 1940s name a
heritage. Porteau Cove was served by steamships until 1955 whe
railway link between Vancouver and Whistler gutted the waterbo
traffic. The route leaves North Vancouver for West Vancouve
waterside vistas and posh residences, Horseshoe Bay and Ho
Sound's craggy shoreline to the watersports paradise at Porteau Cove

Right
The *Pacific Starlight*
Dinner Train

ACIFIC WILDERNESS RAILWAY✥✥✥

**Pacific Wilderness
Railway $$$**
*1208 Wharf St,
ria; departures from VIA
Station; tel: (250) 381-
0, tollfree (800) 561-
0; web: www.
ficwildernessrailway.com
artures June–Sept 1100
1400. Return trip 1.5
rs.*

Route: Victoria–Aerie Resort–Victoria.

Journey back in time and travel in grandeur on restored 1930s-era open window coaches and 1950s-era long distance coaches. A maximum of 24 passengers make the 1-hour journey in grand style to the top of Malahat Mountain and Milepost 20 where you are chauffeured to Aerie Resort, a Relais and Chateaux property which is frequently named one of the best small hotels in the world. After a four-course luncheon, guests catch the return train to Victoria.

OCKY MOUNTAINEER RAILTOURS✥✥✥

**Rocky Mountaineer
Railtours $$$**
*0 Station St, Vancouver;
(604) 606-7200, tollfree
0) 665-7245; web:
v.rockymountaineer.com
s May–early Oct, with
winter trips.*

Route: Calgary–Banff–Kamloops–Vancouver or Jasper–Kamloops–Vancouver.

The *Rocky Mountaineer (RM)* tours live up to their billing as the 'Most Spectacular Train Trip in the World', travelling a route abandoned by VIA Rail. The heavily booked tourist train offers good steward service, food and, above all, stunning scenery. Expect occasional stops or slow-downs for wildlife spotting. The *RM* waits for commercial traffic, so schedules are not precise, enhancing the feeling of travelling back in time when nature (avalanche, flood or rockslide) or business (a freight train with more priority) could affect railway operations.

Goldleaf Service, with roomy seats, has much-coveted dome car views, whose windows are kept clean despite often misty or rainy weather. White linen and flower-vase dining is below the dome car level. Signature Service passengers benefit from access to landings between cars, a spot favoured by photographers. Meals served at your seat are box lunches of excellent quality. Snacks are non-stop.

The *RM* provides a tabloid newspaper upon boarding, a Mile Marker by Mile Marker key to the routes, scenery, engineering feats, commercial development and ethnology the train passes through. With the tabloid guide, it is impossible to be lost even though the *RM* traverses about 1000km and seven (roughly) 200km divisions over track controlled by two railway companies – Canadian National and Canadian Pacific.

The *RM* trains from Calgary and Jasper follow the same route to Vancouver from Kamloops. As the train leaves Kamloops and criss-crosses the Fraser and Thompson river canyons, who can resist the sight of an occasional raft upriver from Suicide Rapids or the evocatively named Jaws of Death Gorge? The *RM* travels down the Fraser River Canyon, gathering a collective gasp at gondolas moving

Opposite
Heading into the Rockies

across the river almost into the train at Hell's Gate Gorge. The tr
continues west through the sprawling suburbs, across the Alex Fra
Bridge and into Vancouver's Pacific Central Station.

Calgary–Kamloops: the *RM* leaves urban density behind for
rolling foothills as the Rocky Mountains loom larger with each pass
mile. The train pulls into Banff townsite where passengers n
continue on or take an exhausting but rewarding all-day motorco
tour to the Columbia Icefields, with stops at Athabasca, Sunwa
Falls, Peyto Lake and Lake Louise. The tour is also available fr
Jasper. Return to the train and continue on to Kamloops.

Jasper–Kamloops: Mount Edith Cavell is on the left as the tr
leaves Jasper townsite. Yellowhead Pass, used by the Grand Tru
Pacific and Canadian Northern Railway (predecessors to Canad
National Railway), is the crossing rejected by the CPR as not southe
enough to protect Canadian interests against American railways. T
RM stops briefly for photographers at lovely Pyramid Falls and follc
the North Thompson River to Kamloops where passengers disembar

The Skeena***

The Skeena $$$
tel: (604) 640-3741,
tollfree (800) 561-8630;
web:
www.viarail.ca/en.trai.nord.
htm
Runs three times weekly.

Route: Prince Rupert–Jasper.

A stop in Prince George is a welcome pause along the 1160km ro
that follows the track of the early 20th-century Grand Trunk Pac
Railway. *The Skeena* leaves Prince Rupert, threading through
namesake canyon, often giving credence to the Skeena's name, 'ri
of mists', continuing west through the land of First Nations and
Gitxsan, preserving the world's largest collection of standing tot
poles. The route generally follows the Fraser River after Prince Geor
passing by the landmark Mount Robson on the left, over t
Yellowhead Pass and into Jasper National Park and the townsite.

Whistler Northwind***

**Whistler
Northwind $$$**
BC Rail Ltd, 1311 west 1st
St, North Vancouver; tel:
(604) 984-5246, tollfree
(800) 663-8238; web:
www.whistlernorthwind.com
Runs May–Oct.

Route: Vancouver–Whistler–Williams Lake–Prince George.

Following the same route as the *Cariboo Prospector*, this train is a
luxe service which features single-level, full-domed passenger cars. T
3-day journey stops overnight in Whistler and Williams Lake.
meals are served on English fine china with two levels of service:
seat dining on Panorama or dining in a vintage car on Summit servi
where passengers can repair to the round-end club car built in 1939
ride the rails between New York and Miami.

Suggested tour

Time: 4–7 days, depending on connections and season.

Links: For major stations, see Vancouver (*see page 268*), Victoria *page 248*), Kamloops (*see page 191*), Jasper and Banff (*see pages 84* Prince George and Prince Rupert. Central Vancouver Island co᷿ stops on the E&N 'Malahat'. At Prince Rupert, disembarking *Ske* passengers can take an Inside Passage Ferry Cruise (*see page 184* Port Hardy. *The Royal Hudson* takes the Howe Sound and Whis route.

Route: All railway companies offer combination packages with e᷿ other, as well as motorcoach and ferry connections where appropri᷿ Most tourist rail excursions run from approximately May–Se depending on route and snowfall. There are also regular routes suc᷿ VIA Rail's transcontinental 'Canadian' from Vancouver to Toront᷿ cross-Canada railway excursion provides an excellent introductior geography before hiring a car and taking to the road. Rail buffs ᷿ want to take the train to see the two Western provinces with va᷿ scenery and rolling stock.

Rockies to Coast Triangle: Eastern Loop. Take the **ROC᷿ MOUNTAINEER ❶** from Vancouver to Kamloops. Overnight and᷿ board the Rocky Mountaineer to Jasper. The next morning, take **T SKEENA ❷** to Prince George. Board the **CARIBOO PROSPECT ❸** the next morning to Vancouver.

Alternate route: Take the **ROCKY MOUNTAINEER ❺** fr᷿ Kamloops to Banff. Take the bus over the Icefields Parkway to Jas᷿ and catch the return train to Kamloops and Vancouver.

Interior to Coast: Western Loop. Take a BC Ferry from Vancouve᷿ Victoria and board the E&N 'Malahat' ❹ to Courtenay , the᷿ motorcoach to Port Hardy at the north end of Vancouver Isla᷿ Catch a BC Ferry to Prince Rupert and board *The Skeena* going east ᷿ follow the curves of the broad, high-walled super-scenic Skeena R᷿ Valley to Prince George. Board the Cariboo Prospector to Vancouve᷿

The Silk Trains

Roaring across Canada in the early 20th century, Silk Trains transported bales of Chinese silk from the docks of Vancouver to the silk mills in New York City. The 'Silkers' set speed records that have yet to be broken as speed, security and safety were vital. Canadian Pacific freight trains carried the valuable cargo in up to 15 airtight boxcars. With preference over all trains, a Silker once had priority over Prince Albert, later King George VI, as he and his entourage waited on a siding for a racing train. Man-made fibres and the advent of air travel ended the exotic Silk Train-era during the Second World War.

Ferry cruises

Ratings

History	●●●●●
Mountains	●●●●●
Nature	●●●●●
Scenery	●●●●●
Wildlife	●●●●●
Children	●●●●○
Food and drink	●●●○○
Villages	●●●○○

Operating one of the biggest fleets in the world, Ferries' 40 vessels navigate the province's varied wat with ferries ranging from the 34m *Nimpkish* to the jum 170m *Spirit of Vancouver Island*. Strictly speaking, the ferr are transportation for vehicles and passengers but even most everyday ferry run can take on the air of a cruise wh the sun shines bright and temperatures rise. On the no coast, a ferry trip is more adventure than transportatic Navigating the waters of the Inside Passage from Bella Coc Prince Rupert and Port Hardy, a ferry voyage is the best w and often the only route, to enjoy some of North Americ most awesome coastal vistas. Expect to see snow-capp peaks dropping steeply into icy fiords lined with dark gre forests, and do not be surprised to see nothing at all i storm blows through.

BELLA BELLA/McLOUGHLIN BAY ✢

**Bella Bella/
McLoughlin Bay
Heiltsuk Band
Administration**
*tel: (250) 957-2381. See
Quest Adventures, tel: (250)
957-2774.*

The Heiltsuk, based at Bella Bella (Waglisla), are opening the door tourism slowly and cautiously. While hospitable, the Heiltsuk rest tourists generally to McLoughlin Bay, 3km south of the village. purser may say that Bella Bella is too far to walk during the short p call but it is not too far for several local artists to set up shop on dock when the *Queen of Chilliwack* calls, including famed silversm Peter Gladstone. McLoughlin Bay is also a popular stop for kayak setting off for or returning from camping trips through the Ha Recreation Area (*see page 182*). If the weather is reasonable, that anything blowing less than a full gale, walk a few hundred met down the crushed shell beach to the traditional-style longhouse. B by Heiltsuk carvers Frank and Kathy Brown, the longhouse i combination local history museum, Aboriginal art gallery and sim restaurant specialising in salmon roasted on cedar plants over an o

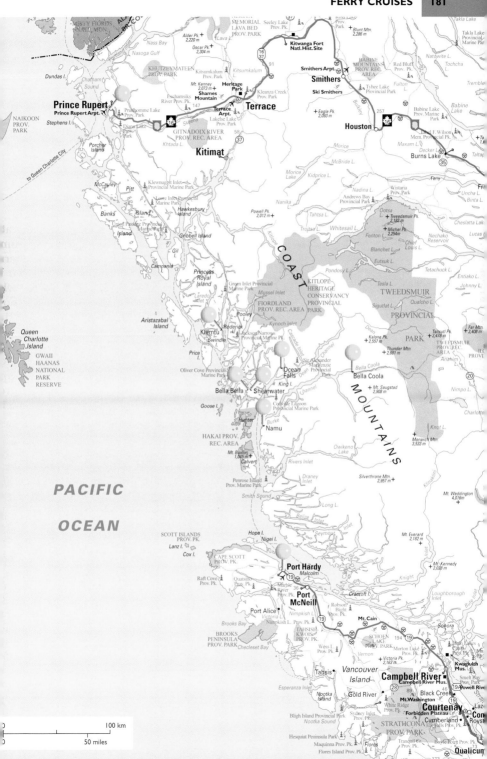

MISTY FJORDS NATL. MON.

Nass Bay

Nasoga Gulf

Alder Pk.
2,220 m

Oscar Pk.
2,304 m

MEMORIAL
LAVA BED
PROV. PARK

Lava L.

Seeley Lake
Prov. Pk.

Kitwanga Fort
Natl. Hist. Site

Blunt Mtn.
2,286 m

Takla Lake

Takla L.

Takla Lake
Provincial
Marine Park

Natwite L.

Tochcha
L.

Tremble

KHUTZEYMATEEN
PROV. PARK

Kitsumkalum L.

Kitsumkalum

16
37

91

BABINE
MOUNTAINS
PROV. REC.
AREA

Red Bluff
Prov. Pk.

Dundas I.

Chatham
Sd.

Mt. Kenney
2,073 m

Shames
Mountain

Heritage
Park

Kleanza Creek
Prov. Park

Smithers Arpt.

Smithers

Ski Smithers

Tyhee Lake
Provincial Park

Fulton

Babine
Lake

Tweedsmuir
L.

Tochcha L.

NAIKOON
PROV.
PARK

Prince Rupert
Prince Rupert Arpt.

Pschamsiks
River Prov. Pk.

147

Terrace
Arpt.

Terrace

Skeena

Eagle Pk.
2,093 m

Bulkley

Houston

257

Babine Lake
Prov. Marine Park

Lord E. Wilson
Mem. Provincial Pk.

Porcher
Island

to Queen Charlotte City

Prudhomme Lake
Prov. Park

Diana Lake
Prov.
Park

GITNADOIX RIVER
PROV. REC. AREA

Lakelse Lake
Prov. Park

58

37

Morice

McBride L.

Maxam L.

Decker L.

35

Burns Lake

Fr

+Ta
L.

Stephens I.

Khtada L.

Kitimat

Morice
Lake

Kidprice L.

Ferry

Uncha L.

Binta L.

McCauley

Pitt

Klewnuggit Inlet
Provincial Marine Park

Powell Pk.
2,012 m

Nanika

Nadina L.

Andrews Bay
Provincial Park

Wistaria
Prov. Park

Cheslatta L.

Lucas L.

Banks
Island

Lowe Inlet Provincial
Marine Park

Hawkesbury
Island

Ootsa

Tweedsmuir L.
2,182 m

Nechako
Reservoir

Union Passage Provincial
Marine Park

Gribbell Island

Powell Pk.
2,012 m

Tahtsa L.

Whitesail L.

Fenton

Michel Pk.
2,254m

Chief
Louis L.

Eutsuk L.

Campania
I.

Gil
I.

C
O
A
S
T

Tropsa L.

Blanchet L.

Tetachuck L.

Entiako L.

Johnny L.

Queen
Charlotte
Island

Aristazabal
Island

Princess
Royal
Island

Laredo
Inlet

Green Inlet Provincial
Marine Park

Mussel Inlet

Pooley

Kynoch Inlet

KITLOPE
HERITAGE
CONSERVANCY
PROVINCIAL
PARK

Pondosy L.

Siguttlat L.

Tesla L.

TWEEDSMUIR

PROVINCIAL

Qualcho L.

Kalone Pk.
2,557 m

Tsaitsutl Pk.
2,478 m

Far Mtn.
2,408 m

TWEEDSMUIR
PROV. REC.
AREA

Anahim

PROVI

GWAII
HAANAS
NATIONAL
PARK
RESERVE

Price

Swindle

Roderick

Jackson Narrows
Provincial Marine Park

FIORDLAND
PROV. REC.
AREA

King I.

Sir Alexander
Mackenzie
Provincial
Park

Thunder Mtn.
2,681 m

Monarch Mtn.
3,533 m

Nimpo L.

Charlotte

Klemtu

Oliver Cove Provincial
Marine Park

Ocean
Falls

Mt. Saugstad
2,908 m

Bella Coola

20

PACIFIC

OCEAN

Goose I.

Bella Bella

Shearwater

Codville Lagoon
Provincial Marine Park

Burke
Channel

HAKAI PROV.
REC. AREA

Hunter

Namu

Owikeno
Lake

Kitlatla

Knot L.

M
O
U
N
T
A
I
N
S

Mt. Baxton
1,045 m

Calvert
I.

Rivers Inlet

Silverthrone Mtn.
2,957 m

Mt. Waddington
4,016m

Penrose Island
Prov. Marine Park

Draney
Inlet

Smith Sound

Long L.

Belize Inlet

SCOTT ISLANDS
PROV. PK.

Lanz I.

Cox I.

Hope I.

Nigei I.

Seymour
Inlet

Mt. Everard
2,182 m

Mt. Kennedy
2,028 m

Loughborough
Inlet

CAPE SCOTT
PROV. PARK

Raft Cove
Prov. Park

Quatsino
Prov. Pk.

Port Hardy

Malcolm

19

Marble
River
Prov. Pk.

36

Port
McNeill

Craycroft I.

Robson
Bight
Prov. Pk.

Knight

Inlet

BROOKS
PENINSULA
PROV. PARK

Port Alice

Brooks Bay

Victoria L.

Nimpkish L.

Nimpkish R.

19

Mt. Cain

SCHOEN
LAKE
PROV. PARK

194

Mt. Cain

19

Sonora

Small Lakes
Prov. Pk.

Kwaguilth
Mus.

Checleset Bay

TAHSISH-
KWOIS
PROV. PK.

Woss L.
Prov. Pk.

Vernon

Victoria L.

Morton Lake
Prov. Pk.

89

Tahsis

Esperanza Inlet

Nootka
Island

Vancouver
Island

Gold River

Mt. Washington
1,163 m

Campbell River
Campbell River Mus.

28

Black Creek

46

Powell Riv

19A

Maquinna Prov. Pk.

Bligh Island Provincial Park
Nootka Sound

Sydney Inlet
Prov. Pk.

White Ridge
Prov. Pk.

STRATHCONA
PROV. PARK

Mt. Washington

Courtenay
Forbidden Plateau
Cumberland

Coy

Roys

Laz
Co

Hesquiat Peninsula Prov. Park

Tranquil Cr.
Prov. Pk.

Boyle Point Prov. Pk.

Epper Passage Prov. Pk.

Flores Island Prov. Park

Flores
I.

Clayoquot
Sd.

Qualicum

173

fire. Brown also takes passengers on a 1-hour paddle in the Glwa traditional Heiltsuk canoe carved from a single cedar log. The t passes old totem poles, deserted fish canneries, ravens, eagles, ord herons, dolphins and often bear and deer before rejoining the *Queer Chilliwack* in the next port, Shearwater. On ferry trips that stop Shearwater but not McLoughlin Bay, Brown brings his authentica carved canoe out to meet the ship and take on paddlers. Seats on canoe are limited and popular with repeat passengers, so sign immediately after boarding the *Queen of Chilliwack*.

DISCOVERY COAST PASSAGE: BELLA COOLA TO PORT HARDY ✦✦✦

Discovery Coast, Bella Coola–Port Hardy $$$ web: *www.discoverycoast.bcferries. bc.ca The summer-only route operates mid-June–early Sept.*

BC Ferries *1112 Fort St, Victoria; tel: (250) 386-3431 or (888) 223-3779; web: www.bcferries.bc.ca*

Hakai Recreation Area *tel: (250) 398-4414.*

Unlike most BC Ferries that cater to commuters, commercial tra and local residents, the Discovery Coast Passage route was created tourists. The summer-only service aboard the *Queen of Chilliwack* named 'Discovery' after Alexander Mackenzie, who, in 1793, was first European to cross North America north of Mexico. Macker emerged from the mountains at Bella Coola to discover that he l finally found the Pacific Ocean. There are more ghost towns tł modern settlements along the route, but the often-narrow, alwa scenic channels are seldom empty. Cruise ships and fishing bc make regular runs between Alaska, to the north, and Seattle a Canadian ports to the south. Pleasure craft throng the protected in and passages of the **Hakai Recreation Area**,✦✦✦ a popular area for kayaking.

The entire voyage takes 15–33 hours, depending on how many five potential port calls the *Queen of Chilliwack* makes. Allow about hours for a return voyage from either Bella Coola or Port Hardy. ship stays reasonably close to schedule but do not expect slav devotion to the timetable. The 115m car ferry also carries kayaks a other small craft that can be dropped off and picked up at irregu stops along the trip. There may be detours when the captain spo pod of orcas or a breaching humpback whale nearby. For the ł sightseeing, sail the Discovery Coast southbound, Bella Coola–F Hardy, to enjoy the panorama of mountains surrounding No Bentinck Arm (near Bella Coola) in daylight. For easier driving, tał northbound sailing, Port Hardy–Bella Coola. In Bella Coc passengers board at the ferry dock but vehicles must check in a staging area near the Cedar Inn, about 2km from the dock, to pick a boarding pass before driving to the dock. In Port Hardy (*see p 229*), passengers and vehicles board at the Bear Cove ferry dock.

Check current procedures with BC Ferries when making yc booking. Boarding starts 60 minutes before sailing at both ports bu is better to board early than late: early arrivals get the coveted se next to the *Queen of Chilliwack*'s oversized view windows. Seating is first-come, first-served, so passengers in the know race aboard to drop a jacket or a backpack on their preferred window seat, usually in the forward lounge. Hotels, motels and B&Bs at either end of the route can arrange transportation to and from the dock for passengers on foot. Reservations are required for vehicles and are highly recommended for foot passengers: space is limited and the season short. There may be space on the first few and the last few sailings at the last moment, but book four to six months in advance for June–Aug trips. Reservations can be changed (if space is available on the new date) but each change costs $50 per segment. You can check availability, make reservations and buy tickets by credit card online or by telephone.

Summer weather is usually good but the coastal climate is fickle. Rain, fog and wind are at least as common as sunshine, which comes and goes almost without warning. Stick to comfortable, layered clothing and flat shoes for walking about on deck, up and down outside stairways and on shore. Long trousers, long sleeves, closed shoes and a warm jacket with a hood are likely to be as useful as sunglasses and sun block, even if the weather forecast predicts nothing but sunshine. Seas will probably be calm no matter what the weather. Except for a short stretch of open water in the Queen Charlotte Sound north of Port Hardy, a maze of islands protects the entire route from ocean swells and large wind waves.

The Discovery Coast is a tourist cruise but the *Queen of Chilliwack* is no cruise ship; no disco, no casino, no swimming pool, no sauna, no beauty parlour, no dressy dinners. There is a gym, a couple of stationary bicycles on the solarium deck, as well as a full-service cafeteria, bar, lounge, laundry, showers, video arcade and gift shop. There is also plenty of outside deck space to enjoy the passing scenery while looking for orcas, humpback whales, eagles, seals, dolphins and passing vessels of all sizes. Binoculars and telephoto camera lenses are a must. The *Queen of Chilliwack* has no passenger cabins but the reclining seats are comfortable for night-long napping. Blankets, sheets and pillows can be hired

on board, or bring your own. You can also hire tents on board, or pitch your own on the outer decks (or perhaps indoors, depending on weather). A popular option is to overnight in Klemtu, Ocean Falls or Shearwater and pick up the ship on a later sailing, but rooms on shore

t
whale breaching

are limited. Book shoreside accommodation first (and explain that
are arriving aboard the *Queen of Chilliwack*), then book passag€
match your dates ashore. Port calls stretch from 30 minutes to h₅
day, depending on the port and day of the week.

Arrival and departure times are posted near the Purser's Of
forward of the cafeteria. There are shore excursions in most p€
usually walking tours, traditional dancing, salmon feasts or pa€
trips. Buy shore tours as soon as possible after boarding. The better
weather, the earlier the excursions sell out. You can also exp
ashore on your own, but watch the time. The *Queen of Chilliwack* ₍
not wait for late returns. The only departure warning is a long wh₅
blast 15 minutes before pulling away from the dock.

INSIDE PASSAGE: PRINCE RUPERT TO PORT HARDY✢✢

**⊘ Inside Passage,
Prince Rupert–Port
Hardy $$$**
*1112 Fort St, Victoria; tel:
(250) 386-3431 or (888)
223-3779; web:
www.bcferries.bc.ca*

Eagles, whales and mouth-dropping scenery on all sides make this
year car-ferry route the most popular 15-hour cruise in Canada. L€
for sheer mountains cloaked with red cedar and Sitka spruce ris
from glacier-carved channels, low islands swept clean by winter sto
and lighthouses marking channels less than 250m wide. The en
trip takes place during daylight hours mid-May–early Oct, when n
sailings of the 125m *Queen of the North* depart Prince Rupert at 0
and arrive at Port Hardy at 2230 the same day. Check with BC Fe₁
for off-season schedules. Vehicle spaces must be reserved in advar
Foot passengers should also book space, especially June–Aug wh
tour groups flock to north-coast ferry trips. Last-minute vehicle s₁
may be available mid-Sept–mid-May but make reservations
months in advance for summer travel.

In Prince Rupert, follow Second Avenue (Hwy 16) to the ferry d€
In Port Hardy, board at Bear Cove, just south of town. Boarding st
1 hour before sailing. In summer, be prepared to scramble for winc
seats in the forward cabins with the best views or opt for an out€
seat. There is no rush to be first on board to scramble for window s€
in winter, when there are few passengers. Weather is usually w₅
and clear (but not always sunny) in summer, while storms
common in winter. The Inside Passage is calm and well protected
dozens of islands off the coast, but rain, wind, fog and snow b€
down from the Arctic in winter. In any season, most passengers op
spend the trip in comfortable reclining chairs or in the many lou
areas set with tables and chairs. Private cabins are available at
additional charge. There is also a fine dining room, complete v
silver and white linen tablecloths. Most passengers go for the
expensive cafeteria that serves everything from snacks to full me
Ferries also have a licensed lounge, video arcade, children's play a

elevator, washroom for persons with disabilities, games, free videos in public rooms and a well-stocked gift shop.

LEMTU❖❖❖

Klemtu Kitasoo Band Council
(250) 839-1255.

This is one of the most popular overnight stops on the Discovery Coast, thanks to a bed and breakfast operated by the Kitasoo Band: book accommodation first, then the Discovery Coast sailing that matches your stay. Most of Klemtu's 500 or so residents turn out to welcome the *Queen of Chilliwack*. Main street is among the longest boardwalks in Canada, skirting two sides of a bay that is alive with bald eagles, dolphins and orcas on the hunt for salmon and other fish. The most popular activity is a 3-hour walking tour of town with stops at a busy carving shed and a traditional Aboriginal feast guaranteed to finish before the ship sails. BYOK – bring your own kayak – or charter a boat from band operators for fishing, sightseeing, hiking and camping on nearby islands.

NAMU✦✦✦

🚢 **BC Ferries**
tel: (250) 386-3431 or (888) 223-3779; web: www.bcferries.bc.ca

Namu is a rarity along the BC coast: a former fish cannery that st[ill] has a permanent population. The faded white cannery buildings lo[ok] like a cinema set against the dense green shoreline forest after t[he] plant closed down in 1970, but a handful of hardy residents fi[nd] Namu an inviting spot nonetheless. They are not alon[e.] Archaeological digs have found human habitation dating back 10,0[00] years around the tranquil cove, making Namu the oldest continuou[sly] occupied site along the western coast of North America.

OCEAN FALLS✦✦✦

🚢 **BC Ferries**
tel: (250) 386-3431 or (888) 223-3779; web: www.bcferries.bc.ca

Below
Deck bathing

Known for its world-class swimmers (1940s–1960s), Ocean Falls is al[so] known for its mean annual precipitation of 4 386.8mm. Named af[ter] Link Falls, a waterfall that thunders directly into the sea, Ocean Fa[lls] was once a thriving pulp and paper mill-town at the head of Cousi[ns] Inlet. Three thousand people lived here in the mid-20th centu[ry,] enough to fill a hospital, high school, hotel and Olympic-siz[e]

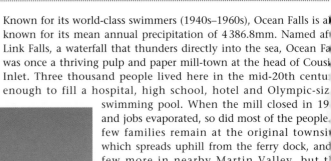

swimming pool. When the mill closed in 19[??] and jobs evaporated, so did most of the people. [A] few families remain at the original townsi[te,] which spreads uphill from the ferry dock, and [a] few more in nearby Martin Valley, but t[he] population more than doubles when the *Queen [of] Chilliwack* passengers hit the streets on walki[ng] tours. Fishing and sightseeing boat charters a[re] also available, as are a few B&B rooms: bo[ok] onshore accommodation first, then matchi[ng] sailing dates. There is home-made soup, ice crea[m] and espresso at the only restaurant in tow[n,] Bernie Bashan's floating café. There are a fire ha[ll,] modern school and the mouldering remains o[f a] long-closed hotel, but most of Ocean Falls [is] vanishing beneath a creeping carpet of alde[r,] blackberry bushes and seedling pines. It is hard [to] miss the occasional splash of colour, usually [a] bright blue hydrangea in what was once [a] carefully tended front garden. Today's reside[nts] would not change much about their town. [The] hydroelectric dam built for the mill still chur[ns] out power, but with no logging and no toxic p[ulp] waste pouring into the ocean, salmon, halib[ut,] eagles, dolphins and other wildlife have returne[d.]

Inside Passage

The domain of basking seals, breaching killer whales and schools of playful dall porpoises, the Inside Passage is a majestic panorama of natural beauty protected by offshore islands and tempered by the *Kuroshio* (Japan Current). A vast archipelago of deep channels, quiet bays and forested islands makes up one of the most scenic and interesting waterways in the world. Sparsely populated, the area has been inhabited by Coast aboriginals for some 10,000 years. Fewer than 5000 live on the coast, half of them at Bella Coola (*see page 133*) and another quarter in Queen Charlotte City in the Queen Charlotte Islands. Two hundred years ago, the waters and islands between Prince Rupert and Port Hardy were the realm of aborigines who lived well off the bounty of the rich sea and the temperate coastal forests. A century ago, the same waters teemed with floating logging camps, pulp mills and fish canneries. Changing economic conditions closed most of the outside industries, leaving the Inside Passage once again a largely aboriginal area where humans are vastly outnumbered by the wildlife, and the scenery draws visitors from around the world.

ow
ce Rupert harbour

Shearwater/Denny Island❖❖

Shearwater/Denny Island Shearwater Marine Resort
tel: (604) 270-6204, tollfree: (800) 663-2370; web: www.shearwater.ca

Flying boats based at Denny Island, opposite Bella Bella, on patrolled the Queen Charlotte Channel during the Second World W watching for Japanese submarines. The base is long gone, as is an ea 20th-century fish-packing plant, but with the newer name Shearwater, the sheltered bay has become a base for tourism, sp fishing and maritime traffic. The Shearwater resort includes a sm hotel, fishing charters, restaurant, pub, marina and B& accommodation. Look for commercial fishing boats, sailboats a luxury motor yachts tied up to the dock. Crew and passengers most likely tied up to the bar inside, the only full-service stop betwe Bella Coola and Port Hardy. The *Queen of Westminster* ties up lo enough for a meal or a drink at the resort. The alternative is to spe several days cycling and hiking the island or boating nearby waters.

Suggested tours

Time: Allow up to 15 hours to travel the Inside Passage betwe **Prince Rupert ❶** and **Port Hardy ❸**, or 33 hours to travel t Discovery Coast between **Bella Coola ❷** and Port Hardy.

Links: Prince Rupert is the mainland terminus of the Yellowhe Highway, which continues westward to the Queen Charlotte Islar or eastward to the Rocky Mountains and Jasper National Park (*see p 87*). Both ferry routes meet at Port Hardy (*see page 229*), at the no end of Vancouver Island, for the drive south toward Victoria (*see p 248*). From Bella Coola (*see page 133*), it is possible to drive t Cariboo–Chilcotin to Williams Lake (*see page 137*) and either north Prince Rupert or south toward Vancouver (*see page 268*).

Route: Both ferry trips fit into a circular driving tour from Vancouv then north by mainland to Bella Coola or Prince Rupert, then sou by ferry to Port Hardy on Vancouver Island, then south by highway Victoria and by ferry to Vancouver. Allow 7–10 days for the ent route. It is possible to combine both ferry voyages by driving to eith Bella Coola or Port Hardy, taking one ferry route into Port Hardy a then taking the second route back to the mainland. Allow 10–14 da for the two ferry trips, plus long-distance driving on the mainland a any excursions on Vancouver Island. Both routes are served by ferries but do not take 'car' too literally. If it is street-legal in BC, Ferries will carry it: cars, vans, RVs, motor coaches, motorcycl bicycles, trucks and foot passengers. Both tours can be taken in eith direction and both can be made with a combination of train, coa and air connections to avoid driving altogether.

Cowboy Country

Ratings

Cowboys	●●●● ○
First Nations	●●●● ○
History	●●●● ○
Outdoor activities	●●●● ○
Scenery	●●●● ○
Sport	●●●● ○
Children	●●● ○ ○
Museums	●●● ○ ○

There's a kind of time warp that happens in this a⟩ region of rolling hills and grassland, like returning t⟨ more rural existence when transportation meant a horse, ⟩ an RV or 4x4. There are certainly towns (and Kamloops i⟩ large city in BC terms) but this is unquestionably 'c⟨ country' as it was when the BC cattle industry was born⟩ the 1860s. In its beginnings, the hot summers and op⟩ ranges seemed like a good 'fallback' position after the g⟨ rush petered out. Unlucky prospectors, too tired or poor⟩ go home, purchased farmland and put down roots for n⟨ communities. Among the new settlers were Engli⟩ gentlemen farmers and remittance men who rais⟩ gamecocks and galloped about the hills to the sounds⟩ hounds and hunting horns. Today, more than a thousa⟩ ranches give the area its dominating flavour.

CACHE CREEK❖❖

ⓘ Cache Creek Chamber of Commerce *1389 Quartz St; tel: (250) 457-6237.*

🏛 Historic Hat Creek Ranch *11km north of Cache Creek at junction of Hwys 12 & 97, then west 5km; tel: (259) 457-9722; tollfree: (800) 782-0922; e-mail: gail.dennison@ gems 5.gov.bc.ca*

🛍 Cariboo Jade Shoppe *1093 Todd Rd in downtown Cache Creek.*

With its large cattle ranches worked by real cowboys and its grassla⟩ filled with grazing beef cattle, Cache Creek is the Wild West revisit⟩ The **Historic Hat Creek Ranch**❖❖❖ is the last intact stopping house⟩ the Old Cariboo Waggon Road and interpretive tours here provid⟩ glimpse of what ranching was like from 1860 to 1915, along wit⟩ history of the area's First Nations people. This is still a working ra⟩ but one that offers visitors nature walks, trail rides, wagon to⟩ blacksmith and farm machinery displays and a bunch of spec⟩ events. Good sport fishing and a place to find jade which you ⟨ watch being cut and polished in the **Cariboo Jade Shoppe.**❖

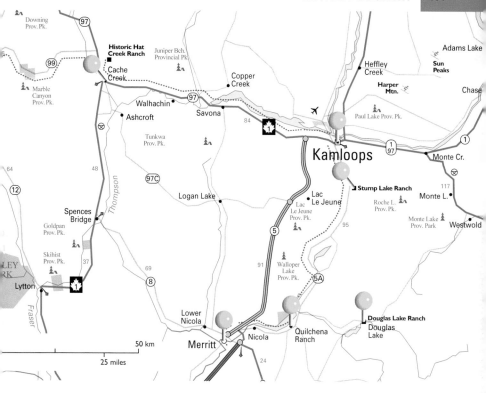

OUGLAS LAKE RANCH✦✦✦

**Douglas Lake
Ranch $$** *turn east off
5A at Douglas Lake Rd,
nue 26km to main
ance of ranch; web:
.douglaslake.com*

First set up in 1884, the Douglas Lake Ranch is the largest working
cattle company in Canada and offers a well-established tour
programme that looks at the rich history, traditions and lifestyle on
the ranch. All of the tours take in the home ranch, the company town,
general store, calving barn, quarter horse barn, feedlot and school.

AMLOOPS✦✦

**Kamloops Info
Centre**
) west Hwy 1; tel: (250)
-3377; tollfree (800)
1994; web:
.venturekamloops.com;
 daily mid-May–mid-
rest of year Mon–Fri.

This is BC's fifth largest city (and its biggest at least in terms of area)
but there's still an Old West, 'cowboy' feel to much of it. As it has for
almost 150 years, Kamloops still serves as a watering hole for the area's
ranch hands who come in from the 1100 ranches largely near the city.

Kamloops takes its name from a Secwepemc native word meaning
'where the rivers meet', a place where the ancestors had their
gathering place. Downtown, well-kept turn-of-the-century brick
buildings rub shoulders with art galleries and theatres near the

Tranquille Marsh
10km west on Tranquille Rd from North Kamloops.

Kamloops Art Gallery $
465 Victoria St; tel: (250) 828-3543. Open Tue–Sat 1000–1700, Thur until 2100, Sun 1000–1600.

Kamloops Museum and Archives $
207 Seymour St; tel: (250) 828-3576. Open Tue–Sat 0930–1630.

Kamloops Wildlife Park $ *15 minutes east of Kamloops city centre off Hwy 1; tel: (250) 573-3242; fax: (250) 573-2406; web: www.kamloopswildlife.org; e-mail: info@kamloopswildlife.org*

MV Wanda-Sue $
moored at the foot of 10th Ave; tel: (250) 374-7447. Cruises daily May–Sept.

Secwepemc Heritage Park and Museum $
355 Yellowhead Hwy; tel: (250) 828-9801; web: www.secwepemc.com Open daily.

Sun Peaks $$
24.5km east of Hwy 5 via Heffley–Louise Creek Rd, then 9km on Sun Peaks Rd; tel: (250) 578-7842; tollfree (800) 807-3257.

Farmers Market $
two locations: Victoria St, 4th–5th Aves, Wed 0800–1200; St Paul and 3rd, Sat 0800–1400.

beaches on the low banks of the South Thompson River. T Kamloops Museum and Archives** has three floors of displays t explore local Secwepemc First Nations history, local Chinese cultu Victoriana and natural history. The museum's collection Secwepemc baskets is one of the best in the province. The exhib include an 1842 log building from the Hudson's Bay Company fort what is now the Kamloops Indian Reserve on the north bank of South Thompson River, two Victorian-era house interiors and mo Just on the outskirts of town, the **Secwepemc Heritage Park a Museum***** expands on the history of the First Nations people w have lived in this area for thousands of years. There is a 2 000-year-archaeological site in the 5ha park and four reconstructed win homes showing building styles over time. Summer dwellings, uni ethno-botanical gardens, and a wildlife marsh with many bird spe are other features of the site. Outdoor performances are held fr time to time. The museum exhibits archaeological and ethnograp materials of the Secwepemc (Shuswap people). There is a gift shop.

The **Kamloops Art Gallery**** has recently undergone a facelift w a whole new design to enhance the largest public art exhibit in interior of BC. Like many weekly markets, the **Kamloops Farm Market**** began as a produce outlet for local farms but has si expanded to include everything from rabbits and chickens to l music and square dancing. It's a great place to stock up on fragr freshly baked breads, cheeses and vegetables for a weekend picnic spots such as **Sun Peaks Resort,***** a year-round mountain resort t offers good hiking, horse-back riding, mountain biking and more the summer, and excellent skiing in the winter. For a slice of the p a ride on the **MV Wanda-Sue**** is the dream child of a long-ti resident that now takes visitors on a 2-hour river cruise. The 2 sternwheeler carries 100 passengers down the Thompson River.

The biggest event for would-be cowboys is the annual cattle drive each July (*see page 193*) when for six days greenhorns get to drive cattle into Kamloops along with real cowboys. The scenery these 'dudes' ride through is spectacular: rolling grasslands and forest, weirdly shaped hills and hoodoos (rock pinnacles). To the north of Kamloops, the **Tranquille Marsh**** has its own beauty and attracts hundreds of birds to the delight of bird watchers and hikers. Snow geese, herons and trumpeter swans are just a few of the species in this very active waterfowl habitat. The **Kamloops Wildlife Park*****is the area's newest attraction

and allows visitors to have an up-close and personal glimpse at some of the area's animal life. Kids will love riding the park's Wildlife Express, a steam locomotive-driven train that chugs along 1km of track.

Accommodation and food in Kamloops

The Plaza Hotel $$ *405 Victoria; tel: (250) 377-8075; tollfree: (877) 977-5292; fax: (250) 377-8076; web: www.plazahotel.kamloops.com; e-mail: plazahotel@kamloops.com* This 1920s heritage building not long ago entertained bikers not barons and was definitely on its way to being seedy. After a total restoration, it now has charming, individually decorated rooms and exudes the warmth of a country inn.

Rick's Grill $$$ *downtown at 227 Victoria; tel: (250) 372-7771.* As you'd expect in 'cattle country', beef is king in Kamloops and restaurants don't come any better for steaks and prime rib than this one.

Peter's Pasta $$ *149 Victoria St; tel: (250) 372-8514.* You can tell a restaurant that's popular with the locals by the length of the lineup to get in. Run by a welcoming family, this has superb home-made pastas and breads.

The Swiss Pastry $ *359 Victoria St; tel: (250) 372-2625.* Another spot with a heavy emphasis on home-made goodies: soups, sandwiches, breads and desserts. Open for lunch only.

The Kamloops Cattle Drive

Like the three greenhorns in the movie *City Slickers*, almost anyone can join a cattle drive, maybe even save the day and come home with a pet calf. The famous annual Kamloops Cattle Drive has been luring would-be cowboys since 1990 for a 5-day ride in mid-July through the open rangelands of BC's breathtaking ranch country. Even if you haven't ridden before, professional cowboys will teach you the ropes so that before long anyone with a touch of stamina will be riding high in the saddle. Starting at the Crater Valley Ranch, every day begins with a campfire breakfast and the scent of sage before heading out onto the range behind the herd. In the evening, it's tasty 'grub' with foot-stompin' campfire tunes provided by the cowboys. This is a Western odyssey at its best.

For more information contact **Cattle Drive 2002** *PO Box 1332, Kamloops, BC, V2C 6L7; tel: (250) 372-7075; tollfree (800) 288-5850; fax: (250) 372-0262; web: www.cattledrive.bc.ca*

MERRITT✦

ⓘ Merritt Information Centre 1950 Mamette Ave; tel: (250) 378-5634; tollfree (877) 330-3377; e-mail: manager@ocis.net Open daily all year.

ⓕ Merritt Mountain Music Festival tel: (604) 525-3330 or web: www.mountainfest.com

☾ Coldwater Hotel $ 1901 Voght St; tel: (250) 378-2821; e-mail: coldwaterhotel@uniserve. com

This town of 7 631 people sits in the valley at the confluence of the Nicola and Coldwater rivers and serves as a transportation hub for ranching country. It's a centre for five aboriginal communities and marks the spot where the territories of the Nlaka'pamux First Nation people and Okanagan First Nation people meet. For a nostalgic look at cowboy history, spend a little time in the shrimp-pink **Coldwater Hotel✦✦** with its balconies and copper-domed turret. When it was built in 1908 for $6 000 it was considered the finest hotel in the BC Interior since it boasted rooms with attached bathrooms. Couples could be married in hotel and then rent a room for $1.50 including breakfast. On Satur nights, cowboys would come in from the hills and sit on the balco watching the women stroll by. The area is a major draw for fisherm with 150 lakes filled with rainbow and cutthroat trout, kokanee Dolly Varden char. The biggest event is a 4-day **Merritt Mount Music Country and Western Festival✦** in July.

Right
Nicola Valley wooden church

Opposite
Stump Lake Ranch

QUILCHENA RANCH✦✦✦

☾ Quilchena Hotel $$ on Hwy 5A north of Merritt; tel: (250) 378-2611; fax: (250) 378-6091; web: www.quilchena.com; e-mail: hotel@quilchena.com Open end Apr–Thanksgiving weekend.

Like a lot of stories in BC, that of the Quilchena Ranch starts dur the gold rush when four brothers named Guichon from Sav France, came to seek their fortunes. Ultimately, two of the broth acquired land in the area and the Guichon Cattle Company was set in 1890. The Quilchena Cattle Company today is one of the lar working cattle ranches in BC, runs about 4 500 head of cattle a and is operated by the third and fourth generation of Guich descendants. The **Quilchena Hotel✦✦✦** is set right in the heart of ranch against a backdrop of gently rolling ranges and overlo beautiful Nicola Lake. A full slate of activities (hiking, horseb riding, biking) as well as excellent food in a Victorian house.

UMP LAKE RANCH✦✦✦

Stump Lake Ranch
$$–$$$ *take Hwy 5A*
from Kamloops for 25
tes to gates of Stump
Ranch; tel: (250) 372-
5; web:
.stumplake.com; e-mail:
@stumplake.com

The Stump Lake Cattle Company was established in 1883 and continues today, tucked into the rolling hills of the Nicola Valley, as both a working cattle spread and a guest ranch. This tradition of hospitality began many years ago when earlier ranchers decided to combat loneliness by encouraging visitors to get a feel for the cowboy lifestyle through helping with the daily work. **Stump Lake Ranch✦✦✦** sits on 32,000ha with three miles of frontage on Stump Lake and even

more on four other lakes. The property is a network of habitats *
include grasslands, creeks, forest, lakes and wetlands that attrac
wide range of birds and other animals. Guests at the ranch
participate in all the daily chores but there's also an active program
of horseback riding lessons, fly fishing, guided hikes and wild
viewing. At any time, moose or black bears can wander by the ra
house and deer, eagles and coyote are regular visitors. Accommodat
is de luxe to luxurious but there are also seven canvas tents for visi
who like to experience native traditions.

Suggested tour

Total distance: 318km.

Time: 4 hours' driving time with up to 8 hours with stops.

Route: This is a circular driving tour starting and ending
KAMLOOPS ❶. Follow Hwy 5A to stay at either the STUMP LA
RANCH ❷ or at the QUILCHENA RANCH ❸ and Hotel.

Detour: Just north of Quilchena on Hwy 5A, take the Douglas Lake
east for 26km and turn right into the main entrance of DOUGI
LAKE RANCH ❹ for a complete look at Canada's largest work
cattle ranch. Be sure to phone first since it's a gated ranch.

Continue on to MERRITT ❺. From Merritt, take Hwy 8 going v
heading toward Lower Nicola. From here, swing north on Hwy ⬝
toward **Logan Lake**. This is an instant town created for employees ⬝
vast copper mining operation 16km west of the community centre
Hwy 97C (heading toward Ashcroft). The big attraction here is ⬝
Highland Valley Copper Mine which is the largest copper min⬝
North America. The mine has tours and there's splendid photogra⬝
of the lake. It's a beautiful drive west toward **Ashcroft** ❻ (*see ⬝*
140). After a stop at historic **Ashcroft Manor** for tea, continue al⬝
Hwy 97C to join up with Hwy l. Continue north to CACHE CR⬝
❼.

Turn east here on Hwy 97 heading toward Savona. About 16km eas⬝
Cache Creek, you pass the tiny community of Walhachin with gr⬝
and-pink clapboard houses that's the site of a former town built ⬝
group of English investors who dreamed of an orchard paradis⬝
1908. When the settlers returned home during the Second World ⬝
to enlist, storms destroyed the irrigation system and the orchards d⬝
The few families who returned immediately turned around and w⬝
home again. All that's left of the dream is a dilapidated irriga⬝
system. Continue on to Kamloops.

Prov. Pk.

99

Marble
Canyon
Prov. Pk.

**Historic Hat
Creek Ranch**

Cache
Creek

7

Juniper Bch.
Provincial Pk.

Copper
Creek

Adams Lake

Heffley
Creek

Sun
Peaks

Chase

Walhachin

97

Savona

84

Harper
Mtn.

Paul Lake Prov. Pk.

6 Ashcroft

12

48

97C

Tunkwa
Prov. Pk.

1 Kamloops

1
97

Monte Cr.

97

2 Stump Lake Ranch

Monte L.

Logan Lake

Lac
Le Jeune

Lac
Le Jeune
Prov. Pk.

Roche L.
Prov. Pk.

117

Monte Lake
Prov. Park

Westwold

Spences
Bridge

Goldpan
Prov. Pk.

37

5

95

Skihist
Prov. Pk.

69

8

91

Walloper
Lake
Prov. Pk.

5A

Lytton

1

Lower
Nicola

Merritt

5

Nicola

3 Quilchena

4 Douglas Lake Ranch
Douglas
Lake

50 km

25 miles

24

5

Pennask L.
Prov. Pk.

Okanagan Valley

Ratings

Beaches	●●●●
Children	●●●●
Food and drink	●●●●
Wineries	●●●●
History	●●●○
Outdoor activities	●●●○
Parks	●●●○
Scenery	●●●○

The Okanagan Valley is a 20km-wide strip that lies in t rain shadow of the Cascade Mountains creating a h sunny, dry climate and BC's most important fruit and grap growing area. The Valley stretches from the US border a continues north following a series of lakes strung togeth like pearls on a string. Canada's only real desert is here, t most northerly tip of Mexico's Sonoran, but aside from ca and a few scorpions it's a little hard to find. Only sm patches remain because of farming and irrigation, hence t name 'pocket desert'. Lush orchards and burgeoni vineyards extend throughout the Valley, transforming wh used to be hot sand into one of Canada's most fertile regio For visitors, the lakes linked by the Okanagan River are summer playground, and in winter the mountains offer d snow and skiing called BC's 'best kept secret'.

OLIVER✧

ⓘ Oliver Info Centre
36205 93rd St; tel: (250) 498-6321. In 1923 CPR railway station.

➲ Oliver Hiking and Bicycling Trail
from the McAlpine Bridge where Hwy 97 crosses the river just north of Oliver to Osoyoos Lake.

Fairview
4.5km southwest of Oliver on the steep Fairview Rd at junction of White Lake Rd.

This town of less than 5000 people is surrounded by more th 9000ha of such productive orchards south on Hwy 97, it's called ' golden mile'. Some of the Okanagan Valley's most product vineyards supply nine local wineries and you'd need a full day to v the lot. Among the best are **Tinhorn Creek✧✧** with its flavourful r and **Gehringer Bros✧✧✧** with their traditional German-style win Oliver, also known as the Cantaloupe Capital of Canada, has fruit a vegetable stands all along Hwy 97 with either picked or U-pick (pi your-own) fruit available.

For hikers and mountain bike enthusiasts, the **Oliver Hiking a Bicycling Trail✧✧✧** provides dikes and an old railway right of w 10km of paved trail and 8km of prepared road bed on the Okana River. **The Oliver and District Heritage Society Museum a Archives✧** is in a former 1924 headquarters of the BC Provincial Pol

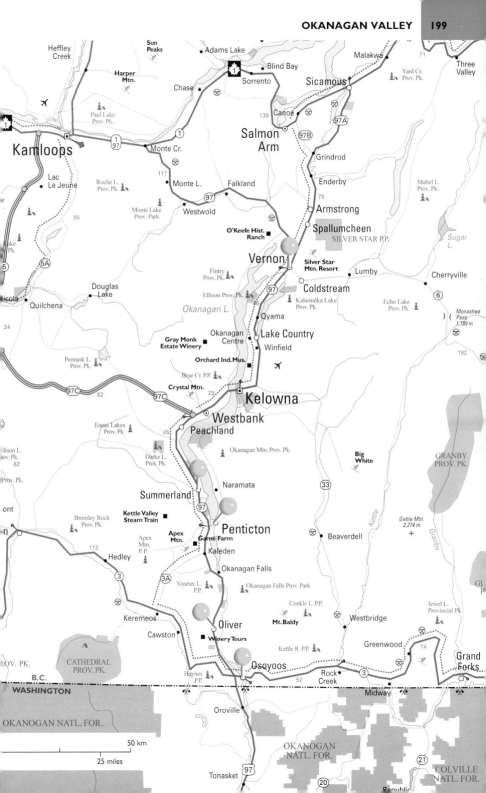

Heffley Creek
Sun Peaks
Adams Lake
Malakwa
Yard Cr. Prov. Pk.
Three Valley
71
Harper Mtn.
Blind Bay
Chase
Sorrento
Sicamous
Paul Lake Prov. Pk.
Canoe
97A
97
Kamloops
Monte Cr.
1
97
139
Salmon Arm
97B
Grindrod
117
Lac Le Jeune
Monte L.
Falkland
Enderby
Roche L. Prov. Pk.
Mabel L. Prov. Pk.
95
97
Westwold
75
Armstrong
Monte Lake Prov. Park
Sugar L.
5
5A
O'Keefe Hist. Ranch
Spallumcheen
SILVER STAR P.P.
Silver Star Mtn. Resort
Douglas Lake
Fintry Prov. Pk.
Vernon
Lumby
Cherryville
icola
Quilchena
Ellison Prov. Pk.
Coldstream
6
Okanagan L.
Kalamalka Lake Prov. Pk.
Echo Lake Prov. Pk.
Monashee Pass 1,189 m
24
Qyama
Pennask L. Prov. Pk.
Okanagan Centre
Lake Country
192
97C
82
Gray Monk Estate Winery
Winfield
Orchard Ind. Mus.
97C
Bear Cr. P.P.
23
Crystal Mtn.
Kelowna
Ennis Lakes Prov. Pk.
Westbank
GRANBY PROV. PK.
45
Peachland
lison L. ov. Pk.
62
Darke L. Prov. Pk.
Okanagan Mtn. Prov. Pk.
Big White
Prov. Pk.
ont
Naramata
33
Summerland
Bromley Rock Prov. Pk.
Kettle Valley Steam Train
97
Gable Mtn. 2,274 m
n
113
Apex Mtn. P. P.
Apex Mtn.
Penticton
Beaverdell
Granby
Hedley
Game Farm
GL
3
Kaleden
3A
Okanagan Falls
Jewel L. Provincial Pk.
Vaseux L. P.P.
Okanagan Falls Prov. Park
Conkle L. P.P.
Westbridge
Keremeos
Mt. Baldy
74
Cawston
Oliver
Kettle R. P.P.
Greenwood
Grand Forks
OV. PK.
CATHEDRAL PROV. PK.
Winery Tours
60
Osoyoos
Rock Creek
B.C.
Haynes P.P.
52
Midway
WASHINGTON
OKANAGAN NATL. FOR.
Oroville
OKANAGAN NATL. FOR.
21
50 km
25 miles
COLVILLE NATL. FOR.
Tonasket
97
20
Republic

Tinhorn Creek Winery $
Road 7; tel: (250) 498-3743.

Gehringer Bros Winery $ Road 8; tel: (250) 498-2784.

The Oliver and District Heritage Society Museum and Archives
$ 9728 356 Ave; tel: (250) 498-4027. Open Tue–Sun in summer; varied winter hours.

and has exhibits on local agriculture and irrigation plus early min artefacts and the jail from a ghost town called **Fairview.**[*] There's much left of a town that was said to be the biggest city north of Francisco in 1893 with 500 people. In 1902 the grand Teepee H burned down and by 1908 Fairview, once awash in gold, had beco a ghost town.

Right
Okanagan cowgirl and cowboy

Osoyoos[**]

Osoyoos Information
Info Centre at Hwy 3 and 97 junction; tel: (250) 495-7142; tollfree: (888) 676-9667; fax: (250) 495-6161; web: www.town.osoyoos.bc.ca; e-mail: tourism@ osoyooschamber.bc.ca
Open May–Aug, daily 0800–1900; rest of year Mon–Fri 0900–1700.

As one of Canada's hottest spots, this little town in the fertile deser both a 'fun place' and a fruit basket with Canada's earliest fruit cro In the summer, swimmers and water-skiers fill the four beaches town and visitors come from all over to buy bushels of fruit a tomatoes at roadside stands. The name Osoyoos means 'narrows of lake' and refers to Lake Osoyoos[**] in the centre of town, a lake t stretches 17km from Canada into the US and is called Canad warmest lake. To get a little background, the **Osoyoos Museum** (called the best small town museum in BC) has an excellent a eclectic collection that includes aboriginal artefacts, antique vehic period clothing, pioneer treasures, police archives, an original 18 log schoolhouse and even liquor distilling apparatus from bootlegging days. The museum gets rave reviews.

The Spotted Lake
8.8km west of Osoyoos
Hwy 3.

e Osoyoos Oxbows
h and Wildlife
nagement Reserve
r Oliver, 7.5km north of
yoos, turn east onto Road
and follow 1km to kiosk.

Osoyoos Museum $
on beach at end of
n St; tel: (250) 495-
2. May long weekend
I end of Sept; afternoons
I June then daily
0–1600.

oyoos (Pocket)
sert Centre $
5 Ave & Hwy 97; tel:
0) 494-2470; tollfree:
7) 899-0897; web:
w.desert.org; e-mail:
l@desert.org
en mid-Apr–mid-Oct,
y; in winter walks are
ry second Sun.

ynes Point
ovincial Park
m south of town on
yoos Lake; tel: (250)
4-6500 or (604) 689-
25. Reservations for 41
np sites on (800) 689-
25.

The dunes of the **Pocket Desert**✤ are a bit hard to find but worthwhile for anyone interested in rare and endangered ecosystems. There are species here found nowhere else in Canada such as the pallid bat, shy night snake and the ground mantis. **The Osoyoos Desert Society** has guided boardwalk tours daily from Easter to the end of Sept. **The Spotted Lake**✤ (8.8km west of Osoyoos) is another natural phenomenon that is on private property but is still visible and highly photographable from the highway. The lake has the world's highest concentration of minerals so that bizarre white-ringed circles form when the water evaporates under the hot summer sun. Ancient tribes were said to soak away aches and ailments in the healing mud and waters of 'Klikuk' as they called it.

Haynes Point Provincial Park✤✤✤ is 2km south of town on Osoyoos Lake and is a popular swimming and camping site. Canada's tiniest bird, the Calliope hummingbird, can be seen buzzing flowers, along with orioles, Eastern kingbirds and California quail. **The Osoyoos Oxbows Fish and Wildlife Management Reserve**✤✤ provides a glimpse into what is left of crucial wildlife refuges. Road 22 continues on through vineyards and Inkaneep First Nation reserve land where there are real sand dunes and natural landscape.

Accommodation and food in Osoyoos

Newton Observatory B&B $$ *3 Observatory Rd; tel: (250) 494-6745; web: www.jacknewton.com* This 4-star unusual B&B has a dramatic view of the lake and promises 'out of this world hospitality'. Owner Jack Newton is a passionate amateur astronomer so each guest gets a free lesson in astronomy along with a bed and breakfast. Open May–Oct.

Campo Marina $$ *Richter Pass Motor Inn, Hwy 3; tel: (250) 495-7650.* Excellent Italian cuisine.

Osoyoos Golf Club $$ *12300 Golf Course Drive; tel: (250) 495-7118.* Good food and good view.

ENTICTON✤✤✤

Tourism Penticton
888 Westminster Ave
st; tel: (250) 490-2464;
ree: (800) 663-5052;
: www.penticton.org;
ail: tourism@img.net
mer Info Centre is on
y 97, 5km south of
ticton.

City boosters insist that the translation for the aboriginal name 'Penticton' means 'a place to live forever', and anyone visiting in the spring particularly when thousands of fruit trees are in bloom would be easily convinced. Like its sister cities in the Okanagan, Penticton has fruit and wine in abundance but its biggest appeal is to families who like active vacations. The city lies between the sands of two lakes joined by a narrow channel so beaches are everywhere. **Okanagan Lake**✤✤✤ with its park and marina is joined to **Skaha Lake**✤✤✤ by the 7km-long

Okanagan Lake *for access follow Lakeshore Dr.*

Skaha Lake *is at end of Channel Parkway with access via Lee Ave.*

Skaha Climbing Bluffs *south of town, left off South Main onto Crescent Hill Rd.*

Wonderful Waterworld $ *Skaha Lake Rd at Yorkton Ave; tel: (250) 493-8121.*

Apex Mountain Resort $$ *32km southwest of Penticton (about 45 minutes) to Green Mountain Rd; tel: (250) 292-8126; tollfree: (800) 387-2739.*

Penticton (AT Atkinson) Museum and Archives $ *785 Main St; tel: (250) 490-2451. Open Tue–Sat 1000–1700.*

SS Sicamous $ *on Okanagan Lake off Lakeshore Dr.; tel: (250) 492-0403. Open mid-June–mid-Sept, daily; Mon–Fri from Oct–May.*

man-made Channel Parkway. Sun worshippers will bathe and swim one lake and then 'tube' down the channel to the other. It's beach at its best. For younger kids, there are water parks such as **Wonder Waterworld** with everything from giant squirt guns to pea shaped concession stands; older kids find an even longer list activities: guided horseback riding or overnight trips, mount. biking, parasailing, water skiing, jet skiing, kayaking and hou boating. In the winter **Apex Mountain Resort** has a quad chair t takes skiers and snowboarders up the slopes, and in the summer hik ride up to alpine meadows. The **Skaha Climbing Bluffs** are a ser of granite slabs, faces and overhangs that offer challenges to be amateur and experienced rock climbers as well as trails for hikers the sage and ponderosa pine forests. For the more sedentary, 1 **Penticton (AT Atkinson) Museum and Archives** displays 1 history of First Nations people in the area, pioneer artefacts a military memorabilia. The **SS Sicamous** is in restoration and example of the sternwheelers that once plied the lakes between 19 and 1935. There's a good model of the Kettle Valley Railway he Penticton is famous for its festivals all year round with everythi from tributes to ale and Triathlons to Meadowlark and Square Dai Festivals.

Accommodation and food in Penticton

Bear's Den B&B $$ *189 Linden Ave, Kaledan; tel: (250) 497-6721; f (250) 497-6453; web: www.bearsdenbb.com; e-mail: stay@bearsdenbb.c* Set in a garden with spectacular lake views 10 minutes south Penticton. Hot tub, videos, library, minutes to the beach and ted bears everywhere.

Eden House B&B $$ *104 Arlayne Rd, Kaleden; tel: (250) 497-83. tollfree: (888) 497-3336; fax (250) 497-8535; web: www.edenhouse.ca, mail: edenhouse@telus.net* A gem of a B&B in a professionally decorat log home overlooking Skaha Lake about 10km south of Pentictc Bedrooms are themed, some have jacuzzi *en suite* and a swimmi pool was recently added.

Lavender Lane Guesthouse $$ *3005 DeBeck Rd; tel: (250) 496-57 fax (250) 496-5741; web: www.bctravel.com/lavenderlane; e-mc leechman@telus.net* Nestled in the hills between orchards a vineyards, this beautifully decorated home has European antiques a modern amenities. Gourmet breakfasts served on a balco overlooking the lake with the scent of roses and lavender.

Penticton Lakeside Resort and Casino $$ *21 Lakeshore Drive west; (250) 493-8221; tollfree (800) 663-9400; fax (250) 493-0607; w www.lakeside@rpbhotels.com; e-mail: lakeside@rpbhotels.com* Lakes resort with 204 rooms in several categories, fitness and busin

right
ticton beach

centre, in-room jacuzzis.

1912 $$$ *100 Alder Ave, Kaleden; tel: (250).497-6868.* Specialises in excellent regional cuisine with fresh ingredients.

Granny Bogner's Restaurant $$ *302 Eckhardt Ave; tel: (250) 493-2711.* Northwest cuisine prepared by a European-trained chef. Serves a good list of local wines.

Chinese Laundry and Szechuan $ *123 Front St; tel: (250) 492-2828.* Good northern Chinese menu with antiques from historical Chinese

UMMERLAND✜✜

Summerland Chamber of mmerce *15600 Hwy (north end at Thompson ; tel: (250) 494-2686; (250) 494-4039; web: merlandchamber.bc.ca; ail: schamber@vip.net*

Summerland was the brainchild of a creative Baptist miner-turned land developer looking to lure settlers from the more frigid parts of Canada. He subdivided lakeshore properties, put in irrigation and launched the slogan 'Heaven on earth with summer weather forever!' To ensure the prosperity of their community, settlers in Summerland fought long and hard to ensure that the Kettle Valley Railway (KVR) line from Nelson to Hope passed near town despite geographical obstacles. The result was the McCulloch Trestle, the KVR's largest steel girder bridge and North America's third largest. Today you can board the **Kettle Valley Steam Train**✜✜✜ and see for yourself. Ride the train on a 90-minute journey through orchards, vineyards, over dramatic

Kettle Valley Steam Train $
from Hwy 97, take either the Rosedale Ave or Prairie Valley Rd exits and follow signposts or call for detailed instructions; tel: (250) 494-8422; tollfree in BC (877) 494-8424; web: www.kettlevalleyrail.org; e-mail: kvr@telus.net Open end of May–mid-Oct, primarily weekends, departs 1030 and 1330.

Kettle Valley Dried Fruit Company $
14014 Hwy 97N; tel: (250) 494-0335.

The Pacific Agri-Food Research Centre $
4200 Hwy 97S (across from Sunoka Beach); tel: (250) 494-9554. Gardens open daily; interpretive centre weekday afternoons.

Summerland Museum $ *9521 Wharton St; tel: (250) 494-9395. Tue–Sat afternoons year round; June–Aug Mon–Sat 1000–1600.*

Summerland Sweets $ *Canyon View Rd; tel: (250) 494-0377. Open July–Aug, daily; rest of year Mon–Sat.*

trestles and bridges and spectacular scenery. Today, Summerland riv
Kelowna as a major fruit-processing centre and is home to numere
fruit packing companies such as **Summerland Sweets**✲✲ and the **Ket
Valley Dried Fruit Company**.✲✲ The **Pacific Agri-Food Resear
Centre**✲✲✲ is known locally as the Research Station Gardens a
combines a good history of fruit development and experimentation
the area with a garden experience. The Interpretive Centre
surrounded by 6ha of English-style flower beds, lawns and wooc
forest pathways. Also check out the **Summerland Museum**✲✲ with
video presentations of Summerland history and the KVR.

Accommodation and food in Summerland

Summerview B&B $$ *3792 Gartrell Rd; tel: (250) 494-1914; w
www.bbcanada.com/2159; e-mail:summer@vip.net Friendly, great vie
of Okanagan Lake, close to beaches, wineries and the KVR.*

Cellar Door Bistro $–$$ *located at Sumac Ridge Winery, 307 Hwy
north of town; tel: (250) 494-0377 or (250) 494-3316. Has a great me
of French-inspired regional dishes with wine sampling as a bonus.*

Right
Okanagan Valley vineyards

ERNON❖❖

Vernon Tourism
6326 Hwy 97 north;
(250) 542-1415; tollfree:
0) 665-0795; fax: (250)
-3256; web:
v.vernontourism.com;
ail:info@vernontourism.
,
n daily.

**Floral Clock in
Polson Park**
h Ave & 32nd St.

**Historic O'Keefe
Ranch $** on Hwy 97,
ut 1km east of Westside
tel: (250) 542-7868;
: www.okeeferanch.bc.ca;
ail:
_chin@junction.net
en May–Oct, daily;
0–1700.

**eater Vernon
seum and Archives**
009 32nd Ave; tel: (250)
-3142. Open Mon–Sat in
mer; rest of year
–Sat.

**Sen Klip Theatre
Company $$**
(250) 549-2021 or
0) 549-4100 for
formances.

At the northern edge of the great fruit belt running down to the US border, Vernon makes up for a slightly cooler climate (and therefore less fruit) with a more trendy, 'with it' kind of appeal. This is the oldest city in BC's interior with perhaps its most 'cowboy' history thanks to Cornelius O'Keefe, a 19th-century cattle entrepreneur who drove his herds north to provide beef for hungry gold miners. You get the full story at **Historic O'Keefe Ranch**❖❖❖ which began the year Canada became a nation. The ranch was the largest in the region and a town in itself with church, general store and post office. The ranch is now the area's most popular museum with authentic store, church and mansion that tells the story through video and highly informed guides. You can follow this up at the **Greater Vernon Museum and Archives**❖❖ which elaborates on Lord Aberdeen (an early Governor-General) and his involvement in vast orchard plantings. Vernon sits between three beautiful lakes, the Kalamalka, Okanagan and Swan, all of which provide sandy, warm beaches. History buffs can sign up at the Vernon Info Centre for walking tours and photographers love the **Floral Clock in Polson Park.**❖❖ The 10m powered floral clock is one of only a few in Canada. For a glimpse into how First Nations people fit into the story, the **Sen Klip Theatre Company**❖❖❖ presents an excellent show that looks at traditional themes in a modern way.

Accommodation and food in Vernon

**The Castle on the Mountain B&B $$$** 8227 Silver Star Rd; tel: (250) 542-4593; tollfree: (800) 667-2229; web: www.monday.com/castle; e-mail: castle.eskila@telus.net This 4$\frac{1}{2}$-star B&B has a great location and view of the lake, lovely rooms and art studio on site.

Harbour Lights B&B $$ 135 Joharon Rd; tel: (250) 549-5117; fax: (250) 549-5162; web: www.bbexpo.com/harbourlights Panoramic view of the lake, spacious rooms and friendly hosts.

The Vernon Lodge $$ 3914 32nd St; tel: (250) 545-3385. A hotel with a real stream, the BX Creek, running through the dining room which is a tropical forest with two-storey-high trees. Restaurant serves Italian-influenced cuisine.

Italian Kitchen Company $$ 2916 30th Ave; tel: (250) 558-7899. An award-winning Italian menu that has been voted Vernon's best restaurant.

Johnny Appleseeds $ 3018 30th Ave; tel: (250) 542-7712. The place to go for healthy juices, home-made cookies, muffins and gourmet sandwiches.

Above
Okanagan Valley fruit stall

Suggested tour

Total distance: 174km.

Time: 3–4 hours' direct driving time but allow 2–5 days for touring.

Links: The Okanagan Valley connects west to the **Gold Rush Tr**
(*see page 140*) from **Kelowna** (*see page 208*) via Hwy 8 and Hwy
From there on to **Hope** (*see page 223*) and the Fraser Valley. Fro
Vernon (*see page 205*) continuing north, Hwys 97/97A lead to t
Shuswap Lakes (*see page 160*).

Route: After visiting the attractions around **VERNON ❶**, head sou
on Hwy 97 and follow the signs to **Kalamalka Lake Provincial Pa**
for wild flowers, unspoiled swimming beaches and excellent bi
watching. Kalamalka Lake is called the 'Lake of Many Colours' becau
of the striking blue-green cast to the water caused by glacial silt.

Detour 1: Head east 17.5km off Hwy 97 for **Silver Star Mounta**
Resort ❷, the region's most northerly ski area with 84 runs and a v
area for snowmobiling, cross-country skiing and more. In the summ
the resort turns its chairlift to ferrying visitors up to the summit of t
mountain for great views, hiking in alpine meadows and mounta
biking. Silver Star features a turn-of-the century mining town to visit

Returning to Hwy 97, continue south to **Kelowna ❸** with a turn off
Winfield for some wine tasting at the **Gray Monk Estate Winery (**
From Kelowna, continue south along Hwy 97 with a stop at t
Mariners Reef Waterslides, about 1km east of **Westbank** for anyo
with children. Continuing south past Peachland, where alas, there
no peach orchards, to **SUMMERLAND ❺** and its various attractio
This is the place to take a ride on the **Kettle Valley Steam Train**
and to stop at a **viewpoint** overlooking Rattlesnake Island and Squa
Point on the east side of the lake 6km past Okanagan Lake Pa
Legend has it that Ogopogo, the sea serpent, lives in an underwa
cave just off the point and has been sighted here. All along this rou
and heading south, stands overflowing with fruits and vegetables
everywhere. Just north of **PENTICTON ❼**, photographers should lo
west for a series of hoodoos formed 10,000 years ago as glaci
retreated.

Detour 2: At **Kaleden**, take White Lake Rd, 9km from Kaled
Junction to the **Dominion Radio Astrophysical Observatory** for
little sci-fi experience (*tel: (250) 493-4355, open daily*). This is one
the world's best radio astronomy sites and its visitors' centre explai
the use of radio telescopes for gathering astronomical data. Wh
Lake, at the same location, has sand hill cranes, curlews, shrikes a
sage thrashers.

From Kaleden, continue south on Hwy 97 to **Okanagan Falls** where there are interesting stops at the **Bassett House and Museum**, a restored residence of the pioneer Bassett family and the **Memorial Rose Garden.** Just south of OK Falls, **Vaseux Lake Provincial Park ❽** is a good place for wildlife with bighorn sheep often on the highway. The Wildlife Centre is at the north end of Vaseux Lake and is one of the best places in North America to see California bighorn sheep. Lots of trails, bird watching hides (blinds) and about 350 of those sheep. Continue on to **OLIVER ❾** and **OSOYOOS ❿** with lots of stops for seasonal fruit. For a camping and bird watching experience, drive 2km south of Osoyoos to **Haynes Point Provincial Park ⓫** .

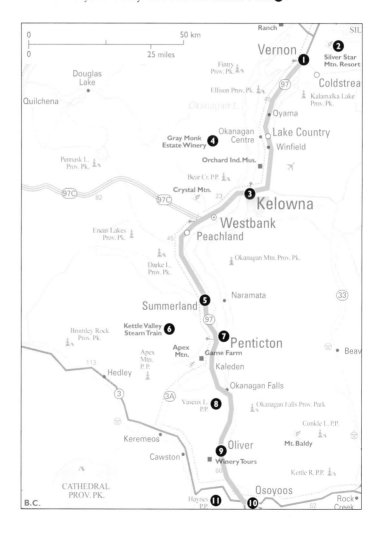

Kelowna

Ratings

Beaches	●●●●
Children	●●●●
Orchards	●●●●
Outdoor activities	●●●●
Wineries	●●●●
Museums	●●●
Nature	●●●
Sport	●●●

Kelowna proudly announces that its lifestyle is 'the best Canada' and it presents a convincing list of reasons w this is so. First of all, it sits on Okanagan Lake, a 150km-lo stretch of vibrantly clean, clear water surrounded mountains and wilderness. Coastal and Cascade mounta ranges protect the city from all the coastal rain so summ are hot and dry and winters are mild. What this means warm water for swimmers who flock to the sandy beaches the summer and powdery-dry snow for skiers in the wint The seductive climate is also ideal for all sorts of fru including grapes, so Kelowna has become the hub of a v region producing prize-winning wines. While other cit will argue similar virtues, Kelowna has the ultimate prize friendly but shy lake monster known as Ogopogo, frequen glimpsed and occasionally photographed. Well, maybe.

Sights

ⓘ Kelowna Visitor Information Centre 544 Harvey Ave (Hwy 97); tel: (250) 861-1515; tollfree (800) 663-4345; web: www.kelownachamber.org Provides information and maps. Open daily.

🛏 Big White Ski Resort $$ lies just 55 km east of Kelowna,: tel: (250) 765-3101; tollfree (800) 663-2772; web: www.bigwhite.com

Big White Ski Resort✦✦✦

Outside of BC Big White is one of the skiing world's 'best kept secre a ski area that keeps getting accolades as North America's 'best val or 'best place for families' or even 'one of the best ski resorts in world'. The reasons for all the hype are many: the mountains h have massive snowfalls of light, dry champagne powder. Combine t with one of the most ambitious development plans in res development anywhere and you get BC's second largest ski villagε much less cost than Whistler/Blackcombe, BC's No 1 resort. Τ season runs late Nov–Apr with an average annual snowfall of o 295in (750cm) spread over 755 groomed acres (305.7ha), 1 325 alp and gladed acres (131.6ha) and 38 illuminated acres (15.3ha) for ni skiing.

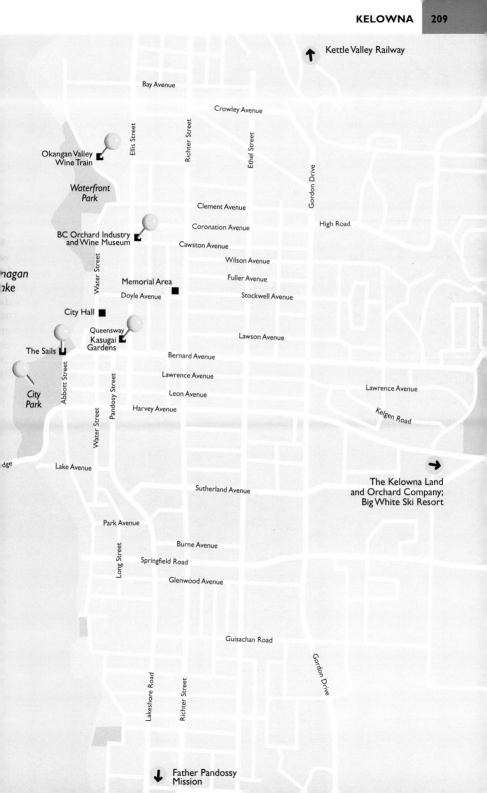

Kettle Valley Railway

Bay Avenue

Crowley Avenue

Ellis Street

Richter Street

Ethel Street

Okangan Valley
Wine Train

Gordon Drive

*Waterfront
Park*

Clement Avenue

Coronation Avenue

High Road

BC Orchard Industry
and Wine Museum

Cawston Avenue

Wilson Avenue

Water Street

Fuller Avenue

Memorial Area

Stockwell Avenue

Doyle Avenue

*nagan
ake*

City Hall

Queensway

Lawson Avenue

Kasugai
Gardens

The Sails

Bernard Avenue

Abbott Street

Lawrence Avenue

Pandosy Street

Leon Avenue

*City
Park*

Harvey Avenue

Lawrence Avenue

Water Street

Kelgen Road

dge

Lake Avenue

The Kelowna Land
and Orchard Company;
Big White Ski Resort

Sutherland Avenue

Park Avenue

Long Street

Burne Avenue

Springfield Road

Glenwood Avenue

Guisachan Road

Gordon Drive

Lakeshore Road

Richter Street

Father Pandossy
Mission

🄸 **The BC Orchard Industry and Wine Museum** *1304 Ellis St; tel: (250) 868-0441 or (250) 763-0433. Orchard museum open Tue–Sat; wine museum every day.*

Father Pandosy Mission
$ *3685 Benvoulin Rd; tel: (250) 860-8369. Open Apr–Oct daily.*

Kettle Valley Railway
contact Kelowna Tourism for detailed instructions to the three access points.

The BC Orchard Industry and Wine Museum✦✦

Set in a former packing house, this museum provides a go background on Kelowna's early days as a century-old fruit-growi area with lots of photos and hands-on displays. The Wine Museu section has wine-making exhibits, a wine shop and information abo touring local wineries.

Father Pandosy Mission✦✦✦

The site of the first European settlement in central British Columb founded by Father Charles Pandosy of the Oblate missionaries 1859. One of the Father's best gifts to the area was the introduction apple and grape growing to the Okanagan Valley, making him larg responsible for its becoming a major fruit-producing region. Fo original log buildings (one a tiny chapel) stand on the 4-acre (1.62) site as well as a farmhouse and settler's cabin. All the buildings furnished as they would have been in the 19th century. The Missi was declared an official heritage site in 1983 following the discov of Father Pandosy's grave in an abandoned cemetery near his missio

Kettle Valley Railway✦✦✦

This is not really a railroad anymore but actually a 16km section abandoned track that once linked Nelson and Hope. Just north

Right
Father Pandosy Mission

Kelowna, the track now serves as a dramatic way to see Myra Canyon on mountain bikes, horseback, hiking or on 4x4 adventure tours. There are 18 railway trestles in all, which link the sheer rock walls of the Canyon providing incredible views. There are several ways to access the KVR, but the main three are June Springs, Myra Canyon and Chute Lake. Kelowna has many other hiking trails for all levels including Gallagher's Canyon, Big White Mountain for beginners, Black Knight Mountain, Kelowna Crags and Blue Grouse Mountain for intermediate hikers, and Wild Horse Canyon and Terrace Mountain for advanced hikers.

Okanagan Valley Wine Train✦✦✦

This 1950s vintage Super Continental train combines a scenic excursion through BC's lush wine and orchard country from Kelowna to Vernon along Kalamalka Lake. The round trip includes wine tasting on board, a meal and a Las Vegas-style show.

Okanagan Valley Wine Train $$$
(250) 712-9888; tollfree ⊔) 674-8725. Runs ⊔ends 30 June–30 Sept.

Orchard tours and agri-tourism✦✦✦

There are no end of farms in the area to tour, from apples and alpacas to bees and emus, but one of the best is the **Kelowna Land and**

City Park *extends from the foot of the floating bridge to the large sculpture, The Sails, 1km away.*

The Mission Creek Greenway *is an 18km linear trail extending from Lakeshore Rd to Ziprick Rd with access at Lakeshore and Truswell Drives.*

Bill's Honey Farm Vacation $
2910 north, Glenmore Rd; tel: (250) 762-8156. Open May–Sept with tours daily at 1300 with reservations. Provides honey tasting, bird watching and canoe trips.

The Geert Maas Sculpture Garden
250 Reynolds Rd; tel: (250) 860-7012. Open May–Oct Mon–Sat; varied hours rest of year.

Kelowna Alpaca Farm
$ 3960 Todd Rd; tel: (250) 860-5503; web: www.kelownaalpaca.com Call for tours.

Kelowna Land and Orchard Company $
2930 Dunster Rd; tel: (250) 763-1091; web: www.k-l-o.com Open daily from mid-Apr with one tour a day until May, then three times daily.

Orchard Company✦✦✦ which is the home of the famous Fuji ap that is grown using an old Asian technology in a bag right on the t The orchard has operated since 1904 and offers visitors today about everything you might want to know about apple growing: for example they get the clever logos 'tattooed' onto the apple. A fe store on the site sells everything from apples (of course) to apple cream and a tea house is open for lunch and dinner. There are b self-guided walking tours to the orchard and animal farm or a wa tour. For a taste of honey, **Bill's Honey Farm**✦✦ is a combi B&B/working bee farm and the **Kelowna Alpaca Farm**✦✦ is home to alpacas and their babies. Owner Kelly Cummings welcomes visitors

Parks and gardens✦✦✦

Kelowna calls itself a walker's paradise with numerous enhanced a for people who like to stroll. **City Park**✦✦✦ that starts from the foo the floating bridge across Lake Okanagan has a lakeside walk stretching 1km to the Rotary Marshes at the foot of Knox Mount It's paved and a favourite with rollerbladers as well. **The Miss Creek Greenway**✦✦ is the first children's interpretive trail in BC v signage accompanied by inspired artwork and poetry of local yo artists. This 18km linear corridor is a multi-use trail t accommodates wheelchair users, pedestrians, cyclists and horseb riders. Along the way, visitors enjoy ponds, rich foliage suc

Right
Kasugai Japanese Garden

Kasugai Japanese Garden *is located beside City Hall.*

⊃x Mountain Nature k *is at north end of Ellis*

Gray Monk
23km from Kelowna at 5 Camp Rd; tel: (250) -3168; web: v.graymonk.com ·n daily summer ·0–1700; winter ·–Sat 1100–1700, Sun ·0–1600.

sion Hill Winery $ *·n from Kelowna at ·0 Mission Hill Rd; tel: ·) 768-3168 or (250) ·-7611; web: v.missionhillwinery.com ·n daily 0900–1700; July ·ug 0900–1900.*

ail's Winery Gate ·eyard and Estate *·ut 10km from Kelowna ·303 Boucheire Rd; tel: ·) 769-4451; tollfree ·) 420-9463; web: v.quailsgate.com ·n summer 0900–1900; ·er 1000–1700.*

nmerhill Estate nery $ *20 minutes from ·wna, 4870 Chute Lake · tel: (250) 764-8000; ·ee: (800) 667-3538; ·: www.summerhill.bc.ca ·n daily 1300–1600 all ·.*

cottonwoods and aspens, and wildlife such as marmots, minks, skunks, beaver, deer and coyotes. One of the city's loveliest parks is the serene **Kasugai Japanese Garden**,✦✦✦ a genuine Oriental garden built as a project between Kelowna and its sister Japanese city. The **Geert Maas Sculpture Garden**✦✦ is an outdoor 'art park' and the **Knox Mountain Nature Park**✦✦ draws hikers, picnickers and divers especially to Paul's Tomb where a 7m-long model of Ogopogo lurks 8m below the surface awaiting divers. This is a BC Wildlife Watch viewing site especially for songbirds in the summer.

Winery tours✦✦✦
Since growers in the area began planting quality grapes, local wines have been winning an increasing number of international awards especially for their ice wines. The major showcase for these wines is the Okanagan Wine Festival held each April and in late September, events that have been voted as among the top 100 events in North America several times in recent years. The festival offers upwards of 100 events at venues up and down the Valley including dinners, parades, 'grape stomps' and grape fairs. More than a dozen wineries around Kelowna, the heart of BC's wine country, offer free tours and tastings. **Mission Hill Winery**✦✦✦ with its spectacular setting and wide range of activities after a $27million expansion can cater to large groups. You can sit in their outdoor amphitheatre, visit the underground cellar or dine in a state-of-the-art kitchen. **Summerhill Estate Winery**✦✦✦ is BC's largest producer of sparkling wines and serves excellent lunches featuring Pacific northwestern cuisine for $10 between 1000 and 1500 on the Veranda Bistro. **Quail's Winery Gate Vineyard and Estate**✦✦✦ is another award-winning winery specialising in ice wines; its Old Vines Patio restaurant is run by Chef De Montreuil and serves excellent Pacific Northwestern cuisine from 1100 to dusk. **Gray Monk**✦✦✦ owners were pioneers in the 'estate winery' concept and produce a long list of award winning wines.

Accommodation and food

Kelowna has a good range of hotels, motels, inns and B&Bs from luxury to budget. The city does a good convention business so there can be a rush on rooms at any time and reservations are highly recommended. A good percentage of the properties can be viewed on the Internet before making bookings.

The Cedars Inn $$$ *278 Beach Ave; tel: (250) 763-1208; tollfree (800) 951-0769; fax: (250) 763-1109; web: www.cedarsinnokanagan.com; e-mail: info@cedarsinnokanagan.com* Five-star heritage home in lovely gardens with pool and outdoor hot tub. Beautifully decorated rooms, seconds to the Lake and easy walk to downtown.

Grand Okanagan Resort $$$ *1310 Water St, tel: (250) 763-45(tollfree: (800) 465-4651; fax: (250) 763-4565; w(www.grandokanagan.com; e-mail: sales@grandokanagan.com* On the l; with a downtown location, this is a 5-star resort with a park, lagoo recreational facilities, pool and full-service European spa. The res has several restaurants and coffee shops.

Manteo Resort Waterfront Hotel $$$ *3762 Lakeshore Rd, tel: 8(1031; tollfree (800) 445-5255; web: www.manteo.com* Right on the l; with exceptional views, a private beach and marina, spa, mo' theatre and all the facilities of a luxury resort hotel.

At Otella's $$ *42 Altura Rd; tel: (250) 763-4982; tollfree: (888) 8.' 8596; fax: (250) 763-4982; web: www.bbcanada.com/otell e-mail: otellas@home.com* Lovely 4-bedroom 4½-star inn on 1 a((0.405ha) park-like setting with European-trained chef who provi(huge gourmet breakfasts. Ask for his home-made chocolate.

Edgcombe House B&B $$ *1923 Abbott St; tel: (250) 712-2231; (250) 712-0381; web: www.bbcanada.com/edgcombehouse; e-m(edgcombe@silk.net* Charming English cottage-style home in a herit; neighbourhood near the beach and downtown. Lovely gardens.

De Montreuil Restaurant $$$ *368 Bernard Ave; tel: (250) 860-5508 mail: demontreuil@home.com* This cosy restaurant in downto(Kelowna is known for its regional specialities and its 'Canadi(cuisine'.

Guisachan House $$–$$$ *1060 Cameron Ave: (250) 862-9368 or (2. 470-2002; web: www.worldclasscatering.com* Located in a BC herit; park that was once the summer home of Lord Aberdeen, a Canadi(Governor-General. European cuisine with everything prepared on s(Ask for their special 4-course lunch.

Kelowna Lands and Orchard Teahouse $$–$$$ *3002 Dunster Rd, (250) 712-9404.* Trendy Cascadian cuisines using lots of organic fr(produce from the region. North Okanagan farms venison i(speciality.

JAKX Neighbourhood Grill $ *203 595 KLO Rd; tel: (250) 763-0773.* big favourite with locals, it features a menu made from scratch ser(in healthy portions.

The Jammery $ *8038 Hwy 97 north; tel: (250) 766-1139.* Another lo favourite with the added touch of a tour to see some of the delici(jams served being made in what was the Okanagan's first jam facto Hearty lunches and afternoon tea plus an ice cream parlour featuri(specials such as blueberry/amaretto ice cream. The gift shop sell(wide range of speciality jams.

Suggested tour

Total distance: 4km.

Time: 1 hour.

Links: From Kelowna, Hwy 97 north connects to **Vernon** (*see page 205*) as well as **Salmon Arm** (*see page 162*). Hwy 97 south links to **Penticton** (*see page 201*) and **Osoyoos** (*see page 200*).

Route: Heritage walking tour of downtown starting from **The Sails ❶**, a well-known sculptural Kelowna landmark in the **Capozzi Fountain**, follow the path south to the entrance of **City Park ❷** where you will get great views of the lake and see trees imported from different areas around the world. Continue south to the **Okanagan Lake Bridge ❸**, built in 1958 with a 1300m span. The design of the bridge allows for the rise and fall of lake levels and for high winds through the valley. Follow Harvey Ave northeast to Water St, turn north two blocks for the town's **Firehall** (1616 Water St). The original wooden building was replaced in 1924 by the current brick structure. Just up the street, at 1580 Water, is the **Courier Building** where the town's original newspaper was published. Turn right on Bernard three blocks to the **First United Church** built in 1909. Backtrack and turn northeast on Ellis to the **Kelowna Centennial Museum** to learn more about the area's first settlers. Stroll over another block to see the **Okanagan Military Museum**. Here you will see historical artefacts that created Okanagan military history. Continue northeast on Ellis St to Doyle and turn south for half a block. Take the path that leads behind City Hall to the serene **Kasugai Garden ❹** that represent the relationship between Kelowna and her sister city, Kasugai in Japan. A half block west at Pandosy St and Queensway Ave, the Bennett Clock is a carillon clock tower erected in the memory of WAC Bennett, one of BC's longest serving Premiers. The clock tower's seven steps represent the number of terms he was re-elected as Premier, while the 20 spires recognise each year of service as Premier.

Continuing on in your car, head south on Pandosy taking KLO to Benvoulin and follow it to the intersection of Casorso. Here you will find **FATHER PANDOSY MISSION ❺**, site of Kelowna's first white settlement on Mission Creek. This is a completely refurbished historical mission containing Kelowna's oldest structures. You can also visit **Benvoulin Heritage Church** at 2279 Benvoulin Rd, a Gothic revival-style church that dates back to Kelowna's earliest days. To end the day, take a ride on the **MV *Fintry Queen***, a circa 1948 paddle wheeler that still plies the waters of Okanagan Lake. Meals are served on board along with entertainment.

Also worth exploring

Agricultural tours

Dozens of fruit, vegetable and flower markets along with ot[ ] farming operations welcome visitors to Kelowna. The products offe[ ] range from ginseng and lavender to honey and emu meat. A g[ ] number are located on Benvoulin, KLO or Casorso roads and Tour[ ] Kelowna will provide complete guides. Note: many farms were clo[ ] to visitors during 2001 because of the various animal health epiden[ ] but these will all resume as soon as possible.

The tours available depend on the season, with Blossom Tours tak[ ] place during April and May for plums, apples, apricots, cherr[ ] peaches and pears, and harvest tours from early July to m[ ] September. The **BC ORCHARD INDUSTRY AND WINE MUSEUM** located in an historic packing house (1304 Ellis St) is a good place see some of the history of fruit production in the area along w[ ] artefacts of packing and preserving. There's a gift shop on site as v[ ] as a 50ft (15.24m) model railroad. **The Kelowna Land and Orch[ ] Company ❼** (3002 Dunster Rd) is a 140-acre (56.7ha) family-own[ ] historic orchard that welcomes visitors with wagon tours daily dur[ ] the peak season. The **Gatzke Farm Market** on Hwy 97 in Oyama, [ ] 20 minutes north of Kelowna, overlooks beautiful Kalamalka a[ ] Wood lakes and has 52 varieties of fruit trees in its orchard tour al[ ] with antique farm implements and a petting zoo. You can watch fr[ ] jam making at **The Jammery** on the way.

Right
MV *Fintry Queen*

Kettle Valley Railway

Bay Avenue

Crowley Avenue

Ellis Street

Richter Street

Ethel Street

Gordon Drive

Okangan Valley Wine Train ■

Waterfront Park

Clement Avenue

Coronation Avenue

High Road

BC Orchard Industry and Wine Museum **6**

Cawston Avenue

Wilson Avenue

Water Street

Fuller Avenue

Memorial Area ■

Doyle Avenue

Stockwell Avenue

City Hall ■

Queensway Kasugai Gardens **4**

Lawson Avenue

The Sails **1**

Bernard Avenue

Abbott Street

Pandosy Street

2 *City Park*

Lawrence Avenue

Leon Avenue

Lawrence Avenue

Water Street

Harvey Avenue

Kelgen Road

ridge

Lake Avenue

7

Sutherland Avenue

The Kelowna Land and Orchard Company; Big White Ski Resort

Park Avenue

Long Street

Burne Avenue

Springfield Road

Glenwood Avenue

Guisachan Road

Gordon Drive

Lakeshore Road

Richter Street

nagan ake

5 Father Pandossy Mission

Mighty Fraser Country

Ratings

Children's activities	●●●●●
Gardens	●●●●●
History	●●●●●
Outdoor activities	●●●●●
Parks	●●●●●
Scenery	●●●●●
Beaches	●●●○○
Museums	●●●○○

In 1808, when explorer Simon Fraser guided his can through canyons and rapids to the mouth of the brow river that would bear his name, he launched a kind *tsunami*. Within a few years, trading posts sprang followed by settlers, prospectors, railways and waves immigrants. At first people came to farm the rich soil b today it's the beauty of the Fraser Valley and the mounta beyond that lures. The Fraser is one of the world's great salmon-producing rivers and pulls fishermen from arou the world to cast their lines here and in surrounding lak Latter-day explorers are keen on other adventures the riv and its mountains offer: white-water rafting, skiing, he hiking, mountain biking and camping. Near the Fras ancient petroglyphs and buried log houses are pote reminders thousands of years old that the river witness tenants long before Simon Fraser.

ABBOTSFORD❖❖

ⓘ **Abbotsford Information**
Info centre at 2462 McCallum Rd; tel: (604) 859-9651; fax: (604) 850-6880; web: www.abbotsfordchamber.co m; e-mail: acoc@telus.net Open all year Mon–Fri 0900–1700 and all week July & Aug.

➔ **Clayburn Village**
is just off Hwy 11 between Abbotsford and Mission.

Right
Abbotsford Air Show

Often called 'the hub of the Fraser Valley', Abbotsford is an umbre city that takes in eight communities and is the centre for a vast area fertile farms ranging over 357 sq km that include everything fro corn mazes and cheese to blueberries and llamas. As North Americ second largest producer of raspberries, Abbotsford is called 'the raspberry capital of Canada' but cows, daffodils, kiwi fruit, ostrich and apples are also produced in abundance. Tours to many of the farms are normally offered but have been suspended until the threat of 'mad cow disease' has passed.

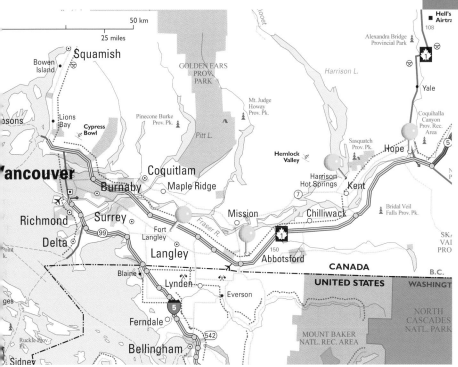

Abbotsford International show $ is held at the ﹒otsford Airport on Mount ﹒man Rd, 3km south of ﹒y l; info from Abbotsford rnational Airshow Society, ﹒6 Tower St, Unit 4, ﹒otsford V2T 6H5; tel: ﹒4) 852-8511; fax (604) ﹒-6093; web: ﹒.abbotsfordairshow.com. ﹒ond weekend in Aug.

﹒eater Vancouver ﹒ological Centre $ ﹒he Aldergrove off Hwy 1, ﹒8 264th St, Aldergrove ﹒V 1N7; tel: (604) 856- ﹒5; web: www. ﹒atervancouverzoo.com ﹒en 0900 to dusk.

The biggest event of the year is North America's best air display, the **Abbotsford International Airshow,***** that draws military, civilian precision aerobatics teams, historical and experimental aircraft and stunt flyers from around the world. **Old Clayburn Village*** is the site of a 1910 brick manufacturing company and visitors come to see historic brick houses, the schoolhouse, village church and old mill site. The **Clayburn Village Store**** with its antiques is a slice of the past and has a charming tea shop with home-baked pastries and sandwiches. Fifteen minutes from Abbotsford at the Aldergrove exit, the **Greater Vancouver Zoological Centre***** has more than 900 animals (200 species) from around the world plus a petting zoo and train rides.

﹒ove
﹒nties, Abbotsford

Clayburn Village Store $ *is at 34810 Clayburn Rd; tel: (604) 853-4020. Open Tue–Sat 0900–1700, Sun 1200–1700.*

Accommodation and food in Abbotsford

Counting Sheep Inn $$ *8715 Eagle Rd, Hatzic, halfway betwe Vancouver and Hope; tel: (604) 820-4148; fax: (604) 820-5149; w www.countingsheep.com; e-mail: vcesheep@uniserve.com* A cosy B&B w a big plus: lots of sheep and other animals for kids and 'kids at hea who like to play at farming. Gift shop with wool products.

Sobieski Restaurant $$ *32071 S Fraser Way; tel: (604) 864-80* Connected to a new computer ordering service called 'Let's Dine Line' where meals can be pre-ordered. Open daily with excelle meals, international cuisine.

FORT LANGLEY✦✦✦

Fort Langley Information *Info Centre, 23245 Glover Rd, Langley; tel: (604) 513-8787. Open May–Sept, daily; off-season call: (604) 888-1477.*

Fort Langley National Historic Site $ *23433 Mavis St; tel: (604) 513-4777; fax (604) 513-4788; web: www.parkscanada.pch.gc.ca*

Paddle Wheeler River Adventures $$ *139 810 Quayside Drive, New Westminster; tel: (604) 525-4465; tollfree (877) 825-1302; fax (604) 525-5944.*

The BC Farm Machinery and Agricultural Museum $ *9131 Kings St, downtown Fort Langley, tel: (604) 888-2273. Open Apr–mid-Oct, daily.*

Canadian Museum of Flight $ *5333 216 St, tel: (604) 532-0035. Open year round.*

This rural village is where BC began as a Hudson's Bay Compa trading post in 1827 when Europeans started to stake territory in t province. Fort Langley was also a jumping off point for prospect heading to the Fraser River gold fields during the late 1850s' rush. T **Fort Langley National Historic Site,**✦✦✦ surrounded by a wood palisade, is a museum today with authentic buildings that provide glimpse into a pioneering past. In the summer months, costumed st demonstrate how pelts were traded, blacksmithing, barrel making a pioneer cooking from the mid-19th century. A novel way to reach t Fort is via **Paddle Wheeler River Adventures**✦✦ who have an c paddle wheeler that drops visitors near the Fort. In Langley near **The BC Farm Machinery and Agricultural Museum**✦ has a la display of 20th-century tractors and threshers, logging and fishi equipment and household furnishings from all over BC, while t **Canadian Museum of Flight**✦✦ holds one of the largest and m diverse collections of aircraft and other vehicles in Canada.

ARRISON HOT SPRINGS**

Harrison Hot Springs Chamber Commerce *499 Hot ngs, Rd; tel: (604) 796- *5. Open May–Oct, daily; kdays rest of the year.*

Harrison Public Hot Pool $ *Harrison Springs Rd and anade Ave. Open daily.*

by Historic Store d Farm $ *PO Box 55, rison Mills V0M 1L0; tel: 4) 796-9576; fax (604) -9592; web: w.heritage.gov.bc.ca/kilby; ail: info@kilby.ca for current opening rs.*

nter Gardens $ *52892 ker Rd, near Hwy 9, just h of Hwy 1; tel: (604) -7191; tollfree (888) -8377; fax: (604) 792- 3; web: w.mintergardens.com; ail: minter@minter.org n Mar–Oct, daily.*

squatch Provincial rk *6.5km beyond rison Hotsprings on kwell Drive; tel: (604) -2300; tollfree (800) -9025.*

orld Championship nd Sculpture mpetition *PO Box 266, rison Hot Springs V0M ; tel: (604) 796-3224; : www.harrisand.org or ail: info@harrisand.org d the second weekend in t.*

The tiny resort community of Harrison Hot Springs sits on the edge of Harrison Lake which is 60km long, ringed with sandy beaches and surrounded by mountains. In those mountains, people have reported spotting hairy and elusive humans called Sasquatch, legendary creatures related to Bigfoot and Yeti. Sceptics say these reporters may have just stayed in Harrison's equally legendary hot springs too long and were having hallucinations. The first hotel was built here in 1886 to make use of two springs that register at 58°C (136.4°F) and 62°C (143.6°F). Non-guests can use the **Harrison Public Hot Pool.** The mountains around are rich in wildlife and a favourite with rockhounds who can find jade, garnets, agates, fossils and even gold. **Sasquatch Provincial Park** (1 217ha) is a favourite for canoeing, fishing, swimming, hiking, camping and wildlife viewing. Beaver, deer and squirrels are plentiful, along with mountain goats on the Slollicum Bluffs.

The biggest annual event is the **World Championship Sand Sculpture Competition** that draws artists from as far away as Russia and the Netherlands to create masterpieces that are kept on exhibit for a month. Using Harrison as a base, there are a number of short excursions to places like **Minter Gardens,** one of BC's best-known gardens with its mazes, aviaries, Chinese gardens, topiary animals and much more. Bridal Veil Falls Provincial Park nearby has a 25m waterfall cascade down a rocky mountain face and strolls through a forest of cedar and fir. For history buffs, **Kilby Historic Store and Farm** is a look at the role the general store played in settlement in BC. Thomas Kilby was a veritable packrat who saved a vast collection of memorabilia, from eggbeaters to long-gone tinned goods. The hands-on exhibits let you press apples or crank up old wall phones.

Accommodation and Food in Harrison Hot Springs

Harrison Hot Springs Resort $$$ *100 Esplanade; tel: 604) 796-2244; tollfree (800) 663-2266; fax (604) 796-3682; web: www.harrisonresort. com; e-mail: info@harrisonresort.com* Newly remodelled spa with a wide range of services.

Rowena's Inn on the River $$$ *14282 Morris Valley Rd, Harrison Mills; tel: (604) 796-0234; tollfree (800) 661-5108; web: www.rowenasinn.com; e-mail: rowenas@uniserve.com* Intimate luxury inn on 160 acres (64.8ha) with pool, hot tub, excellent dining.

OPE✢✢

Hope Information,
Info Centre 919 Water
el: (604) 869-2021;
:
v.hopechamber.bc.ca;
ail:
echmb@uniserve.com
n year round.

Memorial Park ($)
and Japanese Gardens
ntown Hope, Memorial
:, 3rd & Park streets.

Hope Museum $
919 Water St; tel:
4) 869-7322. Open
—early Sept.

quihalla Canyon
:reation Area and
ello Tunnels *10km*
from Kawkawa Lake;
'604) 824-2300. Open
' but closed if icy
litions exist.

This little town with its optimistic name nestles against the Cascade Mountains at the point where the Fraser River turns north, a kind of doorway to the Canadian Rockies. Hope is a folksy place known as the Chainsaw Carving Capital because of giant wooden sculptures erected downtown that were carved by local artists. Self-guided walking maps are available from the Hope Information office. **Memorial Park✢✢** downtown features 22 stumps carved into animal forms, and next to this the Japanese Gardens✢✢ are dedicated to the Japanese-Canadians placed in the Tashme internment camp during the Second World War. The **Hope Museum✢✢✢** explains more about the sad history of Japanese-Canadians interred at the camp (24km east) as well as Sto:lo natives and pioneer life in the area. The **Coquihalla Canyon Recreation Area and Othello Tunnels✢✢✢** about 15km east of the town has spectacular gorge scenery that has drawn Hollywood to make films several times including the first *Rambo* flick. The famous Kettle Valley Railroad's Othello Tunnels, blasted out of solid granite 1910–16, were considered one of the world's greatest engineering feats and today are certainly Hope's top attraction. The 2.8km return walk includes four tunnels and dramatic views of the Coquihalla River rushing below. Tunnels and stations are named after both the chief engineer's daughters and Shakespearean characters.

Accommodation and food in Hope

Quality Inn $ *350 Old Hope Princeton Way, tel: (604) 869-9951; fax: (604) 869-9421; web: www.bctravel.com* On the outskirts, has kitchen, pool and whirlpool sauna.

The Home Restaurant $ *665 Hope–Princeton Hwy; tel: (604) 869-5558.* Has made a BC magazine's Top Ten list for its home-cooked meals and huge portions; recently opened a second restaurant in Hope.

Dee's Riverview Café $ *875 Water St; tel: (604) 869-5534.* Excellent coffee, soups, sandwiches and home baking.

Suggested tour

Total distance: 175km.

Time: Straight driving time from Hope to New Westminster is about 2 hours. Allow 2 hours to half a day for each of Minter Gardens, Harrison Hot Springs and Fort Langley.

Links: This route links Hope, the Cascade Mountains and the Gold Rush Trail going west to New Westminster.

posite
al Veil Falls

Route: From **HOPE** ❶ follow the TransCanada Highway westbou
until signs for Hwy 9. Turn north and watch signs for Minter Gard
❷.

Detour 1: Turn south off Hwy 1 and follow signs to **Bridal Veil F**
❸. From Minter Gardens continue north past Agassiz to **HARRIS**
HOT SPRINGS ❹.

Detour 2: Head northeast 6.5km on Rockwell Drive to **Sasqua**
Provincial Park ❺. Take Hwy 7 going westward to **Harrison Mills**
for the **Kilby Historic Store and Farm** ❼. Continue along Hwy 7
about 35km to **Hatzic Lake** to the right of the highway. Just beyo
this, 2.5km before the city of **Mission**, signs will indicate the **Xa:yt**
(Hatzic Rock) National Historic Site and Interpretive Centre (
604-820-9725). Situated on this site is an immense triangular rock t
is sacred to the Sto:lo First Nations people who settled here 9000 ye
ago. The cedar **Xa:ytem Longhouse Interpretive Centre** presents
history of both traditional and contemporary Sto:lo people. T
historic significance of the rock was discovered just before it was to
destroyed for a planned development. The village that belonged
Sto:lo ancestors was emptied by smallpox in the mid- to late-18C
Just beyond this, Mission's **Westminster Abbey** is the namesake
the city and now a Benedictine monastery that sits high on a
overlooking the valley. The Abbey with its 64 stained-glass windo
12-bell tower and tranquil farm welcomes visitors Mon–
1330–1600, Sun 1400–1630. The area's biggest event is the **Miss**
Annual Powwow that draws participants from all across No
America each year in early July to celebrate native heritage in so
dance and drumming competitions.

Drive through Mission and follow signs leading to the Mission Bri
crossing the Fraser River on Hwy 11 toward **ABBOTSFORD** ❽. Wa
for signs indicating the road to the **Clayburn** ❾ turnoff on the I
Return to Hwy 11 and continue to Abbotsford where signs will h
you back onto Hwy 1. Follow for 15km and at the **Aldergrove** turr
(264th Ave) exit and follow signs for the **Greater Vancou**
Zoological Centre ❿.

Return to Hwy 1 and continue to the **FORT LANGLEY** ⓫ turr
(232nd Ave), following signs to the town and the Fort along Glc
Rd. Return to Glover Rd and continue south to Langley for
Museum Of Flight and **BC Farm Machinery Museum**.

Return to Hwy 1 and follow to **New Westminster** ⓬. Known as
'Royal City', New Westminster is older than Vancouver and was o
a boom town populated by gold prospectors. The city has th
interesting museums; the **New Westminster Museum and Archi**
302 Royal Ave; tel: (604) 527-4640, with artefacts and local hist
displays; the Museum of the **Royal Westminster Regiment** .
Queen's Ave; tel: (604) 526-5116, with military artefacts dating bacl

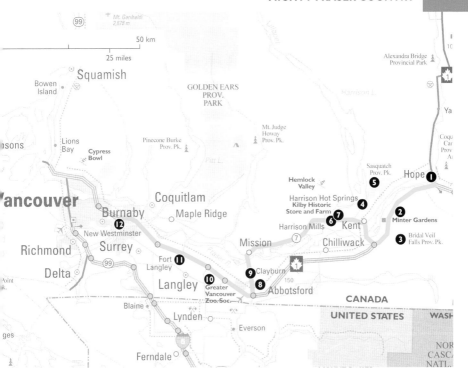

1863; and the **SS *Samson V* Maritime Museum** on the Waterfront between the Public Market and the Inn, *tel: (604) 522-6894*. This was the last working sternwheeler on the Fraser River, operating until 1980.

ght
rch, Fort Langley

North Vancouver Island

Ratings

Beaches	●●●●
Children	●●●●
First Nation art	●●●●
Mountains	●●●●
Nature	●●●●
Outdoor activities	●●●●
Scenery	●●●●
Wildlife	●●●

There's a huge immediate difference driving north fro the southern parts of Vancouver Island as towns a population thin out dramatically. Less than three per cent the island's residents live up here, leaving just wilderness challenge and explore. On the roads, you'll see loggi trucks and heavy machinery reflecting the area's tradition history as a timber, mining, milling and fishing base. N that BC is trying to move beyond its reputation as resource-based economy, many of the towns are quick trying to convert to soft-adventure tourism. The north great assets are its waters and forests with a gold mine of s mammals cruising up and down the Inside Passage betwe Vancouver Island and the mainland. For divers a 'watchers', there seems to be no end to the whales because resident pods that stay year round. This is also a centre First Nations cultural tourism.

ALERT BAY✦✦

ⓘ **Alert Bay Information Centre** *62C Fir St; tel: (250) 974-9911; tollfree: (877) 974-9911; fax: (250) 974-5899; web: www.alertbay.com; e-mail: adventures@alertbay.com Open Mon–Fri year round, daily July–Aug.*

⮎ **'Namgis Burial Ground** *to the right of the ferry dock. Not open to the public but can be seen clearly from the street.*

Located on the beautiful BC Inside Passage, this community blend of native and non-native peoples sits on tiny Cormorant Island j off the coast. Unlike many places, the 'Namgis people of t Kwakwaka'wakw First Nations only moved here in the 1870s fro their original home on the Nimpkish River following a church missi and the establishment of a salmon salt plant. Everything in Alert E is within walking distance and a good place to start is the U'mi **Cultural Centre,**✦✦✦ a building modelled after a traditional Big Hou There are excellent ceremonial masks here, ancient baskets and oth artefacts confiscated in 1922 after colonial laws banned potlat ceremonies. The treasures were returned in 1978 after years of dispu The most visible landmark in town is the Sun Mask at the top of T Totem: at 52.7m it held the Guinness record 1972–94 when a tal pole was set up in Victoria. The **'Namgis Burial Ground**✦✦✦ has m poles that are oddly haunting in the century-old cemetery.

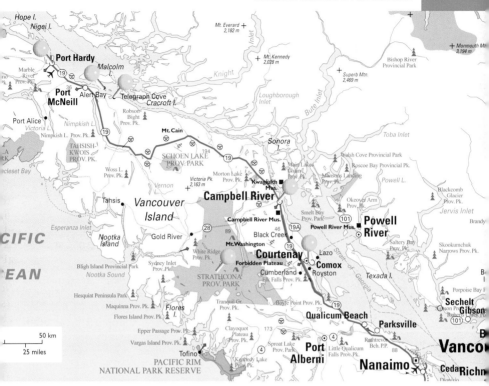

U'mista Cultural Centre $ on Front St
*h of the ferry landing; tel:
) 974-5403. Open
—Sept, daily; rest of the
Mon–Fri. Ask about
cial tours.*

Accommodation and food in Alert Bay

Janet's Guest House $ *667 Fir St; (250) 974-5947; e-mail: janets@island.net* Friendly B&B.

Nimpkish Hotel $ *318 Fir St; tel: (250) 974-5716.* The largest hotel and restaurant on the island.

Orca Inn $ *291 Fir St; tel: (250) 974-5322.* A busy local favourite with great water views.

MPBELL RIVER**❖❖**

Campbell River may have been one of the world's most famous fishing spots years ago but the bloom has faded from the rose somewhat recently. After Roderick Haig-Brown's books on fishing lured such famous fishermen as John Wayne, Bob Hope and Bing Crosby to Campbell River, everyone wanted to come to 'the Salmon Capital of the World'. You can recapture this era in the **Haig-Brown House**

ⓘ Campbell River Tourism
1235 Shoppers Row, Tyee Plaza; tel: (250) 286-1616; tollfree: (800) 463-4386; web: www.campbellrivertourism. bc.ca; e-mail: info@campbellrivertourism. com

ⓒ Haig-Brown House Education Centre $
2250 Campbell River Rd; tel: (250) 286-6646; web: www.haig-brown.bc.ca
Has accommodation in newly restored home of the writer as well as a good library. Seminars and education programmes from end of Feb on environmental issues and gardening.

ⓝ HMCS *Columbia*
scuba divers should ask at the Info Centre for charters and rentals.

Snorkel with Salmon $$
tel: (0250) 923-0848; tollfree (800) 897-2872; web: www.paradisefound.bc.ca; e-mail: info@paradisefound.bc.ca
All instruction and equipment supplied.

Museum at Campbell River *470 Island Hwy at the south entrance to town; tel: (250) 287-3103; web: www.crmuseum.bc.ca Open May–Sept, daily; Oct–Apr Tue–Sat.*

The Kwagiulth Museum *on Quadra Island, Cape Mudge Village; tel: (250) 285-3733. Open June–Sept, daily; Oct–May Mon–Sat.*

Above
Kayak training

Education Centre,** the former home and grounds of the conservationist and writer. Tyee salmon are still here but legendary catches such as the 32kg chinook (caught in 1968) are no longer found and the coho and sockeye fisheries are closed. The bigger industry here today is what you can see rather than catch: orcas from a kayak, scuba diving to see Pacific octopus or hikes along forested trails. Campbell River is a hub for most North Island eco-tourism so there are scores of charter companies and shops that cater to divers who come to expl sunken ships such as the **HMCS *Columbia*.*** For something tot different, water babies can don wet suits and swim with salmon they migrate from early July to late October with **Snorkel w Salmon.*****. In town, the **Museum at Campbell River*****. tells ab early European exploration, pioneer life and First Nations histo Check out the excellent First Nations multimedia presentation. **Kwagiulth Museum**** on Quadra Island is housed in a sea-sh shaped building and holds potlatch artefacts that were seized in 1 and only returned in 1980.

Accommodation and food in Campbell River

April Point Lodge and Marina $$$ *900 April Point Rd; Quadra Isla tel: (250) 285-2222; tollfree: (800) 663-7090; fax: (250) 285-2411; e-m info@obmg.com* This legendary lodge is on Quadra Island but caters t wide range of tours and specialises in fishing. Excellent dining ro and sushi bar. Free shuttle to Campbell River.

Painter's Lodge and Fishing Resort $$$ *1625 McDonald Rd; tel: (2 286-1102; tollfree: (800) 663-7090; fax: (250) 286-0158; e-m info@obmg.com* Ocean and garden view rooms and dining. Tours be set up at the hotel.

Town Centre Inn $$ *1500 Douglas St; tel: (250) 287-8866.* Cle quiet, well-kept motel.

Chateau Restaurant $$ *3 1170 Island Hwy; tel: (250) 287-4143.* One the best views in town; steam and seafood menu.

San Marcos $$ *988 Shoppers Row; tel: (250) 287-7066.* Greek, piz seafood and steak, all good.

Moxie's Restaurant $ *1360 Island Hwy; tel: (250) 830-1500.* A lo favourite, good food and good prices.

OURTENAY AND COMOX VALLEY✵✵✵

**Comox Valley
Chamber of
nmerce** 2040 Cliffe
tel: (250) 334-3234;
ee: (888) 357-4471;
(250) 334-4908; web:
.comoxvalleychamber.
e-mail: chamber@
oxvalleychamber.com
n daily.

**Courtenay
Museum $** 360 Cliffe
tel: (250) 334-3611.
n May–Sept, daily;
-Apr Tue–Sat.

**Forbidden Plateau
Ski Area $$**
minutes' drive west of
tenay in Strathcona
ncial Park; tel: (250)
4428. Open year round.

unt **Washington Ski**
a **$$** 25km west of
tenay, follow signs out of
; tel: (250) 338-1386.
n year round.

t
orest flora

The Comox Valley lies in the rain shadow of the Vancouver Island Range and the peaks around offer the best skiing on Vancouver Island. **Forbidden Plateau Ski Area**✵✵✵ has all the facilities with double chair lifts, 24 runs and extensive cross-country trails. A fascinating native legend claims it got its name from evil spirits who consumed women and children foolhardy enough to venture onto the mountain. **Mount Washington Ski Area**✵✵✵ offers the highest vertical drop on the island, spectacular views, high-speed quad and other chairs plus a ski school, rentals and all the facilities. The Valley also has the most sunshine on the Island along with fertile soil, making the area one of the best agriculturally on Vancouver Island. Today Courtenay is one of Canada's fastest growing urban communities, but 80 million years ago it was a popular stomping ground for giant long-necked elasmosaurs. Fossils of this swimming reptile have been found here, the first of its kind found west of the Rockies. You can see these in the **Courtenay Museum**✵✵ as well as First Nations artefacts and settlement histories.

ORT HARDY✵

**Port Hardy
Chamber of
nmerce** 7250 Market
el: (250) 949-7622.
n June–Sept, daily; rest
e year Mon–Fri.

Scuba diving $$
check in town for
res that take divers out
oice diving areas.

**Port Hardy
Museum and
hives $** 7110 Market
el: (250) 949-8143.
n daily during the
mer months.

Port Hardy has seen better days as a town but it still serves as supply centre in the north island and is a good base for hiking, fishing and kayaking adventures as well as First Nations cultural experiences. As a **scuba dive centre,**✵ Port Hardy is world famous for its clear waters, coral, white-sided dolphins and wolf eels. A number of soft-adventure operators are based here to take visitors caving, kayaking and animal watching to see grizzly and black bears, Roosevelt elk, orcas, grey whales and humpbacks. There's a good stroll along a paved seaside path to watch for bald eagles and other birds. **The Port Hardy Museum and Archives**✵ gives a glimpse into Kwakwaka'wakw history.

STRATHCONA PROVINCIAL PARK***

Canadian Outdoor Leadership Training (COLT) Centre*** *contact Strathcona Park Lodge or web: www. strathcona.bc.ca/outdoor_ leadership/colt_location*

Strathcona Park Lodge $–$$ *Upper Campbell Lake along Hwy 28, 38km west of Hwy 19; tel: (250) 286-3122; fax: (250) 286-6010; web: www.strathcona.bc.ca; e-mail: strathcona@connected.bc.ca Open year round.*

This roughly triangular park is immense, stretching over 250,000ha prime wilderness and including Vancouver Island's tallest moun (Mount Golden Hinde, 2200m) and Canada's tallest waterfall (D Falls, 440m). It was BC's first designated provincial park (establis 1911) and continues to be a hiker's paradise in alpine meadows wit multitude of small lakes for fishing and canoeing and peaks for ski Because of the long separation from the mainland, several ani species such as the Roosevelt elk and the black-tailed deer h evolved differently here. The main centre for ecology is **Strathcona Park Lodge*** which has built an excellent reputat over the years for its wilderness skills programmes, outdoor sum camps and family excursions. The **Canadian Outdoor Leaders Training (COLT) Centre*** has a 105-day intensive programme develop water and land-based outdoor skills and environmen awareness.

TELEGRAPH COVE***

Robson Bight Provincial Park *on the northeast coast, 2km south of Telegraph Cove in Johnstone Strait; web: www. britishcolumbia.com/ parksandtrails. This provincial park is a major whale habitat as well as an ecological reserve protecting rare alpine forests and bogs.*

This town in a teacup (10km off the Island Highway) is about most photographically picturesque you'll find on Vancouver Isla Telegraph Cove booms in the summer months as a major destinat for wilderness seekers, mainly whale watchers who come to see o (killer whales) that rub their bellies on the gravel beaches of **Rob Bight.***

Suggested tour

Total distance: 360km.

Time: In driving time allow 6 hours from Parksville to Port Hardy. could spend weeks here but three days should cover enou adventures.

Links: From Port Hardy, ferry routes lead north to Bella Coola Prince Rupert (*see page 184*).

Route: Take Hwy 19A from **Parksville ❶** north up island, stoppin **Qualicum Beach ❷**, continuing north if you have time and w ocean views. If short of time, take Hwy 19 west of Qualicum Be and continue up to **Fanny Bay ❸** which is famous mainly for excellent oysters.

Detour 1: At **COURTENAY ❹** turn west on 17th Ave for **COMOX** for several interesting parks:

Detour 2: An access point for **STRATHCONA PROVINCIAL PARK** ⑥ and **Gold River**, 89km west of Campbell River.

Returning to Hwy 19, continue on to **CAMPBELL RIVER** ⑦ to the **Fletcher Challenge Elk Falls Pulp and Paper Mill**, *tel: (250) 287-5594* for free tours during the summer. North of Campbell River, signs indicate the ferry to **Quadra Island** ⑧ and the highly recommended **April Point Lodge** as well as its excellent fishing locations.

Returning to Hwy 19, **Elk Falls Provincial Park** is 1km west of the highway and offers good swimming, fishing and biking. You can also see salmon spawning here Sept–Dec. Continuing north, just past Sayward, signs point to **Schoen Lake Provincial Park**, another wilderness park but one requiring a rugged vehicle to reach. Continue on to **TELEGRAPH COVE** ⑨. Just north, the highway passes the **Nimpkish Fish Hatchery**, *tel: (250) 974-9556*, it explains how logging and over-fishing have affected salmon in the area.

East off Hwy 19, take the ferry to **ALERT BAY** ⑩ for its totems and historical sites.

Detour 3: Sointula is on tiny Malcom Island that can be reached by ferry from Port McNeill and Alert Bay as well. Continue north to **PORT HARDY** ⑪.

South Vancouver Island

Ratings

Food and drink	●●●●●
Beaches	●●●●○
Nature	●●●●○
Parks	●●●●○
Scenery	●●●●○
Children	●●●○○
History	●●●○○
Wineries	●●●○○

Until economic conditions and environmental protest ended large-scale logging, southern Vancouver Isla was like a star waiting in the wings. Blessed with a clim so warm and sunny that bananas can actually gr outdoors, it's only been recently that boutique farmers a wine makers have found the proverbial pot of gold. T Cowichan Valley is now heavily dotted with people w have found their calling in specialised food and drin Although the entire island has spectacular scenery, t provincial parks in the south are easily accessible, some rig off the major highways with their virgin forest and ancie petroglyphs. All along the western coastline beaches a steps away from the road for picnicking, tidal pool hunts hikes summer or winter. Some of the best examples of Fi Nations tourism have sprung up in this area to provide enlightened look at the province's original settlers.

CHEMAINUS***

ⓘ Chemainus and District Chamber of Commerce 9796 Willow St (across from Waterwheel Park); tel: (250) 246-3944; fax (250) 246-3251; web: www.chemainus.com; e-mail: ccoc@tourism.chemainus.bc.ca

➲ Waterwheel Park and Chemainus Valley Museum $ in Waterwheel Park in the heart of town.

This is often called 'The Little Town that Did'. When the tow sawmill closed in the early 1980s, Chemainus faced slow extincti until an innovative revitalisation programme was launched by peo who loved their town. With so many talented artists in the area, th decided to paint murals telling the town's history on the side buildings. Local and international artists created 33 murals and statues plus a series of footprints for a self-guided tour of the tov Today, more than 300,000 visitors come every year to photograph t immense murals or take in a production at the professio Chemainus Theatre*** where each season comedies and classics dr in huge crowds. Children will love the **Waterwheel Park**** where th can play at being pirates. Nearby is Chemainus Valley Museum* w its archival documents and artefacts.

Chemainus Theatre $$ *corner of Chemainus Rd and Victoria St; tel: (250) 246-9820 for reservations; tollfree: (800) 565-7738.* Offers dinner, theatre and children's shows as well.

Accommodation and food in Chemainus

Bird Song Cottage B&B $$ *9909 Maple St; tel: (250) 246-9910; fax: (2 246-2909; web: www.romanticbb.com; e-mail: birdsong@islandnet.c* Spilling over with romance, this lovely B&B is run by a musician a artist and their touch carries through into the charming rooms.

The Treasure House $$ *11203 Chemainus Rd; tel: (250) 245-8092; fax: (2 245-4045; web: www.bbcanada.com/2471; e-mail: treasure@island.net* the water between Chemainus and Ladysmith. Great breakfasts a lovely home.

The Waterford Inn $$$ *9875 Maple St.* This fine restaurant usua gets a ten out of ten for its cuisine and ambience.

The Willow Street Café $ *9749 Willow St; tel: (250) 246-2434.* Gr muffins and scones; locals love it.

COWICHAN✦✦✦

Cowichan Tourism *25 Canada Ave, Duncan; tel: (250) 715-0709; tollfree: (888) 303-3337; fax: (250) 715-0710; web: www.cowichan.bc.ca; e-mail: tourism@cowichan. com*

Merridale Ciderworks $$ *1230 Merridale Rd, Cobble Hill; tel: (250) 743-4293; tollfree: (800) 998-9908; fax: (250) 743-9310; web: www.merridalecider.com Open Mon-Sat 1030–1630 and also Sun in summer for tour and wine tastings.*

The name means 'warm land' and the bountiful harvests produc here confirm that it's exactly that: tender and tasty cheeses, ciders a wines. Winemakers here say that there are more hours of sunshine the Cowichan Valley than anywhere else in Canada and this, coup with just the right amount of precipitation and glacial deposits excellent soil creates perfect vineyard conditions. The best thing to in this area is follow a map available at Cowichan Tourism and foll the winding roads to sample choice food and drink at boutique farr **Merridale Ciderworks✦✦✦** welcomes visitors to BC's first estate cid where you can check out the special fruit that goes into cider in 1 orchard, chat with cider makers about their craft and walk throu the cider making process. **Cherry Point Vineyards✦✦✦** welcom visitors to try their award-winning Alsatian wines, while **Glente Vineyards✦✦✦** (opened in May 2000) has already won prizes for th Pinot Gris. **Abbott's Choice Fine Cheeses✦✦✦** is Vancouver Islan latest speciality cheese producer with a wide range from Camembert brushed-rind Tommes and fresh Cheddar curd. Visitors are welcome taste the European-style full-bodied cheeses.

erry Point Vineyards
*840 Cherry Point Rd,
ble Hill; tel: (250) 743-
72; fax (250) 743-1059;*
:
*w.cherrypointvineyards.
n; e-mail:
@cherrypointvineyards.
n*
*en daily from 1000 for
tings; tours daily at 1300
t other times if staff
ilable.*

enterra Vineyards $$
*97 Cobble Hill Rd, Cobble
; tel: (250) 743-2330;
ail:
nterravineyards@telus.net
en daily 1000–1800 for
rs and tastings.*

**bott's Choice Fine
eeses $$** *1282 Cherry
nt Rd, Cobble Hill; tel:
0) 715-0563; fax: (250)
5-0564; e-mail:
ots_choice@cowichan.
n*

*ht
eses from Cowichan*

UNCAN❖❖

**Duncan
Information
ntre** *381 TransCanada
y; tel: (250) 746-4636. In
rwaitea Centre Mall.
en Apr–Oct.*

Beginning as a whistle stop for William Duncan's farm in the 1880s, Duncan is now the main centre for the Cowichan Valley's 74,000 residents. It is probably most widely known for the heavy, warm woollen sweaters, mitts, toques and other knitted garments produced by the Cowichan native people who have lived in the area for thousands of years. The **Cowichan Native Village**❖❖❖ (**Quw'utsun Cultural Centre**) presents an excellent up-to-date multimedia presentation blended with stories and dance to tell the story of the

Cowichan Native Village $ *200 Cowichan Way, immediately after crossing the Cowichan River on Silver Bridge; tel: (250) 746-8119; web: www.cowichannativevillage. com; e-mail: info@cowichannativevillage. com Open daily, year round.*

Artists $$ *for more information on galleries and when to visit contact Cowichan Tourism or web: www.cvac.bc.ca*

BC Forest Museum $ *2892 Drinkwater Rd; tel: (250) 715-1113; fax: (250) 715-1170; web: www.bcforestmuseum.com; e-mail: bcfm@islander.com Open early May–late Sept, daily.*

Cowichan people from the beginning of time. Native artists work the Village, knitting or carving on totem poles and canoes: visitors c try their hand at carving as well. During July and August eve Sunday, there's a salmon barbecue done outdoors in the tradition way. Duncan is also home to a number of excellent **artists**** a several who have become internationally known. The **BC Fore Museum***** tells the story of the BC forest industry with indoor a outdoor exhibits including a small village of pioneers' houses, sho and schoolhouses. Kids will love the narrow-gauge steam train th runs through the 40ha site across a trestle and through a farmste and logging camp, plus there's lots of hands-on activities such as le rubbing.

Accommodation and food in Duncan

Summer Place Inn on the River $$$ *5245 Winchester Rd; tel: (25 715-1222; fax: (250) 746-0610; web: www.summerplaceinn.com; e-ma info@summerplaceinn.com* Luxury B&B set on the banks of t Cowichan River and decorated in 'Canadiana' and antiques.

MacMillan Provincial Park***

MacMillan Provincial Park *at the end of Cameron Lake, 31km west of Parksville.*

Cathedral Grove is here with some of the largest Douglas fir tre remaining on Vancouver Island. A parking lot right on the highw leads into the Grove which has trails that wind through stands of tre that are as much as 800 years old. This beautiful rainforest is poignant reminder of what the whole island looked like before loggi introduced clear-cutting practices.

Malahat Drive***

Goldstream Park *off the Malahat about 20km from Victoria city centre; tel: (604) 689-9025 for camping reservations; tollfree: (800) 689-9025.*

Starting at **Goldstream Park***** this 16km drive over Malah Mountain provides glimpses of what looks like Switzerland combin with Norway at times, with magnificent views looking out ov Finlayson Arm. Goldstream has great stands of virgin western r cedar forest along with giant maples and Douglas firs. There are o mine shafts from the late 1800s and excellent hikes through arbut and oak groves. Visitors in the autumn (fall) may catch the annu salmon run (chum, coho and chinook) when the fish spawn here.

Accommodation and food on the Malahat

The Aerie Resort $$$ *600 Ebedora Lane at the Spectacle Lake turnoff on Hwy 1; tel: (250) 743-7115; fax: (250) 743-4766; web: www.aerie.bc.ca; e-mail: aerie@relaischateaux.com* You will swear you've been transformed into an eagle and this is your nest. This luxury hotel with individually designed rooms was ranked No 2 among small hotels in North America and has a dining room with a stunning view of Findlayson Arm. The dining room here is an award winner.

The Prancing Horse Retreat $$ *located just below The Aerie (above); tel: (250) 743-9372; tollfree: (877) 887-8834; e-mail: phorse@islandnet.com* This lovely B&B has the same view as The Aerie but at lower prices. Lovely rooms and excellent breakfast.

PARKSVILLE AND QUALICUM❖❖

Little Qualicum Falls *north off Hwy 4, km west of Hwy 4A.*

glishman River Falls *w signs at Errington Rd 9km to the park.*

Coombs *9km west of Parksville on Hwy 4A. e market is well worth a p for its fresh produce, ing and hearty taurant: as well as tos of the goats on the f.*

ant Goose Feeding ea *just north of Hwy 19A junction at Craig's ssing; tel: (250) 248-7 for information about grammes.*

Known for its beaches, Parksville is tide-pool heaven when hundreds of hectares of beach are exposed at low tide. Children love to search for tiny trapped sea creatures or build castles in the sand. Parksville is best used as a base to explore **Little Qualicum Falls,**❖❖ **Englishman River Falls**❖❖ and **Coombs.**❖❖❖ Little Qualicum Falls is a stretch of rainforest and walkways beside both the Upper and Lower falls. There's hiking swimming, snorkeling and fishing for brown trout in Qualicum River. Englishman River Falls is also a good place to swim, camp and hike by scenic waterfalls and gorges. Coombs is a town of only 840, most famous for its Old Country Market with a herd of goats grazing on the roof. The town grew out of a Salvation Army programme that brought nearly a quarter of a million poor English and Welsh to settle here and live a simple life. The shores of Parksville and Qualicum Beach are on the Pacific flyway for migratory waterfowl and as many as 20,000 Brant geese stop at the **Brant Goose Feeding Area**❖❖ to feed each spring *en route* to the Baja. Many programmes held here include nature talks, bird activities and more.

Accommodation and food in Parksville

Tigh-Na-Mara Resort $$ *1095 east Island Hwy; tel: (250) 248-2072; tollfree (800) 663-7373; web: www.tigh-na-mara.com; e-mail: info@tigh-na-mara.com* Cosy solid log cottages with fireplaces tucked into a forest of fir and arbutus trees plus seafront condominiums. Excellent restaurant with Northwest cuisine and fresh seafood.

ove *w over the Malahat*

Brother Twelve

BC has always attracted odd characters and bizarre cultists among whom Brother Twelve was legendary. Near Nanaimo, a number of houses were once part of a colony set up by a former English sea captain named Edward Arthur Wilson in the late 1920s. Wilson believed himself to be the '12th brother' of The Great White Lodge that guided the evolution of the human race. After a series of visions, he established a small colony comprised of lonely (and wealthy) followers who gave vast sums of money to share in Brother XII's apocalyptic visions. The colony later moved to Valdes Island and then De Courcy where Wilson stashed away a fortune in jam jars. With the police hot on his heels, Brother Twelve and his strange companion, Madame Zee, disappeared with more than $400,000 in bank notes and gold tucked in the jam jars. Rumour said they went to Switzerland but no one knows for sure.

Suggested tour

Total distance: 213km.

Time: Driving time from the outskirts of Victoria to Parksville a vicinity takes half a day but 4 or 5 days would be necessary to see the sights in-between.

Links: Continue north up to Port Hardy with a ferry connection Prince Rupert (*see page 184*). Ferries also go back to the mainland fro Nanaimo to Horseshoe Bay.

Route: Follow Hwy 1 north from Victoria past **Thetis Lake Park Goldstream Provincial Park ❶** where the road becomes t **MALAHAT** Highway ❷. There are numerous lay-bys on this hig level highway with panoramic views of bays and coastline. T Malahat becomes the Island Highway when it heads into t Cowichan area.

Detour 1: The Shawinigan Lake access road west off Hwy 1 leads the Lake and to **Memory Island Provincial Park**. This beautiful isla was purchased by families who lost their sons in the Second Wor War to set up a permanent memorial.

At **Cobble Hill ❸** explore the area's many wineries, cidery a speciality farms with their tasting rooms. Returning to Hwy continue up to **COWICHAN** Bay ❹ east of Hwy 1 for a walk along t **Hecate Regional Park Footpath** that crosses one of several Cowich Tribe reserves and offers bird watching and views of Mou Tzouhalem. Continuing on to Duncan, the **Cowichan Native Villa** ❺ deserves at least a half day for stories, tour, film and barbecue.

Continuing north up Hwy 1, take the signposted cut-off f **CHEMAINUS** ❻ and the world-famous murals. With a number quaint tea rooms and restaurants, this is a good place to stop for a re

Returning to Hwy 1 for another 10km, **Ladysmith** is worth a qu drive around and a peek at some of the shops. Continuing on Hwy **Petroglyph Provincial Park** is well signposted on the highway a worth a short hike to see the ancient carvings. Nanaimo is a town more than 70,000 that serves as a supply centre for the area and fe access to Vancouver. History buffs might check out **The Bastion** the corner of Bastion and Front Sts for its military archives a artefacts. Hwy 1 becomes Hwy 19 at Nanaimo and continues up **PARKSVILLE** ❼.

Detour 2: At Parksville, private boats will take visitors on tours **Lasqueti Island** and **Jedediah Island Provincial Park** where you w see rich marine life and mammals along with a host of birds. This prime ocean kayaking terrain as well.

The Wild West Coast

Ratings

Beaches	●●●○
National parks	●●●○
Nature	●●●○
Outdoor activities	●●●○
Scenery	●●●○
Walking	●●●○
Wildlife	●●●○

It takes some driving: but haven't we been told that t best things in life don't come easily? The scenery unmatchable anywhere, 'drop dead gorgeous' as they wo say here. The West Coast Trail is one of life's gr adventures for the fit and hardy, but even soft-advent seekers find all they could want on the West Coast: kayaki or canoeing through the Broken Group Islands or watchi whales from a Zodiac. It's a superb place to see marine li especially great whales, and some of the world's best scu diving can be found here. The crystal-clear water ho anemones in every shade of the rainbow, the world's larg octopuses and ancient shipwrecks. Beaches here are not swimming but for walking in summer and in winter t when the wild, wild storms hit with fury. The Pacific Co is simply a world in itself.

BAMFIELD✧✧

ℹ Bamfield Chamber of Commerce
right in town; tel: (250) 728-3006; web: www.alberni,net/bamcham; e-mail: bamcham@cedar.alberni.net

🚶 West Coast Trail $
for permits, information and fees, call after 1 Mar for upcoming season; tel: (604) 663-6000; tollfree: (800) 663-6000 or (250) 387-1642 (outside Canada and US); web: www.parkscan. harbour.com/pacrim/hike2

This tiny seaside village is best known as the starting point of West Coast Trail✧✧✧ but it's also a destination for fishermen, kayak scuba divers and whale watchers. In the summer months, government wharves are filled with boats heading out to ca halibut, cod and salmon; or ferrying visitors to the prime view grounds for orcas, sea lions and whales. Salmon fishing causes local population of 338 to jump dramatically in the summer w sports fishermen and kayakers, who use Bamfield as a launching s for tours of the **Broken Group Islands** *(see page 245)*,✧✧✧ archipelago in Barkley Sound. Bamfield looks off-the-beaten-track visitors can brave an unpaved road from Port Alberni or take eithe boat or float plane.

Cumberland
Elk Falls Prov. Pk.
Sydney Inlet
Prov. Pk.
STRATHCONA
PROV. PARK
Texada I.
Boyle Point Prov. Pk.
Mesquiat
ula Park
Maquinna Prov. Pk.
73   19
Qualicum
Beach
Parksville
Flores
I.
Hot Springs
Cove
Tranquil Cr.
Prov. Pk.
Flores Island Prov. Pk.
Epper Passage Prov. Pk.
Clayoquot
Plateau
Prov. Pk.
173
4
Rathtrevor
Bch. P.P.
Vargas Island Prov. Pk.
Sproat Lake
Prov. Park
Port
Alberni
Little Qualicum
Falls Prov. Pk.
88
Tofino
4
Kennedy Lake
Prov. Pk.
Vancouver
Island
Long Beach
PACIFIC RIM
NATIONAL PARK RESERVE
PACIFIC
Ucluelet
Amphitrite
Point Lighthouse
Broken
Islands
18
OCEAN
Barkley Sound
Bamfield
Hitchie Cr.
Prov. Pk.
Nitinat L.
Lake
Cowichan
PACIFIC RIM
NATIONAL PARK RESERVE
Carmanah
Walbran
Prov. Pk.
Port Renfrew
14
102
50 km
China Beach
Prov. Pk.
25 miles
MAKAH IND. RES.
Strait of Juan de Fuca

ACIFIC RIM NATIONAL PARK RESERVE✤✤✤

The Wickaninnish
Centre✤✤ at the end
.ong Beach Rd, beyond
k headquarters. Open
y late spring to autumn
).

This is the umbrella for three parks and a goodly amount of ocean: the **West Coast Trail**✤✤✤ *(see page 245)* , **the Broken Group Islands**✤✤✤ *(see page 245)* and Long Beach,✤✤✤ which runs between Ucluelet and Tofino. This is a vast park (130km long and covering 84,642ha) that was created to preserve wild things in a terrain of beaches, rain forests, bogs and rocky headlands. Long Beach was for years a Vancouver Island secret until a paved road replaced the dirt track linking Port Alberni and the Coast. Today, visitors stream into the area but beaches are still not overcrowded and it's possible to find a deserted cove or lonely stretch of sand. **The Wickaninnish Centre**✤✤ has observation decks with telescopes for looking out to sea. Inside there are exhibits and murals plus films to bring an insight into the local ecology.

Right
The wild west coast,
Wickaninnish Inn, Tofino

Opposite
Tofino beach

TOFINO✦✦✦

ⓘ **Tofino-Long Beach Chamber of Commerce** *Campbell St; tel: (250) 725-3414; fax: (250) 725-3296; web: www.island.net/~tofino; e-mail: tofino@island.net Open July–Aug, daily; weekends May–June and Sept.*

ⓘ **Eagle Aerie Gallery** *$$ 350 Campbell St; tel: (250) 725-3235.*

Hot Springs Cove $$$ *while the bathing is free, the boat or plane rides are not. Contact Remote Passages Marine Excursions; tel: (250) 725-3330; tollfree: (800) 666-9833; fax: (250) 725-3380; web: www. remotepassages.co; e-mail: tofino@remotepassages.com Offers kayaking, whale watching, Hot Springs Cove and other adventures.*

Tucked into a vast rainforest, Tofino is not only the gateway Clayoquot Sound but also the jumping off spot for a score adventures. Aboriginal people have lived in the area for more th 2000 years: a timeline shared by a cedar tree that sprouted on nea Meares Island 20 centuries ago. This village on the edge of a contine has a long history of logging and fishing that still continues, temper nowadays by a powerful cadre of environmentalists. When the Government decided to log Clayoquot Sound in 1993, it spark Canada's largest civil disobedience action. Clayoquot is the larg expanse of old-growth temperate rainforest left in North America a the international protest saved the Sound.

There's a hike along a boardwalk through the ancient cedar a hemlock forests on **Meares Island✦✦✦** where you'll see trees that w alive before the Roman Empire fell. The island is larger than Ho Kong or Bermuda and it was one of the numerous places saved (now) from the chainsaw. From Tofino, there are whale watching a wildlife tours, sea-kayaking adventures, First Nations cultural to and fishing. One of the most unusual is **Hot Springs Cove✦✦✦** wh steaming 50°C (122°F) water percolates from the ground and flo over a waterfall through a series of pools to the sea. You can bathe these natural pools in exquisite scenery. Fans of First Nations art w find the works of Roy Vickers, one of Canada's most success aboriginal artists, at the **Eagle Aerie Gallery✦✦** with its traditio longhouse façade.

Accommodation and food in Tofino

Meares Island *numerous boating and kayaking tours available by operators in Tofino.*

Wickaninnish Inn $$$ *Osprey Lane at Chesterman Beach, tel: (2. 725-3100; tollfree: (800) 333-4604; fax: (250) 725-3110; w www.wickinn.com; e-mail: info@wickinn.com* The luxury and quality this Inn comes as a surprise with one of the finest restaurants Vancouver Island and a luxurious newly renovated spa, the Anci Cedars.

Middle Beach Lodge $$ *400 MacKenzie Beach Rd; tel: (250) 725-29 fax (250) 725-2901; e-mail: lodge@middlebeach.com* Rustic ocean-fr lodges and cabins on the Pacific Ocean with fireplaces and hot tu Good for families.

Pointe Restaurant $$$ *at the Wickaninnish Inn (see abo\ Extraordinary view from the dining room with a menu to match.

Schooner Restaurant $–$$ *331 Campbell St; tel: (250) 725-3444 mail: schooner@island.net* A favourite with locals, good ambience i excellent seafood and healthy dishes.

Breakers Delicatessen $ *131 First St; tel: (250) 725-2558; e-m tdixon@island.net* Great healthy breakfasts and lunches at low prices

The Common Loaf Bake Shop $ *180 First St, tel: (250)725-391\ local hangout, especially on rainy days with great baking, breads i sandwiches.

Below
Whale watching

CLUELET

**Ucluelet Chamber
of Commerce**
*e foot of Government
*rf on Main St; tel: (250)
*4641; fax: (250) 726-
1; web:
*.ucluletinfo.com; e-mail:
@ucluletinfo.com
*n daily in the summer,
of the year Mon–Fri.*

**Amphitrite Point
Lighthouse**
*1e southern tip of Ucluth
nsula.

**Broken Group
Islands $$**
*ous outfitters such as
*estic Ocean Kayaking;
*800) 889-7644; web:
.oceankayaking.com

**1adian Princess
*ort $$**
3 Peninsula Rd; tel:
)) 726-7771; tollfree:
)) 633-7090; web:
*.obmg.com; e-mail:
g@pinc.com
*p on a ship or in
*ets with tour facilities
*t on the resort
perty.

Perched on the tip of a peninsula at the edge of Barkley Sound, Ucluelet faces the ocean with a great rain forest at its back. These woods are filled with trails including the 2km Wild Pacific Trail that starts near **Amphitrite Point Lighthouse.**♦♦ This was built in 1905 and it's the best spot around for viewing sunsets or migrating grey whales in the summer and storms in the winter. Two of the most popular trips out of Ucluelet are bear watching adventures in a guided canoe and kayaking in the **Broken Group Islands.**♦♦♦ He-Tin-Kis Park♦♦ is a boardwalk trail through old growth cedar and spruce forest along a rugged shoreline with views to the Pacific Ocean. In town, the **Canadian Princess**♦♦ is an historic West Coast steamship built in 1932 that's been converted into a hotel, lounge and restaurant.

The West Coast Trail

This world-famous, 5–10-day, 77km trek from Bamfield to Port Renfrew is a test of endurance but offers so many rewards in stunning scenery and adventures that fans of the hike rave about it. The trail was first established in 1907 to create an 'escape route' for survivors of shipwrecks along the coast (known as the Graveyard of the Pacific). The path was so difficult however that some shipwreck victims might have considered jumping back into the water. It's more groomed now but hikers should be fit, well-prepared with all the necessary gear (such as excellent footwear) and have the required permits. Parks Canada only allows 60 hikers to start each day. The trail can be slippery with lots of rain, waterfalls, tricky slopes, streams, bogs and blisters. If you have strong legs and a bit of experience, this is a journey of soul-enhancing bliss you'll never forget.

Suggested tour

Total distance: 42km from Ucluelet to Tofino.

Time: Varies depending on the number of adventures chosen. Allow a full day (travel time and relaxing) for boat or plane trips to Hot Springs Cove. Hikers should allow 5–7 days depending on experience.

Links: Returning from Vancouver Island's west coast via Hwy continue north from **Parksville** (*see page 237*) on Hwy 19 to P Hardy (*see page 229*) and the ferry to **Prince Rupert** (*see page 184*) south to Nanaimo to catch BC Ferries back to **Vancouver** (*see p 268*).

Route: Most visitors will drive to **UCLUELET** ❶ and **TOFINO** ❷ no from Victoria along Hwy 1 to Nanaimo, Hwy 19 to Parksville and th Hwy 4 west, approximately 320km and 4–5 hours driving time.

Detour 1: With a base in Tofino, depending on the season, take one the whale watching or marine watching Zodiac trips offsho Kayaking trips to **Meares Island** ❸ will take about 4 hours includi hiking time on the island. For **Hot Springs Cove** ❹ trips, allow a h to full day.

Driving south on Hwy 4, watch for the sign for **Chesterman Beach** good walks and shell hunting. Returning to Hwy 4 continue south the turnoff for **Radar Hill** (18km from Tofino). This was built by US as part of the Distant Early Warning system in the 1950s and used today as an excellent viewpoint. About 2km down the road sign will indicate **Long Beach** ❺, an ideal spot summer or winter strolls along the surf-pounded beach. The **Wickaninnish Centre** ❻ at the end of Long Beach Rd just beyond the park headquarters. At **Ucluelet–Tofino–Port Alberni** junction, turn west 8km for Ucluelet

Detour 2: Ucluelet is a base for a variety of adventure trips includi bear watching, whale watching or kayaking trips to **The Brok Islands** ❼.

Right
Ucluelet harbour

Sydney Inlet
Prov. Pk.

STRATHCONA
PROV. PARK

Cumberland
Elk Falls Prov. Pk.

Texada I

esquiat
la Park

Maquinna Prov. Pk.

Flores
I.

4 Hot Springs
Cove

Tranquil Cr.
Prov. Pk.

Boyle Point Prov. Pk.

73

19

**Qualicum
Beach
Park**

Flores Island Prov. Pk.

Epper Passage Prov. Pk.

Clayoquot
Plateau
Prov. Pk.

173

Sproat Lake
Prov. Park

4

**Port
Alberni**

Little Qualicum
Falls Prov. Pk.

Rathtrevor
Bch. P.P.

Vargas Island Prov. Pk.

Meares Island

3

2

Tofino

Kennedy Lake
Prov. Pk.

**Vancouver
Island**

PACIFIC RIM
NATIONAL PARK RESERVE

5

Long Beach
Wickaninnish

6

Ucluelet **1**

Amphitrite
Point Lighthouse

7 Broken
Islands

PACIFIC

Barkley Sound

Bamfield

Hitchie Cr.
Prov. Pk.

Cow

OCEAN

PACIFIC RIM
NATIONAL PARK RESERVE

Carmanah
Walbran
Prov. Pk.

Port Renfrew

14

50 km

China Beach
Prov. Pk.

25 miles

MAKAH IND. RES.

ght
d eagle, the Wild West
ast

Victoria

Ratings

Food and drink	●●●●●
Gardens	●●●●●
Museums	●●●●●
Art	●●●●○
History	●●●●○
Outdoor activities	●●●●○
Parks	●●●●○
Shopping	●●●○○

Once upon a time, Victoria was 'more English than the English', a kind of fantasy created by British immigrants who wanted to reproduce a half-remembered home. Like a lot of tags, the impression that Victoria is a little bit of England seems to linger on despite the city's contemporary hip scene. People still come expecting afternoon tea, but they find following Victoria's 'Ale Trail' a lot more fun. They'll take in the museums and history but find themselves surprised at the talent in local theatres and the *au courant* flavour of Victoria's restaurants. The city seems to always have one festival or another going on – music, wine or food and everything from hot jazz to hillbilly pours out of night clubs and bars. If you insist on believing in myths, Victorians will introduce you to 'Caddy', a legendary local sea monster sighted here and there for more than a century.

Arriving and departing

By air: Victoria International Airport is served by Air Canada, Regional, Horizon, Westjet and United Express connecting from Vancouver or Seattle. Flights take about 35 minutes from Vancouver. West Coast Air and Harbour Air provide 35-minute harbour-to-harbour service from downtown Vancouver to downtown Victoria several times a day. Taxis $$$ to downtown Victoria, or the **Airport Bus $$** tel: (250) 386-2526, with coach service every 30 minutes, or **BC Transit $** tel: (250) 382-6161.

By sea: BC Ferries have regular ferries between Tsawwassen on the mainland (1 hour from downtown Vancouver) and Swartz Bay at the north end of the Saanich Peninsula (about 45 minutes by car from downtown Victoria). **Pacific Coach Lines** tel: (250) 385-4411, has buses from Vancouver's Main Terminal via ferry to downtown

ⓘ Tourism Victoria Visitor Info Centre 812 Wharf St; tel: (250) 953-2033; web: www.tourismvictoria.com; e-mail: info@tourismvictoria.com Open daily.

BC Ferries 1112 Fort St; tel: (250) 386-3431; tollfree: (888) 223-3779; fax: (250) 381-5452; web: www.bcferries.com

Butchart Gardens

Topaz Park

Topaz Avenue

Quadra Street

Blackwood Street

Cook Street

Gorge Road

Douglas Street

Hillside Avenue

Blanshard Street

Kings Road

Cook Street

Bay Street

Bay Street

Pt. Ellice Bridge

Queens Avenue

Central Park

kirk ter

ver Farmhouse d Hill and ighthouse Historic Sights

Upper Harbour

Pembroke Street

Government Street

Royal Athletic Park

Pembroke Street

Esquimalt Road

Caledonia Avenue

North Park Street

Chinatown

Johnson Street Bridge

Pandora Street

Johnson Street

Wharf Street

Bastion Square

Douglas Street

Yates Street

Blanshard Street

View   Street

Craigdarroch Castle

Victoria Harbour

Inner Harbour

Broughton Street

Fort   Street

Quadra Street

Vancouver Street

Courtenay Street

Art Gallery of Greater Victoria

Rockland Avenue

Thunderbird Park

Crystal Garden

Fairfield Road

Cook Street

Belleville Street

Parliament Buildings

Royal British Columbia Museum

Helmcken House

Richardson Street

Superior Street

Montreal Street

Superior Street

Michigan Street

Southgate

Street

Fairfield Street

Government House

Fairfield Road

Oswego Street

Simcoe Street

Michigan Street

Heywood Avenue

Linden Avenue

Moss Street

Niagara Street

Menzies Street

Toronto Street

Beacon Hill Park

Emily Carr House

Children's Pool

Douglas Street

May Street

Dallas Road

Children's Zoo

Cook Street

Faithful Street

Government Street

Battery Street

Viewpoint Shelter

an de Fuca Strait

Scenic Marine Drive

Dallas Road

500 metres

500 yards

Harbour Air
tel: (604) 688-1277;
tollfree: (800) 665-0212.
16 flights a day.

Victoria International Airport Willingdon Rd off Hwy 17, Sidney, tel: (250) 953-7500; web:
www.victoriaairport.com
25km from downtown Victoria.

West Coast Air tel:
(604) 606-6888; tollfree:
(800) 347-2222; web:
www.westcoastair.com
for schedules.

Victoria. From Washington State several ferries come into Victor **Black Ball Transport** tel: (250) 386-2202, has service from P Angeles. The **Victoria Clipper** tel: (250) 382-8100; tollfree: (800) 8. 2535; web: www.victoriaclipper.com has daily catamaran service fr Seattle. **Victoria San Juan Cruises** tel: (800) 443-4552, has da service May–Oct with dinner on the return. **Washington State Ferr** tel: (250) 656-1831, has one sailing daily to Sidney from Anacortes.

Getting around

Downtown Victoria is compact and so walking is the best way explore (see Walking tours, page 254). For sights further out, **BC Tran** tel: (250) 382-6161; web: www.transitbc.com provides frequent serv all through the city with special discount passes available throu Tourism Victoria Visitor Info Centre. **Victoria Harbour Ferries** (250) 708-0201, serve the Inner Harbour with various stops and harbour tour.

Driving in the inner city can be difficult because of one-way stre traffic and limited street parking so the best advice is park and wa Limits at meters are strictly enforced with fines so parking garages advised unless you are certain you can return on time. Read the met carefully for hours when coins are required. Downtown traffic usually heavy most of the day but lighter in outlying areas except rush hour (0730–0900 and 1500–1800).

Right
The Empress Hotel

Opposite
Butchart Gardens

Sights

Bastion Square
*Wharf St between
...es and Fort Sts. Open
...ly.*

The Ale Trail $$
*...for more information on
...anised Ale Trail tours
...ld one Sat each month)
customised tours, tel:
...0) 658-5367, or contact
...ividual pubs.*

...tchart Gardens $$$
*...km north of downtown
...toria, 800 Benvenuto Ave;
...(250) 652-5256. Open
...ar round. There is also an
...cellent dining room;
...servations required.*

The Ale Trail**

By all means do have cucumber sandwiches and tea at The Empress in the afternoon but join youthful Victorians too as they sample some of the best brews you'll taste. Following on the heels of 'boutique wineries', beer connoisseurs have set up a whole string of brew pubs serving beverages you won't even recognise as beer. Some of the brew pubs have as many as 40 different beers that range from porters, lagers and ales to ginseng and yeasty wheat brews. Some of the pubs on the tour are: Spinnakers Brew Pub *308 Catherine St; tel: (250) 384-0334*; Hugo's Grill and Brewhouse *625 Courtney St; tel: (250) 920-4844*; Vancouver Island Brewery *2330 Government St; tel: (250) 361-0007*; Harbour Canoe Club *450 Swift St; tel: (250) 361-1940*; and Swans Brew Pub *506 Pandora Ave; tel: (250) 361-3310*. Beer, they all say, is Victoria's latest 'culture'.

Bastion Square*

This was the spot Sir James Douglas, Victoria's first colonial governor, selected for the Hudson's Bay Company trading post with gaol and courthouse to follow. Today the buildings all belong to funky boutiques and restaurants.

Butchart Gardens***

It's just about the most famous garden in Canada and never fails to please no matter what the season. This stunning 50-acre (20.25ha)

Chinatown *between Herald, Government, Pandora and Store streets.*

Craigdarroch Castle $
1050 Joan Crescent (off Fort St); tel: (250) 592-5323; fax: (250) 592-1099; web: www.craigdarrochcastle.com; e-mail: ccastle@islandnet.com Open daily.

garden has been drawing fans from around the world since it w shaped out of a limestone quarry in 1904. The flowers are planted theme gardens – Japanese, Italian or sunken – with fountains, strear and winding pathways. There are musicians and entertainers in t afternoons and everything is illuminated at night. The Christm displays are a special draw.

Chinatown✢✢
When labourers were brought to Canada to build the Canadian Paci Railway in the 19th century, many of them settled in Victoria whe Chinese who had come as gold prospectors had already set up a sm community. It's the oldest and most historically intact Chinatown Canada. The entrance is through an ornate Gate of Harmonio Interest✢ made of ceramic tiles and leads to Fan Tan Alley,✢✢ t narrowest street in the country, once filled with gambling houses ar opium dens.

Craigdarroch Castle✢✢✢
When the wealthiest man in British Columbia decided to build h wife a house, only a castle would do. Coal baron Robert Dunsmu ordered a 39-room stone mansion but died in 1889 before it w completed; Mrs Dunsmuir lived at Craigdarroch until 1908. The hou is now a museum displaying what life for the very rich was like in t late-19th century . Floors are intricate woodwork, windows a exquisite stained glass and the furnishings lavish Victorian. If yc climb the 87 steps to the top of Castle Tower, you're rewarded with

Right
Craigdarroch Castle

Craigflower
Farmhouse $
0 Island Hwy, Admiral Rd
Hwy 1A; tel: (250) 387-
97. Open daily.

ystal Garden $$
3 Douglas St; tel: (250)
1-1213. Open daily.

nily Carr House $
7 Government St; tel:
50) 383-5843. Open mid-
ay– mid-Oct, daily; rest of
e year by arrangement.

rt Rodd Hill and
sgard Lighthouse $
3 Fort Rodd Hill Rd; tel:
50) 478-6481; web:
vw.harbour.com/parkscan/

en daily 1030–1730.
e lighthouse is
cessible from the beach
ea at the Hill.

elmcken House $
Elliot St; tel: (250) 361-
21. Open May–Oct.

rliament Buildings
1 Belleville St; tel: (250)
7-3046. Visitors can
tch politicians scrap
en the House is in
ssion.

great view of the city, the Strait of Juan de Fuca and the Olympic Mountains.

Craigflower Farmhouse❖❖
When Victoria was founded in 1843 by the Hudson's Bay Fur Trading Company, this farmstead was its most successful enterprise. Guides in period costume will take you on a tour of the colonial furnishings as well as the gardens and orchards.

Crystal Garden❖❖❖
When it opened in 1925, Crystal Garden was the largest salt-water swimming pool in the British Empire and an echo of Queen Victoria's palace of glass in London. Today, it's a conservatory filled with exotic flora and fauna with flamingos, macaws, butterflies and many endangered tropical mammals.

Emily Carr House❖❖
This is where Emily Carr, one of Canada's most famous authors and artists, was born (see page 255).

Fort Rodd Hill and Fisgard Lighthouse❖❖❖
This fortress set in 44 acres (17.82ha) of wild-flower meadows and rocky bluffs was originally conceived to defend Victoria and the Esquimalt naval base in the late-19th century. Victoria was then headquarters for the Royal Navy's Pacific Squadron and required massive fortifications including command posts, underground magazines and related buildings. After two world wars (when it was fully staffed), Fort Rodd Hill was in 1962 designated a national historic site and is considered one of the best preserved 19th-century forts in the world. Fisgard Lighthouse was built in 1862 and was the first permanent lighthouse on Canada's West Coast.

Helmcken House❖❖
Built in 1852, this is the oldest house in Victoria and holds the furniture and memories of a pioneer doctor and statesman named John Sebastian Helmcken. An audio tour of the house explains his life, his 19th-century medical tools and the times.

Parliament Buildings❖❖❖
The massive stone Parliament Buildings brooding over Victoria's harbour were designed by a 25-year-old architect named Francis Rattenbury who went on to put his stamp on much of the city including The Empress Hotel and Crystal Garden. His personal life was less impressive. Rattenbury divorced his wife and married a scandalous, cigarette-smoking 'new woman' 30 years younger than him who caused scandals all over town. The architect was murdered in England by his wife's lover in 1934. Statues of prominent 19th-century figures such as Sir James Douglas and Sir Matthew Baille Begbie surround the building. At night, the buildings are lit up by lights outlining the solid Victorian architecture.

Royal British Columbia Museum
$$ 675 Belleville St; tel: (250) 387-3701; tollfree: (888) 447-7977; web: www.royalbcmuseum.bc.ca Open daily, closed Christmas and New Year's Day.

Thunderbird Park
Belleville and Douglas Sts; tel: (250) 387-3701. Open daily.

Walking tours $
for Neighbourhood Discovery Walks, tel: (250) 384-6698 for times and places; for Cemetery Tours, tel: (250) 598-8870; for haunted tours, tel: (250) 726-4224. No reservations needed.

Royal British Columbia Museum❖❖❖❖

It's routinely rated as one of the best museum/research centres in the world for both its permanent collection and its highly praised special exhibitions. These exhibits creatively blend live performers, interactive sets, models and historic materials so appealing that everyone from tots to seniors gets involved. Some of the highlights are: the frontier town with its cobblestone streets, silent movie house and Chinatown, a nostalgic 20th-century gallery; and a natural history gallery with life-like dioramas of the last Ice Age and a submarine journey to the depths of the ocean. The First Nations exhibits are creatively presented and beautifully lit with a genuine Kwakwaka'wakw longhouse, masks and scenes from the daily life of Canada's first people. A six-storey-tall IMAX screen plays the latest and best National Geographic films several times a day.

Thunderbird Park❖❖❖

This is another example of how BC aboriginal peoples are teaching new generations a sense of pride in traditional culture. When the totems in this park next to the museum began to deteriorate with time and weather, the choice was to pull them down or find some way of replacing them. Mungo Martin, the chief of the Kwakwaka'wakw band who was restoring totem poles at the university, found young people and began to teach them the lost art of totem making. The original poles have been taken inside the museum but many of those carved by Martin and his group in the 1950s are now in the park. In the summer months, you can watch carvers at work.

Walking tours❖❖❖

Well-laid-out Victoria with its concentrated attractions is perfect for walkers on their own, but to discover all the local secrets and stories, a guided walk is a treat. Every other Sunday a well-known local historian guides people past places where odd things happened and tells entertaining stories about Victoria's most colourful characters. Another weekly tour takes people through old cemeteries to learn about the city's history, and 2-hour walking tours in the summer explore the many ghosts and haunted houses of Victoria.

Emily Carr: an independent spirit

She was one of those gifted 19th-century women unfortunately born before her time. Today, her talent would bring her a legion of fans: in her day, she was called an eccentric and her genius decried as 'unseemly'. Born in 1871 in Carr House, she studied art in San Francisco and quickly developed her distinctive style. Following a year in France, she found a vigorous post-impressionist style with which to convey the wild beauty of Vancouver Island and vanishing native life. Despite the strength and beauty of her paintings and writings, she was forced to open a boarding house in Victoria to survive. It wasn't until she was 57 and travelled east to meet The Group of Seven that her work began to get critical recognition. After a heart attack in 1937, she devoted her time to writing and today is known for both her books and her art.

Accommodation and food

Oak Bay Beach Hotel and Marine Resort $$$ *1175 Beach Drive; tel: (250) 598-4556; tollfree: (800) 668-7758; fax: (250) 598-6180; web: www.oakbaybeachhotel.bc.ca; e-mail: info@oakbaybeachhotel.bc.ca* Right on the beach in quiet Oak Bay, this Tudor-style hotel with its popular pub and dinner theatre also has a long list of imaginative soft-adventure activities in the islands around.

Sooke Harbour House $$$ *1528 Whiffen Spit, Sooke; tel: (250) 642-3421; tollfree: (800) 889-9688; fax: (250) 642-6988.* This may be the best-known small luxury hotel in BC but it still attracts a large number of celebrities travelling incognito. The hotel and its restaurant (with its adventuresome organic cuisine) are about 44km west of Victoria but it's well worth the drive if only to taste what the chef does with sea asparagus and to sample some of Canada's finest wines.

Amethyst Inn at Regent's Park $$ *corner of Fort and St Charles; tel: (250) 595-2053; tollfree: (888) 265-6499; web: www.amethyst-inn.com; e-mail: innkeeper@amethyst-inn.com* This beautiful new inn was originally the home of a 19th-century newspaper magnate and was recently restored with perfection in every detail. Each room is a delight and the hosts have spared no expense in each individual design.

Millstream Llama Farm B&B $$ *355 Atkins Rd; tel: (250) 744-6420; fax: (250) 478-9194; web: www.millstreamllamas.com; e-mail: mail@millstreamllamas.com* For something totally different, this B&B in the country only 15 minutes from downtown Victoria offers quiet and a 6-acre (43ha) llama farm. Take the llamas for a walk or just enjoy the countryside.

Swan's Hotel $$ *506 Pandora Ave; tel: (250) 361-3310; tollfree: (8*
668-7926; web: www.swanshotel.com; e-mail: swanshotel@swanshotel.c
Restored 1913 heritage buildings with 30 spacious suites a
penthouse all fully equipped and right in downtown Victoria. Gc
restaurant and brewpub.

Blighty Bistro $$ *2006 Oak Bay Ave; tel: (250) 592-5111.* This form
fish 'n' chip shop now serves delicious homestyle cooking i
bohemian atmosphere. Try their splendid herbed chicken.

Café Brio $$ *944 Fort St; tel: (250) 383-0009; web: www.cafe-brio.c*
Italian with a nice outdoor patio and salon art on the walls. Try
Saltspring goat cheese, duck confit and the hearts of romaine salad.

Cassis Bistro $$ *253 Cook St; tel: (250) 384-1932.* Intimate atmosph
with a West Coast menu that features lots of variety and orga
dishes.

Herald Street Caffe $$ *944 Fort St; tel: (250) 383-0085.* West Cc
cuisine with the emphasis on freshness. Cosy atmosphere with flow
and art. A bit off-the-beaten-track and often called 'the best food
town'.

Marina Restaurant $$ *1327 Beach Dr.; tel: (250) 598-8555.* Some
the best sushi in Victoria and an extensive menu of seafood a
pastas. Also views onto Oak Bay marina.

Ooh La La $–$$ *1 63 Fort St; tel: (250) 978-1920.* You'd never gu
from the name but this is a Mongolian Hot Pot dining experien
now the 'hot' dining experience in Asia where you cook fr
vegetables, meats and seafood yourself at the table. Fun and friendly

The Penny Farthing $$ *228 Oak Bay Ave; tel: (250) 370-90*
Authentic English pub with intimate atmosphere, stained glass a
upscale pub fare.

Suggested walking tour of downtown area

Total distance: 16km.

Time: Allow 3 hours with stops.

Links: Victoria connects with the **Gulf Islands** (*see page 260*) via fe
from Swartz Bay and north via Hwy 1 to the **Cowichan Valley**
page 234).

Route: Starting at **BASTION SQUARE** ❶ check out **The Mariti**
Museum of British Columbia for a look at seadogs and seafarers.

Detour: Heading away from downtown along Wharf , turn right

Johnson and then left on Government to reach **CHINATOWN** and **Fan Tan Alley.**

Return via Wharf Street toward the Inner Harbour, and for the kids the **Victoria Bug Zoo** is filled with creepy crawlies and lots of bug information. Continue on Wharf to the **Fairmont Empress Hotel** ❷, the majestic grand dame of the city opened in 1908. Afternoon tea here is an old (but high-priced) tradition, if that's your thing. The Inner Harbour is alive with activity day and evening and a good place to pick up a horse-drawn carriage or pedal-carriage.

Just behind The Empress on the corner of Belleville and Douglas, the glass-roofed **CRYSTAL GARDEN** ❸ is worth a couple of hours itself to see the world's tiniest monkeys and other flora and fauna. Across the street **THE ROYAL BC MUSEUM** ❹ is an absolute must and you could spend an entire day here quite easily if you have the time. Try not to miss the IMAX theatre presentations. Leaving the museum, to the right of the building you'll find **THUNDERBIRD PARK** ❺ with its impressive totem poles, and **HELMCKEN HOUSE** ❻, the oldest house in Victoria along with the tiny 19th-century **St Ann's Schoolhouse.**

Return to Belleville and walk west to the **PARLIAMENT BUILDINGS** ❼ for a stroll through the groomed lawns and flower gardens and also to sit in on one of the combative sessions of the House if it happens to be sitting. Retrace your steps to Douglas and head south to the

Beacon Hill Park
*east of Douglas St,
south of Southgate St.*

spacious lawns of **BEACON HILL PARK** ❽. You can watch the wa
birds on the many ponds, stop at the petting zoo or enjoy a match
the cricket pitch.

From here, continue toward the water at the bottom of the park
Dallas Rd; cross the road and the park where Victorians enjoy walki
their dogs to pick up the **Shore Trail Walk** ❾. This can be a sh
easy stroll or you can follow the coast all the way to **Clover Point**.

At the foot of Government Street, backtrack north to spend a lit
time in the **EMILY CARR HOUSE** ❿.

Driving tour

Starting downtown, take Government Street north and then turn w
on Gorge Road (1A), continuing until you reach Ocean Bouleva
Turn south and follow Ocean Boulevard to reach **FORT RODD HI**
National Historic Park. **Royal Roads University**, BC's famous milit
college, is just west of here. Return to the Island Highway going no
until it intersects with Hwy 1 and follow this east to McKenzie Ro
which leads to Hwy 17 going north. Follow 17 to Keating Cross ro
and turn west for **BUTCHART GARDENS** with a stop at the **Victo
Butterfly Gardens** on the way to see a wondrous display of colour
creatures.

Returning via Benvenuto turn south onto the West Saanich Ro
(17A) and follow to Observatory Road to visit the **Domini
Astrophysical Observatory** where the public is invited for free to
and Saturday night gazing at the heavens, Apr–Oct. Continue sou
on 17A and follow this, turning west on McKenzie Avenue as
becomes Sinclair Rd and then south on Beach Drive. Follow sce
Beach Drive, stopping for tea or a drink at the Snug in the **Oak Bea
Hotel**.

Continue along Beach Drive to Stannard Avenue and turn north
reach **Government House** facing on Rockland Avenue. After a str
through the gardens, take Joan Avenue from the front of the hou
and follow it north to **CRAIGDARROCH CASTLE**. Follow Jo
Avenue to Fort Street and return to downtown Victoria.

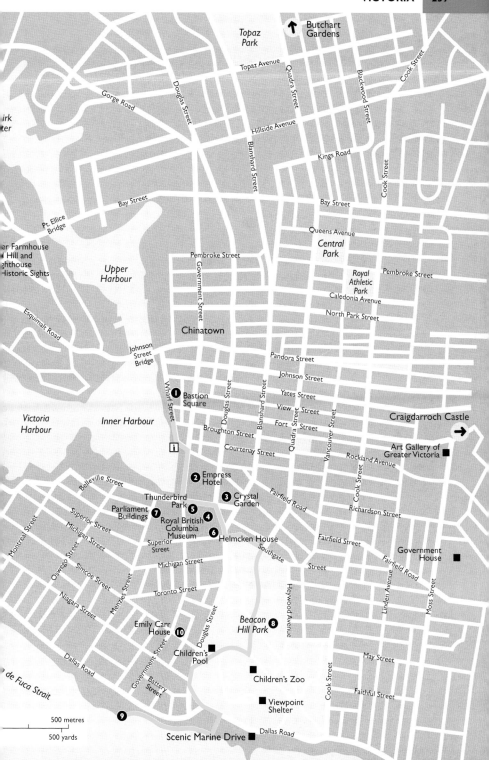

Topaz Park

↑ Butchart Gardens

Topaz Avenue

Gorge Road

Douglas Street

Quadra Street

Blackwood Street

Cook Street

Hillside Avenue

Blanshard Street

Kings Road

Bay Street

Bay Street

Cook Street

Pt. Ellice Bridge

er Farmhouse
Hill and
ghthouse
Historic Sights

Queens Avenue

Central Park

Pembroke Street

Royal Athletic Park

Pembroke Street

Esquimalt Road

Upper Harbour

Government Street

Caledonia Avenue

North Park Street

Chinatown

Johnson Street Bridge

Pandora Street

Johnson Street

Yates Street

Wharf Street

❶ Bastion Square

Douglas Street

Blanshard Street

View   Street

Fort   Street

Quadra Street

Vancouver Street

Craigdarroch Castle →

Victoria Harbour

Inner Harbour

Broughton Street

Courtenay Street

Art Gallery of Greater Victoria ■

Rockland Avenue

ℹ

❷ Empress Hotel

❸ Crystal Garden

Fairfield Road

Cook Street

Belleville Street

Thunderbird Park

❺

Richardson Street

Parliament Buildings

❼ Royal British Columbia Museum

❹

Government House ■

Montreal Street

Superior Street

Michigan Street

Simcoe Street

Oswego Street

Menzies Street

❻ Helmcken House

Southgate   Street

Fairfield Street

Fairfield Road

Linden Avenue

Moss Street

Superior Street

Michigan Street

Toronto Street

Niagara Street

Emily Carr House ❿

Government Street

Douglas Street

Heywood Avenue

Beacon Hill Park ❽

Dallas Road

Battery Street

Children's Pool ■

Children's Zoo ■

May Street

Cook Street

de Fuca Strait

Viewpoint Shelter ■

Faithful Street

❾

500 metres
500 yards

Scenic Marine Drive

Dallas Road ■

The Gulf Islands

Ratings

Art and craft	●●●●●
Nature	●●●●●
Outdoor activities	●●●●●
Parks	●●●●●
Scenery	●●●●●
Coastal villages	●●●●○
Wildlife	●●●●○
Beaches	●●●○○

This archipelago of 200 plus islands lies in the ra shadow of the Vancouver Island mountain ran creating an idyllic climate with low rainfall. Most of t islands are small and uninhabited and have no ferry acce but five of the southern group are home to almost 12,0 permanent residents. These are like miniature countries wi unique histories and personalities. Like islande everywhere, Gulf Islanders are colourful and controvers with a good sprinkling of celebrities and activists. They their own pace and value such things as quality in li organic food, art and crafts, as do visitors who come for t weekend markets. The islands have stunning views, wh crushed shell beaches, protected forest and pastoral valle tucked between mountains and forests. The coastline wi its cliffs, bays and coves draws sea kayakers and hikers well as fishermen on day trips from the mainland.

GALIANO ISLAND✦✦✦

ⓘ Galiano Chamber of Commerce/ Travel Info Centre 2590 Sturdies Bay Rd; tel: (250) 539-2233; web: www.galianoisland.com Open July–Aug, daily; weekends rest of the year.

⊘ Ferries from both the mainland and Vancouver Island arrive on Galiano at Sturdies Bay.

Go Galiano Island Shuttle tel: (250) 539-0202. Operates from the Sturdies Bay Ferry.

Galiano's destiny was determined by its geography: since most of island was unsuitable for farming it attracted artsy a environmentally progressive settlers, followed by tourists with passion for the outdoors. This narrow, hilly island stretches over 5 km with a population of about 1000, most of them involved in a and crafts or tourism. With less than 60cm of rainfall a year, Galia is the driest of the islands which makes it perfect for a multitude sporting activities such as the best-organised mountain bike tr system in the Gulf Islands and a coastline ideal for hiking, kayaki canoeing, scuba diving and fishing. There are seven parks on island where visitors can spin-cast for salmon, hike or train binocul on migrating birds. **Bellhouse Provincial Park✦✦✦** lures photograph with bizarre eroded limestone formations and its dramatic setti overlooking Active Pass. **Bluffs Park✦✦** has spectacular views of mar life, seabirds and eagles, while **Montague Harbour Provincial Marine Park⁺⁺** is known for its ground white shell beaches and enormous Indian middens. **Bodega Ridge Nature Preserve⁺⁺** is part of a new national park and has well-developed hiking trails through grasslands and old-growth Douglas fir forest and along the waterfront. Sturdies Bay is the main commercial centre with several stores, a gas station, restaurants, ferry terminal, info centre and lodge. The island has no transportation system but the Go Galiano Island Shuttle provides tours and taxi service. Shops in town will rent mountain bikes, canoes and kayaks and the island has numerous excellent B&Bs and inns.

AYNE ISLAND⁺⁺

What you find strongest among the 900 residents on Mayne Island (21 sq km) is a powerful sense of 'community' and a pride in the island's history. They'll point out for example that they have BC's oldest continuously operating hotel, the **Springwater Lodge,⁺⁺⁺** built in the 1890s with 'a million-dollar sunset view' from the hotel's massive deck. Food here is excellent and affordable. Miner's Bay,⁺⁺ the main village, looks over Active Pass and is really just a collection of funky little stores and good art and crafts shops. During the Fraser River gold rush in 1858, miners would stop here as a halfway point when they rowed across Georgia Strait from Victoria to the mainland. There are no provincial parks on Mayne but

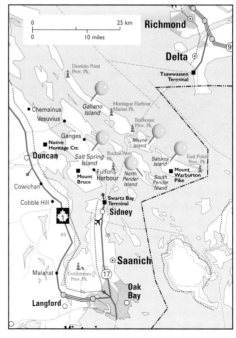

Mayne Island Museum $ *Opposite the community centre off Fernhill Rd; tel: (250) 539-2283. Open daily in the summer 1000–1700; winter Sat 1300–1600.*

Springwater Lodge $ *has good hearty food with the best fish and chips on the island. The cabins, right on the beach, are the best bargain on the Gulf Islands. Located at C-27 Miner's Bay, Mayne Island; tel: (250) 539-5521; fax (250) 539-5521; web: www.gulfislands.com/ springwaterlodge*

neither is hunting allowed so deer can usually be seen calmly graz on local front lawns. A summer farmers' market has just started fresh produce and freshly caught seafood is available in season at Government Dock.** Best attractions for visitors are the May Island Museum,** formerly the local gaol, Active Pass lighthous and the stunning view across the Strait from Mount Parke.*** Th are a number of pleasant beaches and the Georgina Point Herita Park is a good place to check out a wide range of birds and some the 250 varieties of wild flowers. Good photo op: the St Ma Magdalene Church overlooking Miner's Bay.

NORTH AND SOUTH PENDER ISLANDS**

Pender Islands Information *2332 [C]er Bay Rd, North Pender; (250) 629-6541; web: [w]w.penderislands.com or [w]w.gulfislands.net [lo]cated 800m from the ferry [ter]minal. Open June–Sept, [dai]ly.*

Ferries *pull in at Otter Bay in North [Pe]nder.*

Mount Norman *and* **Beaumont Marine [Pa]rk** *from Canal Rd linking [th]e Penders to Ainsley Rd, [the]n follow signs to the [pa]rking lot.*

The Driftwood Centre *at Bedwell [Ha]rbour and Razor Point [roa]ds. Hosts the Saturday [far]mers' market.*

People refer to them just as 'the Penders' but they're actually two islands connected by a one-lane wooden bridge across a narrow canal dug in 1903 to facilitate ship travel in the Gulf Islands. There are around 2 200 full-time inhabitants who have set up a surprising number of amenities (mostly on the North island) but there's no town in the combined 34 sq km islands. **The Driftwood Centre** serves as a hub for post office, bank, gas station, groceries etc., but most visitors hit the many hiking trails or head to the island's 20 lovely beaches. **Mount Norman** (217m) on South Pender has a great overall view of the Gulf Islands as does George Hill** on the north end. The 40-minute **Beaumont Marine Park** trail begins at the same spot as Mount Norman and is well worth the effort. There's a white shell beach here and the marine park is one of the Gulf Islands' most popular. The Penders have numerous small speciality farms that provide produce, cheeses and much more for a thriving weekend market that runs mid-May–1 Sept.

SALT SPRING ISLAND***

Salt Spring Islands Visitor Info Centre *1 Lower Ganges Rd, [Ga]nges, tel: (250) 537-[45]52; fax (250) 537-4276; [em]ail:chamber@saltspring.com; [we]b: www.saltspringtoday.com [op]en daily.*

Ferries *run from Tsawwassen to Long [Ha]rbour, from Swartz Bay [on] Vancouver Island to [Fu]lford Harbour and from [Cr]ofton to Vesuvius Bay. [Th]ere is also a Harbour Air [sea]plane service from [Va]ncouver.*

Salt Spring Island has attracted people wanting to get away from it all ever since nine African-Americans became the island's first settlers in 1857 after purchasing their freedom. Today, it's the most populated of the Gulf Islands and home to internationally known celebrities such as Robert Bateman and Robin Williams, fine craftspeople, boutique farmers and retirees who are passionate about quality in life. The biggest draw is the **Saturday Market** where you can find the most creative crafts imaginable, fresh produce, artistic birdhouses, preserves and live entertainment that draws people from everywhere. The **Sheep Tour** is almost as famous; this is a self-guided tour (maps available from Salt Spring Tourism) to 36 artist studios indicated by a sign with a sheep. The island actually raises a lot of sheep to produce famous Salt Spring Island lamb and wool for the **Gulf Islands Spinning Mill.** Mohair goats, llamas and alpaca are also raised on the island and the mill spins these into products available for purchase. Also check out the **Salt Spring Island Fibre Studios** for demonstrations, workshops and a wide variety of handmade goods made from hand-dyed yarns in sophisticated designs. Ganges, which is not only the

Ruckle Provincial Park can be reached via Beaver Point Rd. **Mount Maxwell** is southwest of Ganges taking Cranberry Rd to Maxwell Rd. **Mount Bruce** is reached from Fulford Harbour, left onto Isabella Point Rd and then via narrow and rough Musgrave Rd.

Ackerman Museum $
2501 Fulford–Ganges Rd, near the ferry; tel: (250) 653-4228. Open by appointment.

Gulf Islands Spinning Mill $$
351 Rainbow Rd, Ganges; tel: (250) 537-4342. Regular tours Tue 1400–1700 or by appointment.

Salt Spring Island Fibre Studios $$ 121 Mountain Rd; tel: (250) 537-2656.

Saturday Market $
held in Centennial Park, Ganges. Open first Sat in Apr–last Sat in Oct.

Sheep Tour $
the artist studio tour is self-guided. Obtain maps and hours at Salt Spring Info Centre.

island's main village but also the largest community in the Gulf Islands, has shops that reflect the exacting tastes of the islanders, excellent bakeries, delis and galleries plus of course the Saturday Market. A glimpse of the island's interesting history can be found in **Akerman Museum✦** that has First Nations and early settlers' artefacts. Salt Spring has dozens of lakes with fine fishing for bass or trout and numerous parks with **Ruckle Provincial Park✦✦✦** the largest. At 486ha this is the largest in the Gulf Islands and embraces a working sheep farm, forest and open fields above a rocky shoreline. Smaller **Mount Maxwell Provincial Park✦✦✦** has a breathtaking view of the islands as does **Mount Bruce,✦✦** the highest point in the Gulf Islands and a popular jumping off point for hang-gliders. Several endangered plants and butterflies can be found here.

Right
Dining out, Salt Spring style

ATURNA ISLAND❖❖

Saturna Island Information
re is no office on the
nd but people at the
thouse Pub and at the
nd's two stores can
vide guidance. There is
o a website:
w.saturnatourism.bc.ca

Ferries to Saturna are
caught from Mayne
ind and dock at Lyall
rbour Government Wharf.

East Point Regional Park follow East Point
**Mount Warburton
ke** can be reached via
ples Rd in the western
tion of the island.

**Saturna Island Vineyard and
inery $$** has 60 acres
4.3ha) of vines under
tivation in four vineyards
d produces a range of
ard-winning white, red
d desert wines; tel: (250)
9-5139, (250) 539-3521
tollfree (877) 918-3388;
: (250) 539-5157; e-mail:
e@saturnavineyards.com

Although Saturna is the closest island to the mainland, it's ironically the least accessible since there are no direct ferries. There's no town, no pharmacy, no bank, few B&Bs, no public campgrounds and you're requested to take your garbage home with you. What it does have is a **vineyard and winery**,❖❖ a totally unspoiled quality and some of the most beautiful scenery on the Islands. There's a view from the top of **Mount Warburton Pike**❖❖❖ (490m) that will simply knock your socks off: and you may also catch a glimpse of wild goats that hang around the Pike. There are only around 315 inhabitants (give or take) on the island but they're an interesting bunch: from a member of the Canadian Senate to tarot card readers and Japanese *raku* potters. Visitors, whether for the day or longer, come to hike, cycle, kayak, fish or take nature walks. **East Point Regional Park**❖❖❖ has a lighthouse built in 1888 that looks toward the Canada/US border from the most easterly point in the Gulf Islands as well as a stretch of strange sandstone formations. This is one of the best places in the Islands to see killer whales in the summer, and spincasting for salmon is excellent, as is bird and mammal watching. You can see seals, sea lions and an endless list of seabirds. The biggest island event is the Canada Day Lamb Barbecue that draws people from all over BC.

Accommodation and food

There are a couple of excellent hotels with international rating and first-class inns and B&Bs plus most islands have budget accommodation and camping facilities. Restaurants vary from pub food to gourmet dining.

Canadian Gulf Islands Reservations *tel: (888) 539-2930; web: www.gulfislandsreservations.com* Provides free bookings and availability information for over 100 of the best B&Bs, inns and cottages on all the Gulf Islands, as well as island hopping packages on Galiano, Salt Spring, Mayne, Pender and more.

Hastings House $$$ *160 Upper Ganges Rd, Salt Spring Island, tel: (250) 537-2362 or (800) 661-9255; fax (250) 537-5333; web: www.hastingshouse.com; e-mail: hasthouse@saltspring.com* This award-winning Relais and Chateaux country house hotel on a 25-acre seaside estate is as good as it gets. Beautiful individual rooms and a dining room that changes its menu daily and serves some of the best food on the islands.

House Piccolo $$$ *108 Hereford Ave, Salt Spring Island, tel: (250) 537-1844, web: www.housepiccolo.com. e-mail: piccolo@saltspring.com* Known for its great wine list and European cuisine in an intimate setting.

Oceanwood Country Inn $$$ *630 Dinner Bay Rd, Mayne Island: t* *(250) 5379-5074; fax: (250) 539-3002; web: www.oceanwood.com; e-ma* *oceanwood@gulfislands.com* Another country hotel run with loads grace and style with the best cuisine on Mayne Island served in waterfront dining room with a spectacular view. Menus change dai with fresh garden ingredients blended into the Pacific Northwest sty accompanied by award-winning West Coast wines.

Sahhali Serenity Inn $$$ *5915 Pirates Rd, Pender Island; tel: (250) 62 3664; tollfree (877) 625-2583; web: www.sahhali-serenity.com; e-ma www.sahhali@gulfislands.com* Sits on 10 acres (4.05ha) surrounded gnarled Garry oaks, ancient firs and arbutus trees. The inn has love rooms with fireplaces, ocean views and jacuzzis.

Woodstone Country Inn $$$ *Georgeson Bay Rd, Galiano Island; t* *(250) 539-2022; tollfree (888) 339-2022; fax: (250) 539-5198; we www.gulfislands.com/woodstone; e-mail: woodstone@gulfislands.com* H 12 spacious guest rooms tastefully furnished in antiques and wick with fireplaces in many of the rooms. Excellent dining room.

Saturna Lodge and Restaurant $$$ *Open Mar–Oct; tel: (250) 539-22 or tollfree (888) 539-8800; fax: (250) 539-3091; web: www.saturn island.bc.ca; e-mail: saturnalodge@hotmail.com* Country inn overlooki Boot Cove with seven charming rooms and an excellent restaura with extensive wine list.

Below
Gulf Islands' sunset

Suggested tour

Time: This will vary widely depending on how many islands are visited and the time of the year (more ferries operate in the summer months). A good routing is from Tsawwassen to **GALIANO ❶**, a 1-hour trip, then to **MAYNE ❷** for 20 minutes more. There are connecting ferries between Mayne and **SATURNA ❸**, then from Mayne to **PENDER ❹** and **SALT SPRING ❺** with the run around 20–30 minutes between the islands. There are direct Tsawwassen to Salt Spring Island ferries without the stops. While you can cover a lot in one day on each of the islands, allow at least 2 or 3 on Salt Spring Island.

Links: BC Ferries from Tsawwassen, the mainland BC link to the Gulf Islands. From Vancouver Island, ferries operate to Fulford Harbour from Swartz Bay and from Crofton to Vesuvius Bay on Salt Spring Island: a 20-minute ferry trip.

Route: For visitors with the time, the most direct route would be from Tsawwassen to Galiano and then Mayne with a side tour to Saturna. From Mayne to Pender and then to Salt Spring Island. If you just have the time for a couple of islands, Salt Spring is a must for the famous market, hiking and some art tours, with perhaps either Galiano or Saturna for hiking and kayaking.

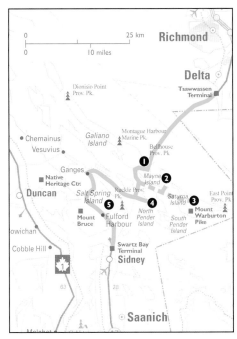

Vancouver

Ratings

Beaches	●●●●●
Food	●●●●●
Outdoor activities	●●●●●
Scenery	●●●●●
Entertainment	●●●●○
Children	●●●●○
Gardens	●●●●○
Shopping	●●●●○

Vancouver is a little like the Sleeping Beauty, blessed a birth by nature with only a tiny curse: winter rain. It si on a point wrapped by high mountains and surrounded b ocean, remains brilliantly green all year round and enjoy the warmest year-round climate in Canada. Because of it youth, clever city planners drew on experience and bestowe upon the city splendid Stanley Park right downtown alon with abundant gardens everywhere. In the spring downtown streets explode with colour as plum and cherr trees turn Vancouver pink. In the summer, everyone flock to beaches that wrap around the extensive shoreline, and i the winter three ski mountains are a short city bus rid away. With the city's cosmopolitan population, restauran run the gamut, serving the freshest seafoods, meats an produce from local farms. Vancouverites love the outdoo and their beloved city in equal measure.

Arriving and departing

i Tourism Vancouver *Plaza level, 200 Burrard St; tel: (604) 683-2000; tollfree: (800) 663-6000; web: www.tourismvancouver.com or www.hellobc.com; e-mail: info@tourismvancouver.com Open mid-May to Labour Day, daily 0800–1900; rest of the year Mon–Sat 0830 or 0900–1700.*

By air: Most flights arrive via **Vancouver International Airpor** (YVR), *Grant McDonachie Way, Richmond, tel: (604) 276-6101, abou* 23km south of downtown off Hwy 99, with **Abbotsford** as a secondar airport. There is a $10 airport-improvement fee charged upo departure for flights to North America and $15 for flights oversea Many international carriers have non-stop flights to Vancouver an numerous smaller airlines service BC. Taxis from the airport to the cit take 25 minutes and cost around $25–$30; the **Airporter Bus** *tel: (60₄ 273-8436; tollfree: (800) 668-3141,* is $12 one way and $18 round tri₱ Limos and car hire are also available.

By rail: **Via Rail** *1150 Station St; tel: (604) 640-3741; tollfree: (800) 56₂ 8630; web: www.viarail.ca* is Canada's national passenger rail servic with trains between Vancouver and Toronto. **Amtrak** *tel: (80C USARail,* has daily trains between Seattle and Vancouver. **BC Rail** *131*

The Georgia Straight *1770 Burrard St; tel: (604) 730-7000.* A free publication available in libraries, cafés and elsewhere that lists everything that's going on in town plus theatre and restaurant information.

Sun and ***Province*** *200 Granville St; tel: (604) 605-2000.* The main daily newspapers.

west 1st St, North Vancouver; tel: (604) 631-3500; web: www.bcrail.co has several trains that explore various sections of the province (s *Train travel, page 170*), including the spanking-new luxury train, th Whistler–Northwind. **Rocky Mountaineer Railtours** *1150 Station S tel: (604) 606-7245; tollfree: (800) 665-7245; web: www.rockymountaine .com* has a luxury 2-day ride through the best of Rocky Mounta scenery.

By sea: BC Ferries *tel: (250) 386-34331; tollfree: (888) 223-3779,* hav numerous ferries arriving from Nanaimo and Swartz Bay o Vancouver Island to Horseshoe Bay and Tsawwassen. Vancouver ha also become a highly popular cruise ship destination with most shi departing from Canada Place but others arriving in from US ports.

By land: Hwy 99 extends from the Canada/US border at Blaine Vancouver. Hwy 1 is the TransCanada Highway spanning the width Canada. Greyhound is the major bus line that connects Vancouv with many cities in Canada and the US.

Getting around

Unlike some cities, Vancouver doesn't have freeways leading into th city so traffic tends to move more slowly downtown. You don't need car in the downtown core since everything is within walking distanc and parking can be expensive. **BC Transit** has a good system of buse trolleys, the **West Coast Express** and an elevated rail system calle **SkyTrain**, plus the SeaBus going across to North and West Vancouve In False Creek the little **Aquabus** takes people from downtown over t Granville Island.

Aside from coping with one-way streets, driving is practical aroun Vancouver although left-turn lanes are not frequent, streets can b narrow with parking on the kerbs and traffic is often heavy during th day. Metered parking is available but can cost as much as $12 per hou in the downtown core. Car parks accept either coins or credit cards.

Sights

Beaches◆◆◆
Beaches are plentiful and crowded in the summer with swimmers, su bathers and volleyball nets. They curve in an arc from English Ba around Stanley Park and from Kitsilano to Wreck Beach (the unoffici nudist beach) near the University of British Columbia (UBC). Le crowded in the winter, the beaches are great for walking an beachcombing.

Canada Place *on the harbour between rrard and Howe Sts.*

Bloedel Floral Conservatory and ueen Elizabeth Park $ *rd Ave and Cambie St; tel: 4) 257-8584. Open daily cept Christmas Day.*

low ada Place from Stanley k

Bloedel Floral Conservatory and Queen Elizabeth Park✦✦✦

Spread over Vancouver's Little Mountain, this is a good place to come if only for a panoramic view of the city. But there's more. The park is second only to Stanley Park in size and it's filled with visitors year round, particularly bridal parties posing for pictures. The Conservatory has more than 500 species of plant with an emphasis on exotic plants, and birds that fly around your head as you wander along circular paths. The nearby Arboretum has almost all the trees native to Canada plus some exotic specimens from other countries.

Canada Place✦✦✦

Like the Sydney Opera House, the sails on the roof of Canada Place have become a symbol for Vancouver. This is multi-use building: it's a convention centre, ship terminal, hotel site and IMAX cinema. All summer long there will be at least a couple of ships docked alongside. This is a photographic 'must' for visitors.

Ⓘ Capilano Suspension Bridge $$
3735 Capilano Rd; tel: (604) 985-7474. Open 0800 to dusk in summer, 0900–1700 in winter.

Dr Sun Yat-Sen Classical Chinese Garden $
578 Carrall St; tel: (604) 662-3207; web: www.discovervancouver.com/ sun; e-mail: sunyatsen@telus.net

Capilano Suspension Bridge***

This is the longest and highest suspended footbridge in the wor spanning 137m across the Capilano River canyon at a height of 70 The original bridge was built in 1889 for men logging on the oth side of the chasm but it was opened to the public later by a wid lonely for company who charged 10¢ to cross to the quiet forest the other side. This is Vancouver's oldest tourist attraction.

Right
Capilano Suspension Bridge

Below
Chinatown market stall

Chinatown**

There's a real feel of authenticity here with even street signs mark with Chinese characters. Vancouver's Chinatown is the third-largest North America and filled with people daily shopping for vegetabl strange dried fish, ducks hanging in glass cases, or having breakfast numerable restaurants. During the summer, there's a great nig market that captures the colour and excitement in the area and th has done a lot to revitalise the area. If you can make it here f Chinese New Year or the Moon Festival, you're in for a special treat.

Dr Sun Yat-Sen Classical Chinese Garden***

This authentic Ming Dynasty garden is the first of its kind to be bu anywhere in the world, including China, since 1492. For authentici most of the materials and traditional construction tools were import

Gastown $–$$$
along Water St
ween Columbia and East
dova Sts.

orge C Reifel Bird
nctuary
stham Island, Richmond,
r the airport; tel: (604)
5-6980.

anville Island $–$$$
the south side of False
ek beneath the Granville
lge. Open daily. The
abus leaves for the Island
n the foot of Hornby St.

ouse Mountain $$
00 Nancy Greene Way,
th Vancouver; tel: (604)
4-0661; web:
w.grousemtn.com
ride leaves every 15
utes 0900–2200.

hthouse Park
Marine Drive at Beacon
e, between West
couver and Horseshoe

from Suzhou, China's foremost garden city. There is such a gentleness and serenity in this tranquil oasis, it's hard to believe bustling Chinatown is just beyond the gate. All through the garden Taoist principals of yin and yang appear in numerous ways: rugged and hard balanced by soft and flowing; dark balanced by light. This is a place to slip into for rest and tranquillity.

Gastown✧✧✧
This is where Vancouver began when a loquacious publican named John 'Gassy Jack' Deighton set up a saw horse with a barrel of whisky and thereby became the city's first businessman. There's a statue to Gassy Jack✧✧ at the corner of Water and Carrall Sts to honour Vancouver's disreputable City Founder. The area now caters mainly to tourists, particularly those off the cruise ships, but there are some good restaurants and pubs. Don't miss the steam clock✧✧ that blows its top on the quarter-hour and makes a wonderful photographic image of Gastown.

George C Reifel Migratory Bird Sanctuary✧
This is a mecca for naturalists from around the world who come for the migratory birds and those that over-winter in this internationally recognised 360ha bird sanctuary. Buy an inexpensive package of birdseed and you'll have flocks around you.

Granville Island✧✧✧
Until the 1960s when a new sense of civic beauty and pride began, this is where tons of metal products and industrial pollutants were manufactured. It was all cleaned up and transformed into an immensely popular centre for live theatre, markets, speciality boutiques and galleries. Emily Carr School of Art and Design✧ is here along with many workshops where potters, glass blowers and designers work at their crafts. It's a place to come to shop for fresh produce, seafood and much more in the Granville Market,✧✧✧ to dine at one of the restaurants, visit the Granville Island Brewery✧✧ or stay at the Island's Boatel.

Grouse Mountain✧✧✧
Take the 125-passenger Skyride to the top of the mountain for a spectacular view on a clear day or to hike the trails around the 1242m summit. This aerial tramway is the largest built in North America and it whisks you from the base to the chalet 1100m above sea level. In the summer a short helicopter ride offers a bird's-eye view, there's a restaurant, a film on Grouse Mountain and lots of sporting activities such as paragliding. In the winter, Grouse is the closest ski area to downtown.

Lighthouse Park✧✧
This park is in West Vancouver and covers 75ha of rainforest. Some of the largest Douglas firs in Vancouver are here, many estimated to be

🛈 Lookout at Harbour Centre $$
555 west Hastings St; tel: (604) 689-0421. For restaurant patrons the elevator ride is free.

Museum of Anthropology
6393 northwest Marine Dr.; tel: (604) 822-3825; web: www.moa.ubc.ca Open mid-May to Labour Day, daily 1000–1700, Tue until 2100; rest of the year closed Mon.

Science World $$
1455 Quebec St near Main at the east end of False Creek; tel: (604) 443-7440; web: www.scienceworld.bc.ca Open Mon–Fri 1000–1700; Sat–Sun 1000–1800.

Stanley Park
follow Georgia St away from the city centre going northwest until you see the park entrance. For the Aquarium tel: (604) 659-3400. Open daily.

more than 500 years old. Trails run through the park with sor leading to the Lighthouse at Point Atkinson✦✦, built in 1912.

Lookout at Harbour Centre✦✦✦

This looks a bit like a flying saucer sitting on top of a high-rise k glass elevators will whizz you up 50 storeys for a panoramic view the city that's hard to beat. On a clear day you can actually see all t way to Vancouver Island. Tickets are good all day so you can con back to see the city at night. There's a revolving restaurant up at t top as well.

Museum of Anthropology✦✦✦

The museum, inspired by West Coast aboriginal longhouses, ho one of the world's finest collections of First Nations art and artefa with both modern and antique totem poles, masks and much mc Outside, there's a life-size model of a Haida village and many mode totem poles.

Science World✦✦

This geodesic dome began life as an Expo '86 pavilion and v transformed into a $50 million science museum with lots of hands-displays explaining science and the natural world for kids and kids-heart. There's lots of interactive exhibits, live performances a special events.

Right
Science World's geodesic dome

Stanley Park✦✦✦

This is deep in the heart of Vancouver and of Vancouverites: a pl you come as a child to ride the Miniature Train✦✦✦ through the fo or pat animals at the Children's Farmyard✦✦✦ and as an adult fo

Steveston Heritage Fishing Village $
outhwest corner of chmond, 8km off Hwy 99 ong Steveston Hwy; tel: 04) 277-8280.

BC Botanical Gardens
niversity of British olumbia, southwest Marine .; tel: (604) 822-9666.

an Dusen Botanical arden $
251 Oak St at 37th Ave; l: (604) 878-9274; web: ww.hedgerows.com pen daily.

aletown runs from False reek to Burrard St on the rthwest and Georgia St on e northeast.

elow uise ship sails under Lion's ate Bridge

thousand and one pleasures. With 1000 acres (405ha), most of it dense West Coast forest, there are dozens of marked trails leading through the 'jungle', lots of beaches, totem poles, cricket pitches, rose gardens and splendid views. Visitors can step onboard a Horse-Drawn Tour✦✦✦ with a professional guide who will relate all the park's favourite stories: from Deadman's Island to the Girl in the Wet Suit. The zoo is now gone but Vancouver Aquarium✦✦✦ with its underwater wonderland remains. The displays are excellent and the whale pool not to be missed especially around feeding time. Underwater windows provide a rare close-up glimpse of these enormous but gentle creatures. Ask at the Aquarium about their special 'Sleeping with the Whales' programme when guests can bunk down in sleeping bags right beside belugas and orcas.

Steveston Heritage Fishing Village✦
Back in the late 1800s, when this was a thriving fishing village, more than 10,000 people lived here and worked a series of canneries. Today, Steveston is still the largest commercial fishing harbour in Canada but it also attracts artists and photographers who come for the rustic buildings, museums, galleries and restaurants. You can buy fresh fish and shellfish right off the boats here.

UBC Botanical Gardens✦✦✦
This is really five gardens in one, making up one of the oldest and finest botanical gardens in Canada. The Asian Garden has a range from magnolias to rare blue Himalayan poppies, the Native Garden displays more than 3500 indigenous plants, the Alpine Garden thrives on imported soil and rare mountain plants from around the world, the Physick Garden re-creates a 16th-century monastic herb garden and the Food Garden is a lesson in efficient planting all on a hectare. Also at UBC is the Nitobe Memorial Garden, a gentle stroll in a traditional Japanese garden.

Van Dusen Botanical Garden✦✦
This vast collection of small gardens was once a Vancouver golf course. Within the 22ha of gardens there are many rare and international species, topiaries, an Elizabethan hedge maze, lakes and children's gardens.

Yaletown✦✦
City planners come from around the world to admire the skill used in redeveloping this part of Vancouver from its former self as a rowdy warehouse area. At one time, Yaletown boasted more saloons per acre than anywhere in the world; today it's filled with galleries, fashionable furnishing shops, architects, designers and filmmakers. It's also a centre for some of the city's most trendy restaurants.

Accommodation and food

Vancouver has the full range of hotels: from the ultra luxurious wit spectacular views to quaint and folksy but easy on the purse. Rates ar considerably higher in the summer at many hotels and inns.

Fairmont Hotel Vancouver $$$ *900 west Georgia St; (604) 684-313.* This is Vancouver's trademark hotel with its famous peaked gree rooftops. Renovated many times and worth its price in comfort an convenience.

Four Seasons $$$ *791 west Georgia St; tel: (604) 689-9333; fax: (60 684-4555.* A name recognised around the world for the best in servic and comfort. This downtown location is perfect for shopping, theatre and dining.

Pan Pacific $$$ *999 Canada Place; tel: (604) 662-8111; we panpac.com/Canada/Vancouver/hotels/hotel* In Canada Place with panoramic view of the harbour.

Sutton Place $$$ *845 Burrard St; tel: (604) 682-5511; we www.travelweb.com/Sutton* A large hotel with an intimate feeling th happens to be a great favourite of celebrities who come to Vancouver

English Bay Inn $$ *1968 Comox St; tel: (604) 683-8002.* A romant and cosy inn just minutes away from Stanley Park and English Bay.

'O Canada' House $$ A beautifully restored 1897 Victorian home i the West End.

West End Guest House $$ *1362 Haro St; tel: (604) 681-2889.* A ho pink Victorian inn with antiques and terrific service.

Buchan Hotel $ *1905 Haro St; tel: (604) 685-5354.* Basic clean roon on a tree-lined street one block from Stanley Park. One of the be downtown bargains.

Eating out in Vancouver is a genuine pleasure with so many differen ethnic restaurants from which to choose in every price rang Vancouver has seen a huge explosion of places to eat out since th wildly successful Expo '86 and the influx of thousands of immigrant particularly from Hong Kong. As a result of this immigratio Vancouver has been blessed with some of the finest Chines restaurants (and Hong Kong chefs) in the world.

C $$$ *2 1600 Howe St; tel: (604) 681-1164.* Wonderful and exot seafood, Zen-like surroundings and a great view of False Creek an Granville Island. This restaurant gets high praise from everyone.

Diva at the Met $$$ *645 Howe St; tel: (604) 602-7788.* Innovative an contemporary cuisine that is as tasty as it is beautiful. The Alaska Blac Cod here is sinfully good.

Right
Vancouver Fountain

Lumière $$$ *2551 W Broadway; tel: (604) 739-8185.* Both chef an
restaurant are highly praised for creative French dishes using loca
ingredients and sinfully good desserts.

Villa del Lupo $$$ *869 Hamilton St; tel: (604) 688-7436.* In
converted historic house with intimate atmosphere and fireplace, thi
is one of the city's best choices for romance.

The Cannery Seafood House $$ *2205 Commissioner St; tel: (604) 254
9606.* A long-time award-winning Vancouver favourite for seafood
Try the house speciality Salmon Wellington.

Meinhardt Fine Foods $$ *3002 Granville St; tel: (604) 732-4405.* This i
the best equipped food store in town but it also offers an excellent de
section for dining in at a counter or taking out for a picnic.

Raincity Grill $–$$ *1193 Denman at Morton; tel: (604) 685-7337
Bright contemporary surroundings, great views and a creative tast
menu. Try the crispy Dungeness crab rolls.

Sun Sui Wah Seafood Restaurant $–$$ *3888 Main St; tel: (604) 872
8822.* Ask anyone about his or her favourite Chinese restaurant i
Vancouver and this usually comes up. Great creative Cantones
cooking at reasonable prices. Another restaurant in Richmond.

Shao Lin Noodle Restaurant $ *548 west Broadway; tel: (604) 873-1816
In addition to great noodle dishes and Dim sum treats, you get t
watch noodle makers spinning and stretching the noodles before you
eyes.

Sophie's Cosmic Café $ *2095 west 4th Ave; (604) 732-6810.* This funk
diner in Kitsilano has good hearty food with lots of vegetarian dishe
Famous for its breakfasts.

La Crêpe Bretonne $ *795 Jervis St; tel: (604) 608-1266.* One of the bes
bargains in town: a French atmosphere with good food and bargai
prices.

Suggested walking tour

Total distance: 16km.

Time: About 3 hours for the walking but could stretch to 8 with stops in Yaletown and on Granville Island.

Links: This city tour links with ferry routes to Vancouver Island from Horseshoe Bay via Hwy 1 westbound and to the Fraser Valley eastbound. From **Hope** (*see page 223*) Hwy 3 goes through the Cascade Mountains to **Osoyoos** (*see page 200*), the starting point for a journey through the Okanagan Valley.

Route: Starting at CANADA PLACE ❶, head east down West Cordova and veer left to Water Street. Turn right on Seymour for **THE LOOKOUT at HARBOUR CENTRE** ❷ for a ride up to an eagle's view of the city. Return to Water Street as this is the start of **GASTOWN** ❸ where Vancouver souvenirs of every sort can be bought or you can just hang around the **steam-powered clock** at Water and Cambie until it puffs out billowing white clouds. Anyone interested in historical architecture should note **Gaoler's Mews** at 12 Water Street and the **Byrnes Block** on the corner of Water and Carrall Streets.

Detour 1: Continuing east along Cordova brings you into Vancouver's Skid Row, not the best place to walk around alone. If you have a companion though you might check out the **Vancouver Police Centennial Museum** at Cordova and Gore just east of Main Street. This museum has a fascinating collection from the city's more notorious crimes including the famous Babes in the Wood murder.

Walk south on Carrall until it hits Pender and you will see the entrance to the **DR SUN YAT-SEN CLASSICAL CHINESE GARDEN** ❹. This serene oasis is worth half a day just for time to rest and contemplate. The free public park next door is also designed as a Chinese garden. A short path through the park will take you to Columbia Street where on the left you find the entrance to the **Chinese Cultural Centre Museum and Archives**, the first museum in Canada dedicated to Chinese-Canadian history. Return to Pender Street and continue west into **CHINATOWN** ❺ where there is good shopping for both eastern and western cooking, and kitchen wares at **Ming Wo Cookware**, 23 East Pender St. For a vast selection of teas, visit **Ten Lee Hong Tea and Ginseng** at 500 Main, and for ceramics and furniture **Yeu Hua Handicrafts Limited** at 173 East Pender.

Following Main Street south, turn right at the **SkyTrain** station and walk toward the huge geodesic dome that is **SCIENCE WORLD** ❻. If you have kids from three up, you'll have to drag them away from here. You can pick up the start of the grand Seawall Trail here and continue by foot around False Creek to Pacific Boulevard and cross to

Maitland. This is **YALETOWN ➐**, a perfect area for browsing having lunch in one of the area's many funky restaurants.

Detour 2: Catch the **Aquabus** at the small dock at the foot of Dav Street for **GRANVILLE ISLAND ➑** where you can spend a couple hours sampling the excellent foods at the Granville Market, wate street performers, visit artists in their studios or just throw chips to the seagulls.

Return to Pacific Boulevard via the Aquabus to Hornby Street, the turn south for two blocks to pick up the Seawall Trail. The Seawa Trail on almost any day of the year will be alive with walkers, cyclis and rollerbladers, mostly Vancouverites who enjoy this easy road fitness. It's a beautiful trail that hugs the shoreline for 10km windir past **English Bay ➒**. The trail goes past several beaches, under the **Lion's Gate Bridge** and by the rock on which **Girl in a Wet Suit** sit Vancouver's answer to Copenhagen's Little Mermaid. The walk offe excellent photo opportunities across **Coal Harbour ➓** over **CANADA PLACE** and the city.

Coming back to the entrance of the park, continue north to the park **rose garden** and then under a viaduct to **Lost Lagoon ⓫**.

What to do on a rainy day

It's rumoured that Vancouverites are actually the ones who spread the myth that it rains in Vancouver all the time: but when it does, here's what to do. You can head out to the Stanley Park Aquarium and even spend the night in your sleeping bag by the belugas if you want. Visit the Bloedel Conservatory in Queen Elizabeth Park for tropical heat and flowers. Enjoy a tranquil tea in the Bacchus Lounge of the Wedgewood Hotel on Hornby Street. Take an X-Tour where the actual scenes were shot for some of the 118 *X Files* episodes filmed in Vancouver. Visit the Vancouver Public Library with its Roman Colosseum design to catch up on your reading. Buy a 'brolly' or have one custom-made in The Umbrella Shop, 1106 West Broadway, then head out to Lighthouse Park for a wilderness walk in the rain with Manfred Scholermann, Rockwood Adventures, *tel: (604) 926-7705*.

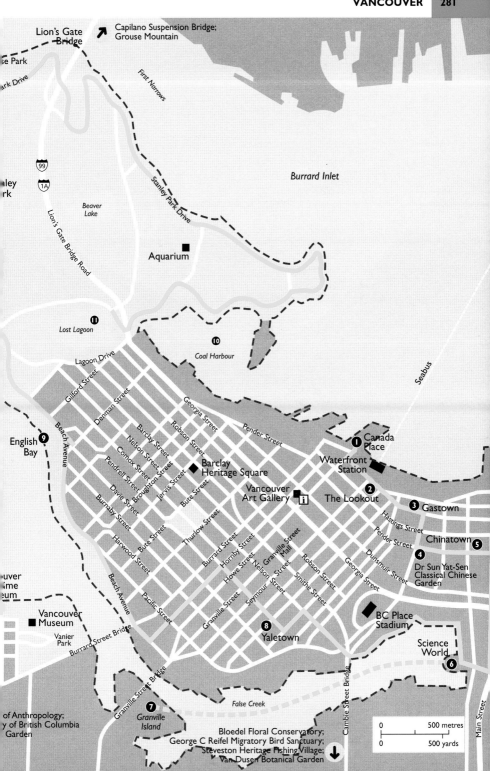

Lion's Gate Bridge

↗ Capilano Suspension Bridge; Grouse Mountain

se Park

ark Drive

First Narrows

99

1A

aley rk

Beaver Lake

Lion's Gate Bridge Road

Stanley Park Drive

Burrard Inlet

Aquarium

11 *Lost Lagoon*

10 *Coal Harbour*

Lagoon Drive

Gilford Street

Denman Street

Georgia Street

Robson Street

Pender Street

Seabus

English Bay

9

Beach Avenue

Barclay Street

Nelson Street

Comox Street

Broughton Street

Pendrell Street

Jervis Street

Bute Street

Barclay Heritage Square

1 Canada Place

Waterfront Station

Vancouver Art Gallery i

2 The Lookout

3 Gastown

Hastings Street

Pender Street

Chinatown 5

Burnaby Street

Davie Street

Thurlow Street

Bute Street

Burrard Street

Hornby Street

Howe Street

Nelson Street

Granville Mall

Robson Street

Dunsmuir Street

Georgia Street

4

Dr Sun Yat-Sen Classical Chinese Garden

uver me um

Harwood Street

Beach Avenue

Pacific Street

Seymour Street

Granville Street

Smithe Street

BC Place Stadium

Vancouver Museum

Vanier Park

Burrard Street Bridge

8

Yaletown

Science World 6

of Anthropology; y of British Columbia Garden

Granville Street Bridge

7

Granville Island

False Creek

Cambie Street Bridge

Main Street

Bloedel Floral Conservatory; George C Reifel Migratory Bird Sanctuary; Steveston Heritage Fishing Village; Van Dusen Botanical Garden

↓

| 0 | | 500 metres |
| 0 | | 500 yards |

ndex

Opposite Lake Louise, 'the Mona Lisa of the Montains'

Acknowledgements

The authors and publishers would like to thank the following people and organisations for the assistance during the preparation of this book: the spirit, inspiration and dedication of Patric and Peggy Telfer; Mona Gauvreau and Carla Moesman of pr works; Maria Crump, Travel Albert Cindy Burr and Mika Ryan, Tourism British Columbia; Marla Daniels, Edmonton Tourisn Danielle Oberle, Calgary Convention and Visitors Bureau; Kimberley Lyall, Alberta Sou Tourism Destination Region; Delta Lodge at Kananaskis; Lisa Kiehl, Fairmont Palliser Hote Panorama Mountain Village; Ramada Hotel, Lethbridge; Anastasia Martin-Stilwell, Fairmo Jasper Park Lodge, Jasper; André and George Schwarz, Post Hotel, Lake Louise; Nora Weber, B Rail; Monica Ott, Okanagan Wine Train; Deirdre Campbell; Grace and Karl Sands, Amethyst In at Regent's Park; The Prancing Horse; WKL Communications; Chris Higgins, Seasmo Communications; Markus Griesser, The Aerie; Laura Serena, Tourism Vancouver; Josette Whis Stump Lake; Beverley Dragseth, Pacific Wilderness Railway; Ali Macaraeg, VIA Rail, Vancouve Janice Greenwood, Rocky Mountaineer Railtours.

We would also like to thank the following for the photographs used in this book, to whom th copyright in the following photographs belong:

Cover photographs: Robert Harding (front); Tim Thompson (back)

BC Ferries: page 180

BC Rail: pages 173, 174

Candace Meyer/BC Rail: page 170

Fred Gebhart: pages 34, 167 (top), 212

The Russ Heinl Group: page 218

Chris Potter: pages 220, 225

Spectrum Colour Library: page 46

Donald L Telfer: pages 3, 6, 7, 13, 14 (upper), 19, 21, 28, 35, 38, 40, 41, 42, 44, 45, 50, 51, 52, 5 55, 56, 59, 62, 64, 65, 67, 70, 72, 74, 77, 79, 81(both), 84, 86, 88, 89 (both), 90, 91, 94, 97, 9 99, 102, 104, 107, 108, 109, 112, 115, 118, 121, 122, 124, 126, 127, 129, 132, 134, 140, 143, 14 145, 146, 147, 148, 156, 160, 163, 165 (both), 167 (bottom), 172, 271

Tim Thompson: pages 12, 14 (lower), 29, 155, 275, 282

Don Wiexl: pages 198, 200, 203, 204, 206, 211

Helena Zukowski: pages 17, 22, 24, 27, 30, 31, 32, 117, 135, 150, 171, 177, 183, 185, 186, 19 192, 194, 195, 197, 208, 210, 212, 214, 216, 218, 219, 222, 226, 228, 229, 232, 235, 237, 24 242, 243, 244, 246, 247, 248, 250, 251, 252, 254, 257, 260, 262, 264, 266, 268, 272 (both), 27 277, 278

Feedback form

If you enjoyed using this book, or even if you didn't, please help us improve future editions by taking part in our reader survey. Every returned form will be acknowledged, and to show our appreciation we will give you £1 off your next purchase of a Thomas Cook guidebook. Just take a few minutes to complete and return this form to us.

When did you buy this book? ....
....

Where did you buy it? (Please give town/city and, if possible, name of retailer)
....
....

When did you/do you intend to travel in the Canadian Rockies?....................................
....

For how long (approx.)? ....

How many people in your party? ....

Which cities, national parks and other locations did you/do you intend mainly to visit?
....
....
....
....

Did you/will you:
❑ Make all your travel arrangements independently?
❑ Travel on a fly-drive package?
Please give brief details: ....
....

Did you/do you intend to use this book:
❑ For planning your trip?   ❑ Both?
❑ During the trip itself?

Did you/do you intend also to purchase any of the following travel publications for your trip?
Thomas Cook Travellers: Vancouver and BC ....
A road map/atlas (please specify) ....
Other guidebooks (please specify) ....

Have you used any other Thomas Cook guidebooks in the past? If so, which?
....
....

Please rate the following features of Signpost Guide *Canadian Rockies* for their value to yo (circle VU for 'very useful', U for 'useful', NU for 'little or no use'):

The Travel facts section on pages 14–21	VU	U	NU
The Driver's guide section on pages 22–5	VU	U	NU
The touring itineraries on pages 36–7	VU	U	NU
The recommended driving routes throughout the book	VU	U	NU
Information on towns and cities, national parks, etc.	VU	U	NU
The maps of towns and cities, parks, etc.	VU	U	NU

Please use this space to tell us about any features that in your opinion could be changed improved or added in future editions of the book, or any other comments you would like t make concerning the book:

....

....

....

....

....

....

....

....

....

....

....

Your age category: ❑ 21-30   ❑ 31-40   ❑ 41-50   ❑ over 50

Your name: Mr/Mrs/Miss/Ms ....

(First name or initials) ....

(Last name) ....

Your full address: (please include postal or zip code)

....

....

....

....

....

Your daytime telephone number: ....

Please detach this page and send it to: The Project Editor, Signpost Guides, *Canadia Rockies*, Thomas Cook Publishing, PO Box 227, Peterborough PE3 6PU, United Kingdom

We will be pleased to send you details of how to claim your discount upon receipt of thi questionnaire.